C000193939

KEY TEXTS

THOEMMES

Printed and bound by
Antony Rowe Ltd., Chippenham, Wiltshire

Classic Studies in the History of Ideas

SOME DOGMAS OF RELIGION

John M. E. McTaggart

With an Introduction by
C. D. Broad

With a new Foreword by
Gerald Rochelle

This edition published by Thoemmes Press, 1997

Thoemmes Press
11 Great George Street
Bristol BS1 5RR, England

US office: Distribution and Marketing
22883 Quicksilver Drive
Dulles, Virginia 20166, USA

ISBN 1 85506 519 3

This is a reprint of the 1930 edition

© *Foreword* Gerald Rochelle, 1997

Publisher's Note

The publisher has gone to great lengths to ensure the quality of this reprint but points out that some imperfections in the original book may be apparent.

FOREWORD

Today we are just as concerned as McTaggart's public with the topics covered by *Some Dogmas of Religion*. These are recurrent human concerns – how we should rate the importance of our beliefs and how we establish them, whether our life is a once and for all incident, whether or not there is a greater power in the universe. The fact that they may remain unsolvable is unlikely to remove them from the human agenda. The intent of McTaggart is that he deals with these fundamental issues clearly, logically and objectively. He guides us through the intrinsic knots and convolutions with care, enthusiasm and humour; and though eventually he arrives at an atheistic scepticism, he also reveals his vision of personal immortality and freedom in a loving and determined universe of spirit. McTaggart's enterprise belongs to a popular philosophical tradition now mostly abandoned.[1]

The first edition of *Some Dogmas of Religion* was published in 1906[2] as McTaggart approached the height of his philosophical career and creative potency. In his mind he had already solved the riddle of our confusing experience of time and linked his atemporal

1 That philosophy could contribute meaningfully to everyday social and personal issues is typified by McTaggart's attempt to bring consolation to those bereaved in the First World War with the reprint of chaps. 3 and 4 of *Some Dogmas of Religion* as *Human Immortality and Pre-Existence* (London, Edward Arnold, 1915).

2 The edition reprinted here is the 1930 edition which incorporates the amendments extracted from McTaggart's own copy by Stanley Victor Keeling.

replacement into an ideal system of mutually perceiving selves existing eternally in a universe that will, after periods of great evil, eventually attain a predominance of good. The following year he presented the framework of his ideas in 'The Relation of Time and Eternity' and in 1908 published the first version of his notorious 'The Unreality of Time'. Time, however, was only one component of his metaphysical search.[3] His philosophy was driven by a faith in an underlying reality which he believed he witnessed in his own experience of love. He was indebted to various sources of inspiration – his idealism he drew from Hegel; Plato provided the model for his logical clarity and his metaphysical vision he owed to his own mystic experience.[4]

Our current philosophical legacy is dominated by a 'technocratic'[5] method while the more holistic tendency of 'continental philosophy', which has its roots in idealism, has been forced to the sidelines. Concerns about the place of mind and the meaning of individuality receive an inflexible response from the modern analytic philosophers, selfhood being no more than a

[3] King-Farlow provides an interesting defence of McTaggart's argument against time as part of a greater scheme, the 'Search for Something Deeper which Underlies our Sense of Time's Passage', as he calls it. See John King-Farlow, 'The Positive McTaggart on Time', *Philosophy*, vol. 49 (1974), no. 188, pp. 169–78.

[4] For a first-hand biographical account of McTaggart see Goldsworthy Lowes Dickinson, *J. McT. E. McTaggart* (Cambridge University Press, 1931). A more recent biography is Gerald Rochelle, *The Life and Philosophy of J. McT. E. McTaggart, 1866–1925* (Lewiston, New York, Edwin Mellen, 1991). For an overview of his important essays and a synopsis of his philosophical system see J. McT. E. McTaggart, *Philosophical Studies*, edited and introduced by Stanley Victor Keeling, with a foreword by Gerald Rochelle (Bristol, Thoemmes Press, 1996; first published London, Edward Arnold, 1934).

[5] Scruton uses this term in Roger Scruton, *Modern Philosophy* (London, Mandarin, 1996), p. ix.

convenient description of higher order physicalness – we are defined by the materialism and rules of science. This view absorbs Darwinism and the achievements of science and casts the evolutionary pinnacle of mind into the electronic 'brain' of the computer.

It is quite natural, and right, that philosophy should avail itself of some of the products of the vast explosion of scientific knowledge that has occurred in the twentieth century; but if this is at the expense of metaphysical enquiry, at the risk of only reflecting the changing face of scientific 'certainty', then the cost is very high. This dominant method of philosophy does little to satisfy the individual's metaphysical needs. Indeed, the sweeping establishment of scientific thinking and the inexorable growth of technology has produced a new Hellenistic religious and cultural vacuum.

As the century closes and suspicions about the infallibility of science grow, in the Western world together with a continuing reduction in belief in the dogmas of religion, a new metaphysical search is gradually under way. Philosophical investigation of mind is again being recognized as central to establishing the nature of consciousness and the connection and meaning this may have to reality. Psychology, as an independent science, has failed to answer the problem of mind – interpreting us as animals with behaviouristic patterns. It has thus abandoned the quest for an understanding of our mental nature that Dewey and James thought fit to deal with, handing it back to science or philosophy. As this happens we are faced again with the philosophical tension between empiricism and rationalism – not so much between science and non-scientific as between science and metaphysical enquiry – and a need to reconsider the elements that caused their partition.

Importantly, McTaggart lived at the time when this original controversy was under the most strain. He experienced the early stresses between Darwinian theory and the accepted tenets of religion, the work of Einstein and the moral and social disturbances that followed in the wake of the First World War. His historical position, together with his profound philosophical power, logical lucidity and mystic intuition make him an obvious focus for any fresh understanding of idealism and the nature of mind.

The original (second) edition of *Some Dogmas of Religion* was well served by Broad's provision of an Introduction which as well as giving biographical detail – much of which was first-hand knowledge – also throws light on McTaggart's thought. Not only does he interpret McTaggart's work on Hegel but he offers an interesting comparison of the two personalities. He affords a brief synopsis of the contents and links this to a useful insight into McTaggart's system as described in *The Nature of Existence*,[6] a work which, as McTaggart's literary executor, Broad brought to final publication. This led him into detailed study of McTaggart's system.[7] Broad was an enthusiastic supporter of science and its place in philosophy whereas McTaggart, though he took an interest in scientific progress, did not consider it philosophically useful. Broad held a materialist view of survival after death –

[6] Further valuable analysis of *Some Dogmas of Religion* can be found in Peter Thomas Geach, *Truth, Love and Immortality* (London, Hutchinson, 1979) where he discusses the 'Importance of Dogma' and 'The Establishment of Dogma' (pp. 22–35) and includes reflection on 'Human Immortality' and 'Human Pre-existence', 'God as Omnipotent', 'A Non-omnipotent God', 'Theism and Happiness' and McTaggart's 'Conclusion' (pp. 162–76).

[7] Charlie Dunbar Broad, *Examination of McTaggart's Philosophy* (Cambridge University Press, 2 vols., vol. 1, 1933; vol. 2 (pts. 1 and 2), 1938).

though his work on psychic phenomena shows that he was no dogmatist about this – and disagreed with McTaggart's denial of the reality of time, embracing instead a dynamic view where temporal 'becoming' feeds the reality which lies only in the past.

Broad was an objective writer whose explanatory powers and attention to detail are beyond reproach (and indeed constantly acclaimed as such); but his aversion to some of McTaggart's ideas occasionally spill out as does the burden of his executive obligation. I disagree with Broad that McTaggart holds 'an extremely Berkelian' view of immortality (or indeed of idealism in general). Though, like Berkeley, McTaggart thinks matter 'present' though not provable, he believes the essential quality of spiritual selfhood is that of 'perceiving' and not 'being perceived'. For McTaggart, consciousness acts like a wedge between the existence of unobserved matter and non-existence without which the distinction dissolves. John Wisdom used to quote Wittgenstein as saying that McTaggart's denial of matter did not mean 'that I don't wear underpants beneath my trousers'.

Now I shall move on to surveying the contents of *Some Dogmas of Religion* taking them chapter by chapter. In his first chapter, 'The Importance of Dogma', McTaggart argues that science is incapable of establishing dogma. He defines metaphysics as 'the systematic study of the ultimate nature of reality', dogmas as 'all propositions which have any metaphysical significance' and religion as 'an emotion resting on a conviction of a harmony between ourselves and the universe at large' (§§ 1–3). Religion is not synonymous with morality; it is not simply feeling good or being in awe of the universe nor is it dependent on a god of science or theology. Its foundations lie in love for others which itself incorporates both reality and harmony. Even though there is some consensus in human views on morality this is not so between dogmas, and, because of their necessary role in the practice of and belief in religion, they seem only to lead to increased religious strife.

The abstract nature of scientific propositions, limited by materialism and mechanics and drawn from only small 'representative' samples, cannot decide any absolute truth in the universe and so cannot be religious dogmas. Only by the practical application of metaphysics can we meaningfully interpret the findings of science and be saved from the anxiety caused by its failures. Though a religion based on science rather than dogma would be more empirically certain and subject to greater consensus, pressing questions of meaning that positively affect our search for happiness and harmony would still remain unanswered.

In the next chapter, 'The Establishment of Dogma', McTaggart concludes, after finding common reasons for holding dogmatic belief unacceptable, that dogmas are not subject to the changing nature of our daily lives and, though demanding moral qualities of us and the faith to trust our conclusions, can only be established by reason without any underlying motives – in other words by the practical application of objective metaphysics.

Dogmatic beliefs are frequently based on immediate convictions. Yet personal certainties like this are also the least reliable foundation for belief; they are neither based on nor shaken by argument, they come in a variety of often contradictory forms, they are believed by more people than actually have the immediate certainty and they cannot be checked nor held a priori. Some people's immediate certainty is widely held by others, but neither is this proof of dogma; there will always be exceptions – and majorities are notoriously wrong. Nor should we rely on miracles to reinforce our certainties; only if god is trustworthy can we find a direct connection between his miraculous ability and our religious credibility and we cannot trust revelation in the first place unless we know to start with that god is good. The belief that dogma is important to our happiness is similarly unacceptable. This belief relies on the nature of, and on the amount of, evil in the universe; and this can be made knowable only by investigating the nature of the universe itself and not the nature of dogma. Any arguments against evil's existence only prove again that we were initially deceived. Nor should faith be used to close the gap between what is actually known and what it is hoped could be known. If we mistrust our capacity to understand, we must also mistrust our capacity to understand what it is we do not understand. We certainly cannot have faith in god to bring about universal good and should not transfer our faith in the basic moral good of people, of whom we have some knowledge, onto god, of whom we have none. Added to which, faith can lead us to love god, then to conclude that he is good – a dangerous recipe for false belief.

McTaggart uses the next chapter, 'Human Immortality', to establish the possibility of the immortal spiritual self by showing that arguments against immortality which support the idea that self is an activity of the body, relies on it for its existence or shares its transitory nature, are all unacceptable. He accepts that there is almost overwhelming evidence from the scientifically validated unified theory that all things are material and that mind is a material manifestation. Still, he believes that science takes a mistakenly metaphysical position that matter is reality even though science's consistency would not be affected by accepting a non-material world.

Our inference of the existence of matter is always distanced by the matter-sensation-inference chain and all we can be certain of as selves is that we are making an inference. Sensations are causally related to both matter and the self but we do not know how the causes are like the sensations. Self cannot be explained in terms of matter and matter cannot be known without consciousness because material qualities are sensational. My self cannot be an activity of my own body because I would then be an event in my own life. Nor could my self be an activity of its body as perceived by another self as this would require the last perception of an unending series to be able to explain the first self and this is nonsense. The self cannot be an activity of the brain; matter cannot be thoughts and sensations if thoughts and sensations are activities of my brain which, if it is matter, will also be thoughts and sensations.

There may be no evidence of selves existing without bodies but all this means is that some body is needed. We may move between one body and another, or the body may only be essential while we are connected to it and drawing sensations from it. The self is a differentiated complex that encompasses a plurality of thoughts, desires and sensations. It cannot exist outside itself nor be part of another self and, as it is not a compound, it cannot cease to exist by separation of its parts.

McTaggart's next chapter, 'Human Pre-existence', stresses that immortality demands existence before this life and describes how the influence of love directs our movement from one life to the next. Pre-existence is implicit in immortality, for if the universe continues to exist then so must the immortal self; and as immortality cannot be expressed in one life, the self must be involved in a plurality of lives. Added to which, annihilation is not consistent with the moral claims of the individual in a good universe which by excluding the degradation of death, a good universe would restore. Love is our best evidence of immortality. Love at first sight and mutual love in general arise from love in previous lives.

Though we derive characteristics from our experience in this life, we do have innate, natural tendencies some of which are hereditary characteristics of our body and some of which derive from the self's experience of previous lives. The self uses hereditary characteristics in its selection of a compatible body for its next life. Loss of memory does not reduce the worth of pre-existence. The nature of the self is to express its attributes, and a self with the same attributes; moving from one body to another, would be the same self irrespective of its loss of memory. We can still be wiser, make judgements and improve our moral character by experience without an endless accumulation of remembered facts. However, we cannot afford to lose the value gained from love when we die; indeed, it must be stronger for the same person in the next life. If improvement is the universal goal, then the universe must rate highly the interests of the self, and because love is of great significance for the self, the universe must be interested in its continuance. Proximity to loved ones is not by chance, it is brought about by love (lovers coming together because of their love for each other) and this process will continue as long as temporal life persists or until an alternative moral direction is revealed.

The next chapter, 'Free Will', is described by Broad as 'very thin and wire drawn'; and Geach does not even consider it, believing that though it 'states determinism clearly...[it] adds little to what other determinists have said'.[8] However, I think this chapter is more substantial than either Broad or Geach concede; it does reinforce McTaggart's main argument that our experiences in this life are so insignificant compared with eternal existence that whether in the end the system is determined or not, from our present position the only way we can view it is as determined. McTaggart's point here is to demonstrate that everyday freedom of choice is compatible with belonging to a system of loving selves moving towards increased good in a determined universe.

As far as McTaggart is concerned, all senses in which we are free to take action – self-determination, self-direction, self-realization and indetermination – are compatible with a determined universe. He defends this view against five indeterminist arguments. The idea that it is valid to hold an immediate certainty that I am free he dismisses as having no logical force. That people feel volition is accompanied by a feeling of freedom he thinks is simply freedom of self-direction – it is a matter of preference and determined by my undetermined will. Judgements about moral obligation which are freely made, though involving our responsibility to other people, god and ourselves and relying on whether something would be good or bad and whether

[8] Geach, *Truth, Love and Immortality*, p. 21.

someone can act on, or will determine some thing, is not in any way affected if determined. The idea that choice is absurd in the absence of freedom is unacceptable because though the determinist determines events by his choice, his choice remains determined. The argument that indeterminacy must be true because of the awful consequences of its being false only points to the determinist being more virtuous than the indeterminist because he can be more intolerant of determined sin and have a higher degree of compassion for the sinner. It is inconsistent to admit validity of morality because the determinist is capable of both fair condemnation and forgiveness. It is inconsistent to attach value to expectation of the way we act, because only determinism can prevent reducing our lives to chaos while providing an appropriate basis for corrective punishment.

McTaggart then passes on to the theme of 'God as Omnipotent'. He uses what he considers an unambiguous and religious (as opposed to a philosophical) definition of god as 'personal, supreme and good' (§ 152) by which he means god must have self-consciousness, be more powerful than any other being and be able profoundly to affect all existence and be more good than evil. He retains (or withholds) the term 'absolute' (meaning true reality) as philosophically separate. Though considering them worthy of discussion, he rejects the arguments from first cause and design. That something is a first cause does not prove its personality or goodness and the idea that a first cause prevents an unending backward series of events in time means only that either god exists in time but had no beginning because he existed in unending time in the past, or that god's existence is timeless in which case there could have been no beginning. The argument from design only proves an 'assembler' of limited power.

In general, McTaggart finds omnipotence, as he rather unconventionally defines it, incompatible with both personality and goodness. Personality requires recognition of the Other (McTaggart uses Hegel's term) either directly (other persons or things) or indirectly (memory or will). Though a non-omnipotent god may find his Other contemplating what he proposes, this would not be so for an omnipotent god because contemplation of the Other implies a separate existence in the future that is beyond the present influence of god and therefore prevents omnipotence. As for goodness, any evil counts as evil and the universe contains evil; and if we think evil is good we cannot trust any ethical judgement and so should not pursue the idea of goodness in god. The idea that we mistake evil in people as good in god is because we associate good with praise and we praise god because we fear the consequent evil if we do not. God is either not bound by universal laws, which leads to contradiction; or he is, which defines him as non-omnipotent. A god who formulates a system with implicit evil or evil which he tolerates or could not change if he wished, is either evil or non-omnipotent, and a non-omnipotent good god is greatly preferable to an omnipotent god who decides to make a universe like this one.

In the next chapter, 'A Non-omnipotent God', McTaggart first considers a creative and non-omnipotent god but finds that because such a god is able to prevent evident evil and does not, he cannot be good. Even though after creation he may regret or wish to change something, his limitations still reside in his original nature which has both started a process towards an end and is also an obstacle to its attainment. Next McTaggart considers a non-omnipotent and non-creative god who has to accept that we (and the universe) exist as a given fact. Such a god is easily conceived as a person and all other persons represent his Other. He is also easily conceived as good (simply trying to do his best to work against evil) and is sufficiently powerful to merit worship. McTaggart's atheism can admit such a god because a god like this is simply a powerful self.

McTaggart does not accept that Berkeley's *esse est percipi* is essential for idealism, instead believing that conscious beings can be the only existents who simply 'know, will, and feel' (§ 209) or *esse est percipere*. If selves are connected in a unity then all that exists will be part of a self, a quality of a self, an event happening to a self or part of a self's relation to another self which in turn, means a relation to all other selves and their parts, qualities, events and relations. On this basis, god could be one of a society of selves, sharing in their imperfection and possibly motivated by increasing evil, limitation or inefficiency. McTaggart believes this is the most likely nature of god and that the only reason left for not believing in his existence is that there is no reason why we should.

In the last chapter, 'Theism and Happiness', McTaggart concludes that atheism is no bar to happiness. If god is omnipotent the eventual outcome of the universe is unknown, so that any optimism we may have is misplaced. If god is non-omnipotent then at best he will achieve little and at worst he will achieve evil. Even though god may be a good model for us of virtue and greater perfection, we lose little by denying his existence. More reliably we can emulate the models of virtue provided by other people and through our love for them experience some of the eternal perfection of which loving is a part.

This godless system of spirit is not our everyday position which either holds the universe to be material and in need of a god, or a mixture of the material and the spiritual and thus directed by god. Nor does it mirror the mechanics of the world of science but, more importantly for happiness than god, it can, by determining the nature of reality, reveal the supremely important immortal loving self. Even so, we lose some comfort or inspiration by rejecting god; and not loving god is a loss because we love one person less. Yet love remains without god; and though 'some love would have been poured out on a dream – or rather a reflexion – which could not return it' (§ 240), as long as there is a future we can still hope that our love for others may compensate for this loss.

In his 'Conclusion' McTaggart explains that metaphysics is the only way to escape the 'dreamy possibilities' of god and because most people do not undertake metaphysical study they have no right to accept religious dogma. However, as religious authority (and therefore the agreed acceptance of prescribed dogma) declines, more people will be unable to hold religious dogma and this may lead to an increased loss of truth and a commensurate growth of evil. Nevertheless, if the universe as a whole is good, this could provide a satisfactory basis for religious belief whether people believed in it or not and ultimately their belief would increase. For example, if immortality is true we will be immortal whether we believe it now or not. Also, any unhappiness brought about by loss of belief in religion would have compensations – for example, in freedom from worship. Metaphysics may become of the greatest practical importance when people realize they cannot have religion without it. Indeed, it may become as certain as physics, immortality being on a par with, say, the law of gravitation. If so, people would then not have to investigate it themselves; they would have ready-made metaphysical dogmas upon which rightly to base a religion. But, in a world that is constantly overturning philosophical opinions this seems only a distant hope.

Even so, McTaggart is cautious about the results of an outbreak of metaphysics; for even if individuals test out metaphysical dogma for themselves, any results may for a long time still lack the consensus which is so important for knowledge. The route to true dogmas is not at all certain. We may die before we attain them or falsely believe we have attained them and never know it. The need for continuing existence therefore seems unavoidable and the question of immortality remains our primary metaphysical concern.

Geach, in his analysis of McTaggart's system, urges us to take the broadest view of events in history and wisely warns against calls for 'agonizing reappraisal' driven by the irrationality of the 'emotional impact of what is near to us in space and time'.[9] *Some Dogmas of Religion* deflects us from the influences of current fashion and fad. It explores the nature of our deeply felt confusions and attempts to expose truths that are often masked by our everyday concerns and influences. It causes us to wonder if we are becoming disproportionately convinced by the dominance of science and the sprawl of information it presents. It even causes us

[9] Geach, *Truth, Love and Immortality*, p. 176.

to wonder whether our being so enthralled by science only takes us a step nearer despair. It challenges us to consider if we are prepared to run the risk of subordinating the possibility of immortality and the fabric of love to the spiritually unproductive style of modern philosophy. It awakens us to the necessity of pursuing truth by metaphysical argument and the rejection of uninformed and ill-founded belief.

Gerald Rochelle
Shropshire, *1997*

BIBLIOGRAPHY

'Trade and the Flag'. Lecture delivered to the Cambridge Economic Club, Lent term 1887, *Economic Club Essays* (Cambridge University Library, 1887), 4pp.

'The Changes of Method in Hegel's Dialectic, I', *Mind*, vol. 1 ns (1892), no. 1, pp. 56–71.

'The Changes of Method in Hegel's Dialectic, II', *Mind*, vol. 1 (1892), no. 2, pp. 188–205.

Review, 'T. Mackay, ed., *A Plea for Liberty*', *International Journal of Ethics*, vol. 2 (1892), no. 3, pp. 391–2.

'Du Vrai Sens de la Dialectique de Hégel', *Revue de Métaphysique et de Morale*, vol. 1 (1893), pp. 538–52.

'The Further Determination of the Absolute', privately published pamphlet (1893). Substantially chap. 9 of *Studies in Hegelian Cosmology*.

'Time and the Hegelian Dialectic, I', *Mind*, vol. 2 (1893), no. 8, pp. 490–504.

Critical Notice, 'E. Caird, *The Evolution of Religion*', *Mind*, vol. 2 (1893), no. 7, pp. 376–83.

'Time and the Hegelian Dialectic, II', *Mind*, vol. 3 (1894), no. 10, pp. 190–207.

Critical Notice, 'F. H. Bradley, *Appearance and Reality*', *Revue de Métaphysique et de Morale*, vol. 2 (1894), pp. 98–112.

'The Necessity of Dogma'. Lecture delivered to the London Ethical Society. *International Journal of Ethics*, vol. 5 (1895), no. 2, pp. 147–62.

Review, 'W. Wallace, *Hegel's Philosophy of Mind*', *International Journal of Ethics*, vol. 5 (1895), no. 3, pp. 393–5.

Critical Notice, 'A. J. Balfour, *The Foundations of Belief*', *Revue de Métaphysique et de Morale*, vol. 3 (1895), pp. 734–53.

Studies in the Hegelian Dialectic (Cambridge University Press, 1896), 2nd ed., 1922, 255pp. Chaps. 1–4 are based on McTaggart's Fellowship dissertation submitted for examination at Trinity College, Cambridge, 1891.

'Hegel's Theory of Punishment', *International Journal of Ethics*, vol. 6 (1896), no. 4, pp. 479–502.

'Hegel's Treatment of the Categories of the Subjective Notion I', *Mind*, vol. 6 (1897), no. 22, pp. 164–81.

'Hegel's Treatment of the Categories of the Subjective Notion II', *Mind*, vol. 6 (1897), no. 23, pp. 342–58.

'The Conception of Society as an Organism', *International Journal of Ethics*, vol. 7 (1897), no. 4, pp. 414–34.

Review, 'J. Watson, *Christianity and Idealism*', *International Journal of Ethics*, vol. 8 (1897), no. 1, pp. 123–4.

'Introduction to the Study of Philosophy'. McTaggart's personal notes of the course of Friday evening lectures held at Trinity College, Cambridge from 1899 to 1924.

'Hegel's Treatment of the Categories of the Objective Notion', *Mind*, vol. 8 (1899), no. 29, pp. 35–62.

'Hegel's Treatment of the Categories of the Idea', *Mind*, vol. 9 (1900), no. 34, pp. 145–83.

Critical Notice, 'J. Royce, *The World of the Individual, First Series*', *Mind*, vol. 9 (1900), no. 34, pp. 258–66.

Review, 'W. R. Inge, *Christian Mysticism*', *International Journal of Ethics*, vol. 10 (1900), no. 4, pp. 535–6.

Studies in Hegelian Cosmology (Cambridge University Press, 1901), 2nd ed., 1918, 293pp.

Review, 'H. H. Joachim, *A Study of the Ethics of Spinoza*', *International Journal of Ethics*, vol. 12 (1902), no. 4, pp. 517–20.

Critical Notice, 'G. H. Howison, *The Limits of Evolution and Other Essays Illustrating the Metaphysical Theory of Personal Idealism*', *Mind*, vol. 11 (1902), no. 43, pp. 383–9.

'Hegel's Treatment of the Categories of Quality', *Mind*, vol. 11 (1902), no. 44, pp. 503–26.

Critical Notice, 'J. Royce, *The World of the Individual, Second Series*', *Mind*, vol. 11 (1902), no. 44, pp. 557–63.

'Some Considerations Relating to Human Immortality', *International Journal of Ethics*, vol. 13 (1903), no. 2, pp. 152–71.

Review, 'F. R. Tenant, *The Origin and Propagation of Sin*', *International Journal of Ethics*, vol. 14 (1903), no. 1, pp. 128–31.

'Hegel's Treatment of the Categories of Quantity', *Mind*, vol. 13 (1904), no. 50, pp. 180–203.

Review, 'R. Adamson, *The Development of Modern Philosophy*', *International Journal of Ethics*, vol. 14 (1904), no. 3, pp. 394–5.

'Human Pre-existence', *International Journal of Ethics*, vol. 15 (1904), no. 1, pp. 83–95.

Review, 'P. S. Tattvabhushan et al., *Aspects of the Vedanta*', *International Journal of Ethics*, vol. 15 (1904), no. 1, pp. 124–5.

Some Dogmas of Religion (London, Edward Arnold, 1906), 2nd ed. (with an introduction by C. D. Broad and including a list of McTaggart's emendations extracted by S. V. Keeling), 1930, 299pp.

Critical Notice, 'A. T. Ormond, *Concepts of Philosophy*', *Mind*, vol. 16 (1907), no. 63, pp. 431–6.

Review, 'E. Westermarck, *The Origin and Development of Moral Ideas*, vol. 1', *International Journal of Ethics*, vol. 17 (1906), no. 1, pp. 125–8.

'The Relation of Time and Eternity'. Address delivered to the Philosophical Union of the University of California, 23 August 1907. *University of California Chronicle*, vol. 10 (1908), no. 2, pp. 127–52. Reprinted as a pamphlet (Berkeley University Press, 1908), 28pp. Reprinted in *Mind*, vol. 18 (1909), no. 71, pp. 343–62.

'The Individualism of Value', *International Journal of Ethics*, vol. 18 (1908), no. 4, pp. 433–45.

'The Unreality of Time', *Mind*, vol. 17 (1908), no. 68, pp. 457–74. Forms the basis of chap. 33, *The Nature of Existence*, vol. 2.

Critical Notice, 'W. James, *Pragmatism, a New Name for some Old Ways of Thinking; Popular Lectures on Philosophy*', *Mind*, vol. 17 (1908), no. 65, pp. 104–109.

'Mysticism', *The New Quarterly*, vol. 2 (1909), no. 7, pp. 315–39.

Review, 'E. Westermarck, *The Origin and Development of Moral Ideas*, vol. 2', *International Journal of Ethics*, vol. 20 (1909), no. 1, pp. 94–9.

Dare to be Wise. Address delivered to the 'Heretics' Society in Cambridge, 8 December 1909 (London, Watts and Co. (for The Rationalist Press Association), 1910), 9pp.

Commentary on Hegel's Logic (Cambridge University Press, 1910), 311pp.

Review, 'Hegel, *Grundlinien der Philosophie des Rechts*, G. Lasson (ed.)', *International Journal of Ethics*, vol. 22 (1912), no. 4, p. 480.

Critical Notice, 'B. Bosanquet, *The Principle of Individuality and Value: the Gifford Lectures for 1911*', *Mind*, vol. 21 (1912), no. 83, pp. 416–27.

Human Immortality and Pre-Existence (London, Edward Arnold, 1915), 119pp. Reprint of chaps. 3–4 of *Some Dogmas of Religion.*

'The Meaning of Causality'. The Henry Sidgwick Memorial Lecture, delivered at Newnham College, Cambridge, 1914. *Mind*, vol. 24 (1915), no. 95, pp. 326–44.

'Personality', *Encyclopaedia of Religion and Ethics*, ed. J. Hastings (Edinburgh, T. and T. Clark, 1917), vol. 9, pp. 773–81.

The Nature of Existence, vol. 1 (Cambridge University Press, 1921), 309pp. Reprinted 1968 and 1988, 330pp.

'Immortality and Monadistic Idealism', *The Monist*, vol. 31 (1921), no. 2, pp. 316–17.

'Propositions Applicable to Themselves', *Mind*, vol. 32 (1923), no. 128, pp. 462–4.

Critical Notice, 'A. S. Pringle-Pattison, *The Idea of Immortality*', *Mind*, vol. 32 (1923), no. 126, pp. 220–24.

'An Ontological Idealism', *Contemporary British Philosophy*, 1st Series, ed. J. H. Muirhead (London, George Allen and Unwin, 1924), pp. 251–69.

The Nature of Existence, vol. 2, ed. C. D. Broad (Cambridge University Press, 1927), 479pp. Reprinted 1968 and 1988, 526pp.

Philosophical Studies, edited and introduced by S. V. Keeling (London, Edward Arnold, 1934), 292pp. Reprinted with a foreword by Gerald Rochelle (Bristol, Thoemmes Press, 1996).

PREFACE

The first chapter of this book is based upon an article entitled 'The Necessity of Dogma' which appeared in the *International Journal of Ethics* (Jan., 1895). The third and fourth chapters appeared in the same magazine (Jan., 1903, and Oct., 1904), but have been rewritten and considerably altered. Part of the second chapter appeared in the *Hibbert Journal* for Oct., 1905, but this also has been rewritten.

I am much indebted to Mr. G. L. Dickinson of King's College, to Mr. G. E. Moore of Trinity College, and to my wife, for their kindness in reading this book in MS. and suggesting many valuable alterations. To Mr. Moore, in particular, I owe the deepest gratitude for criticisms which revealed—and, I trust, enabled me to correct—many lurking errors.

Trinity College, Cambridge,
January, 1906.

TABLE OF CONTENTS

CHAPTER I

THE IMPORTANCE OF DOGMA

A

B

C

CHAPTER II

THE ESTABLISHMENT OF DOGMA

A

B

C

CHAPTER III

HUMAN IMMORTALITY

CHAPTER IV

HUMAN PRE-EXISTENCE

CHAPTER V

FREE WILL

A

B

CHAPTER VI

GOD AS OMNIPOTENT

CHAPTER VII

A NON-OMNIPOTENT GOD

SECT. B PAGE

CHAPTER VIII

THEISM AND HAPPINESS

CONCLUSION

INTRODUCTION

JOHN McTAGGART ELLIS McTAGGART was born in 1866, and educated at Clifton and Trinity College, Cambridge. In 1888 he was placed alone in the first class of the Moral Sciences Tripos. In 1890 he became President of the Union Society. He was elected to a prize-fellowship at Trinity in 1891. Soon after this he paid a long visit to New Zealand. In 1899 he married Miss Margaret Elizabeth Bird of Taranaki. In 1897 he was made College Lecturer in the Moral Sciences, an office which he held until 1923. He then retired, after completing his twenty-five years' service, apparently in perfect health and certainly at the height of his intellectual powers. He still continued to give some of his former courses of lectures, but his main philosophical work after his retirement was the preparation of the third draft of the second volume of his *Nature of Existence.* Beside these professional labours he gave valuable help to Trinity by his active membership of the committee which drew up the new college statutes rendered necessary by the changes which the Royal Commission had imposed on the university and the colleges.

In January. 1925 McTaggart and his wife were taking a holiday in London. He was seeing many of his old friends, and was to all appearance in the best of health and spirits when he was suddenly stricken down. After a short but painful illness, borne with admirable courage and patience, he died on 18th January, 1925, in a nursing home in London at the age of 58; passing, as he firmly believed, to the next stage in the long but finite journey from the illusion of time to the reality of eternal life. He must, it seems, have been suffering for some years from a weakness of the heart, unsuspected by himself or his friends. It was characteristic of him that he left minute instructions for his funeral and for the disposition of his letters, papers, and manuscripts. In accordance with his wishes, his body was cremated; and, instead of the customary religious service, a favourite passage from Spinoza's *Ethics* was read by one of his oldest friends. This passage—*Homo liber de nulla re minus quam de morte cogitat; et eius sapientia non mortis, sed vitae meditatio est*—is engraved on his memorial brass in the ante-chapel of Trinity, which has been fitly placed beside those of his teachers, Sidgwick and Ward. On this brass is an admirable Latin inscription, composed by an old friend who is an eminent classical scholar. At McTaggart's request no specifically Christian symbol or sentiment appears.

McTaggart's life was spent in the service of philosophy, and it is fitting to begin with an account of his philosophical works. While he lived he published the following books: *Studies in Hegelian Dialectic*, *Studies in Hegelian Cosmology*, *Some Dogmas of Religion*, *A Commentary to Hegel's Logic*, and the first volume of *The Nature of Existence.* At the time of his death he had completed the second draft of the remaining volume of *The Nature of Existence* and was engaged in writing the third draft. This volume has been published recently; from the third draft, so far as that goes, and thenceforward from the second.

McTaggart was an extremely careful and conscientious writer and thinker. All his published works had been completely rewritten several times before being sent to the press, and the earlier drafts were submitted to his friends for criticism in respect of logical rigour and literary form. It might have been feared that so much elaboration would lead to a heavy and lifeless production. This is certainly not so with McTaggart, who must plainly be ranked with Hobbes, Berkeley, and Hume among the masters of English philosophical prose. His style is pellucidly clear, yet he never ignores a qualification or over-simplifies a subject for the sake of literary elegance. When he asserts a proposition he generally foresees, emphasizes, and tries to answer the objections which can reasonably be made to it. In this respect he resembles Sidgwick. But Sidgwick's writing, though always clear and dignified, is somewhat heavy; the reader of his works is always enlightened, often elevated, seldom excited, and never amused. There are, e.g., few abler or more conspicuously honest books than Sidgwick's *Methods of Ethics*; yet, after several careful readings of it, one is ashamed to find how little one has remembered of the details. McTaggart, though he never strained after humour or strewed his writings with epigrams, achieved both often enough to lighten the burden of a difficult argument, to fix a doctrine in the reader's mind by an apt illustration, and to deflate a pretentious fallacy by a pointed thrust. The abstractness and complexity of the subjects with which he dealt, and the thoroughness with which he treated them, prevent his books from being easy reading. But, unlike his master Hegel and too many of Hegel's followers, he never added to the intrinsic difficulties of a subject by confused thinking or cloudy metaphorical writing. To McTaggart Hegel played the part of the drunken Helot, whose awful literary example helped to preserve and refine the crystalline clearness of his own style. At times McTaggart's writing rises to heights of intense emotion and great beauty, which are all the more impressive from their rarity and their restraint.

McTaggart's publications fall into three quite distinct, but closely connected groups. The first consists of his three books about Hegelianism. The second contains one work only, viz., *Some Dogmas of Religion*. This is the only book which McTaggart wrote for the educated amateur, as distinct from the trained philosophical specialist. The third comprises the two volumes on the *Nature of Existence*, in which he expounds his own system of constructive metaphysics by his own methods. Something will now be said about each of these three groups in turn.

McTaggart's character combined, as will appear in more detail later in this sketch, many apparently inconsistent features. Perhaps there is nothing at first sight more paradoxical about him than the fact that so much of his life should have been devoted to the study and exposition of Hegel's philosophy. If the style be the man, no two men could have had less in common than Hegel, with his vile technical jargon and his constant abuse of metaphor and verbal ambiguity, and McTaggart, with his short, clear, direct sentences, and his lawyer-like determination to make every clause completely 'water-tight'. If Hegel be the inspired, and too often incoherent, prophet of the Absolute; and if Bradley be its chivalrous knight, ready to challenge all who dare to question its pre-eminence; McTaggart is its devoted and extremely astute family solicitor.

Moreover, Hegel was unlike McTaggart in his merits as well as in his defects. Hegel's strongest point is the comprehensive and intimate acquaintance with science, mathematics, history, law, art, social institutions, and religion, which forms the background of his writings. This gives them a solidity which is impressive even to readers who detest his style and can see nothing but verbal jugglery in his arguments. Such a background is lacking in McTaggart's works. It is of course obvious that he has a wide knowledge and a discriminating appreciation of English literature, and that he felt the interest of a cultured amateur in certain small sections of English history. But he knew little or nothing of science or mathematics, and no more of the classics than he had acquired with pain and disgust at Clifton, whilst he viewed the claims of history to be a serious subject with an amused contempt which some of his colleagues found hard to bear.

Again, McTaggart, in theory at least, was a strong individualist. According to him, social institutions are simply means to the welfare of their members; church and state and family are no more to be regarded as ends than the drainage system or the underground railways. Nothing could be less like Hegel's view. It may, however, fairly be doubted whether the intense emotions of loyalty and patriotism which McTaggart felt towards certain societies, e.g., towards Clifton, Trinity, and England, could possibly have been justified on his own theory, or could have existed unless he had unwittingly thought, felt, and acted in accordance with a view not very different from Hegel's. Closely connected with the difference of emphasis which has just been mentioned is another difference, of profound importance, which was recognized by McTaggart. It is plain that McTaggart's two fundamental convictions were that man is immortal, and that the love of one man for another is of infinite value and profound metaphysical significance. Now he admits that Hegel took so little interest in immortality as hardly to mention it in the course of his voluminous writings. And he admits that there is only one passage, viz., in the account of the *Kingdom of the Holy Ghost* in the *Philosophy of Religion*, in which Hegel seems to ascribe any deep metaphysical importance to love; and, even there it is doubtful whether he means by 'love' what McTaggart meant by it.

Nor do the differences between the two philosophers end even here. Hegel often makes it an objection to other forms of philosophy that they move at the level of Understanding; e.g., that they enunciate a number of alternatives, which are assumed to be severally self-contained, mutually exclusive, and collectively exhaustive, and that they then proceed to knock down all but one of these and to embrace the sole survivor. As against this he holds that philosophy should use Reason, which shows how a number of alternatives that seem to be exclusive and self-subsistent are really but so many different aspects of a single more concrete category. Now, although McTaggart, in discussing Hegel's method, accepts this doctrine, it must be confessed that he paid but little heed to it in his own philosophizing. He is rather conspicuously a devotee of the method of the Understanding, with its characteristic merits and defects; and, if he has a fault, it is a tendency to withdraw his eye from the facts themselves, and to indulge in extremely clever forensic 'logic-chopping' with verbal expressions and uncriticized categories.

Had McTaggart anything in common with Hegel? In temperament they shared one fundamental characteristic. Each consisted of a mystic, kept in perfect control by a sound common-sense citizen of great practical ability who loved order and decency and hated sentimentality and high-flown nonsense of every kind. It is safe to say that McTaggart would have disliked the German romantics of Hegel's time as much as Hegel himself did, and that Hegel would have shared McTaggart's contempt for teetotallers, Nonconformists, pacifists, Irish and Indian Nationalists, and the Labour Party. Now a kind of sentimental and muddle-headed admiration for 'rebels' and 'rebellion', as such, was common form among the comfortably placed bourgeois intellectuals who formed the societies in which Hegel and McTaggart lived. It is natural that both men should have reacted against it. And it is natural that both should often have carried the outward expression of this reaction to extremes which they might have found it hard to justify. Beyond this resemblance the master and the disciple seem to have almost nothing in common except the conviction that the universe is at bottom a spiritual system, and that human reason is competent to discover and to prove many important and paradoxical conclusions about it without the aid of special empirical investigation.

Suppose the following problem in psychology had been propounded: 'Take an eighteenth-century English Whig. Let him be a mystic. Endow him with the logical subtlety of the great schoolmen and their belief in the powers of human reason, with the business capacity of a successful lawyer, and with the lucidity of the best type of French mathematician. Inspire him (Heaven knows how) in early youth with a passion for Hegel. Then subject him to the teaching of Sidgwick and the continual influence of Moore and Russell. Set him to expound Hegel. What will be the result ? Hegel himself could not have answered this question *a priori*, but the course of world-history has solved it *ambulando* by producing McTaggart. It is natural then that McTaggart's interpretation of Hegel should differ greatly from that of other commentators, and that it should often be hard to believe that Hegel had ever imagined, or would have accepted, the doctrines which McTaggart ascribed to him. If McTaggart be challenged on any particular detail he can generally quote one or more almost unintelligible sentences from Hegel, and can triumphantly show that they are capable of bearing the surprising and ingenious interpretation which he has put upon them. And, against critics or rival interpreters of Hegel, he can generally quote passages which are immune to their criticisms and inconsistent with their interpretations. And yet, if McTaggart's account of Hegelianism be taken as a whole and compared with Hegel's writings as a whole, the impression produced is one of profound unlikeness. ' Whatever Hegel may have meant ', the reader says to himself, ' it surely cannot have been this.' 'And,' he hastens to add, ' it was probably nothing nearly so sensible or plausible as this.' If we compare McTaggart with the other commentators on Hegel we must admit that he has at least produced an extremely lively and fascinating rabbit from the Hegelian hat, whilst they have produced nothing but consumptive and gibbering chimeras. And we shall admire his resource and dexterity all the more when we reflect that the rabbit was, in all probability, never inside the hat, whilst the chimeras perhaps were.

McTaggart's first book, *Studies in Hegelian Dialectic*, is an enlargement of the dissertation on which he was awarded his fellowship at Trinity. In it he tries to explain, and to defend against critics, the Dialectical Method, as used in passing from category to category within the *Logic*, and also the transition from the *Logic* as a whole, through *Nature*, to *Spirit*. His account of the Dialectical Method within the *Logic* is, in essence, the following. There is one and only one complete and self-subsisting category, viz., that which Hegel calls the *Absolute Idea*. All other categories are partial factors in the Absolute Idea. Every rational being has an implicit knowledge of the Absolute Idea ; but no human being starts with an explicit knowledge of it, or reaches such knowledge except by the Dialectical Method. If any category, other than the Absolute Idea, be supposed to express adequately the formal nature of Reality, our implicit knowledge of the Absolute Idea forces a certain complementary and opposed aspect of Reality on our attention. On further reflection a more concrete category is presented to our notice, in which these two complementary and opposed aspects are seen to be combined and reconciled with each other. We now try to regard this new category as adequately expressing the formal nature of Reality. The same process takes place as before. Thus we work gradually upward ; our still implicit knowledge of the Absolute Idea reacting at every step with the knowledge of it which has so far been made explicit, until at last all our knowledge of its dragged into the light of clear consciousness.

Assuming that McTaggart's explanation, qualifications, and admissions suffice to remove antecedent objections to the very *possibility* of Hegelianism, the question still remains whether *in fact* Hegel succeeded in passing dialectically from Pure Being to the Absolute Idea. This can be answered only by a detailed investigation into the *Logic* category by category. This McTaggart undertook in his *Commentary to Hegel's Logić*, a work of amazing patience and ingenuity for which all English students of Hegel are deeply indebted to him. The conclusions which he reached may be summed up as follows. Many of the transitions are valid, but several are invalid. Not only are there isolated failures; there are whole sets of categories such that the transitions into, within, and out of the set must be rejected. In the case of isolated failures, McTaggart often suggested an alternative of his own, which he thought would be valid and adequate; in the other cases he did not attempt this. But he records his conviction that Hegel's final result comes nearer to the truth than any other philosopher has reached, and that it could almost certainly be proved from Hegel's starting-point by the Dialectical Method, provided that suitable modifications were made at certain crucial points. The admitted break-down of Hegel's argument at certain points seemed the less serious to McTaggart because he had come to the conclusion, which he admits that Hegel had never contemplated and would probably have rejected, that there might be a number of alternative and equally valid dialectical paths from one category to another.

Studies in Hegelian Cosmology, which was published between the two works which have now been considered, is a series of essays in applied Hegelianism. To the general reader it is far the most entertaining of McTaggart's books on Hegel. Most of Hegel's English followers were interested mainly in his philosophical conclusions and his applications of them to politics, ethics, and religion. These they considered true and important, whilst they abandoned with a smile or a sigh, the Dialectical Method by which he had claimed to establish his conclusions. McTaggart used to call this 'Hegelianism with the proofs left out'. And, for his part, he took exactly the opposite view of Hegel's achievements. He thought that the Dialectical Method and the purely metaphysical results of it were valid and important, whilst he regarded all the concrete applications which had been made of Hegelianism as unjustified and most of them as positively false. Most of the essays in the *Hegelian Cosmology* fall into two classes, viz., those in which McTaggart tries to show that Hegelianism supports the doctrines that he wished to believe, and those in which he tries to show that it does not support the doctrines which other Hegelians wished to believe. In the positive part of the book McTaggart argued that, whatever Hegel himself may have held, his general principles, when fully worked out, imply that the Absolute is not a person but a perfect society of perfect and eternal persons each of whom is in love with one or more of the rest. Moreover, it is probable that each human mind, as it really is, is identical with one of these persons. If so, each of us in reality is eternal, and, *sub specie temporis*, our eternity will probably appear as persistence throughout the whole of time.

In reading the negative part of the book it is worth while to remember that the school of English Hegelianism which flourished during the latter part of the nineteenth century had, as a whole, certain characteristics which filled McTaggart, and would probably have filled Hegel, with an amused annoyance that was quite compatible with genuine respect for and friendship with many of its members. With a very few exceptions, of whom far the most notable was Bradley, it was (if we may say so with becoming submission) a paradise of pompous prigs. 'The sort of people', McTaggart would say, 'who wanted to believe that they ate a good dinner only in order to strengthen themselves to appreciate Dante.' The destructive part of *Hegelian Cosmology* is certainly written with this school and its special foibles in view; and, if a naughty desire to shock Bosanquet never led McTaggart to assert what he did not believe, it almost certainly did influence his choice of subjects, of examples, and of expressions. Thus McTaggart maintains that the state is a means and not an end; that the fact that the Kingdom of Heaven is a perfect society of intimately related persons gives us no guidance whatever in politics or ethics here and now; and that, although neither ethical nor psychological hedonism is true, the hedonic calculus is an adequate guide to conduct and is the only one available to us.

He also stresses every passage in which Hegel minimizes the importance of sin and treats it as a necessary stage in the advance from innocence to virtue. It was indeed his considered opinion that boys and undergraduates should be given ample opportunities to sin and be punished for it. There was no short cut to virtue, and the sins that they were tempted to commit, unlike those of older men, were seldom socially dangerous. Provided they were punished—and this was of course essential—society could afford to treat them as salutary and slightly amusing episodes like mumps or measles. It was in this connexion that McTaggart once formulated the principle that 'every undergraduate should be compelled to satisfy his tutor that he had been drunk at least once a year as a guarantee of good faith that he was not a teetotaller'.

The book ends with a very interesting expository essay in which McTaggart discusses the relations of Hegelianism to Christianity. He points out that, in spite of certain superficial likenesses, the differences are fundamental. And he concludes that, whilst Hegelianism is a most useful ally of Christianity against popular materialism and against Deism or Unitarianism, it is in the end the most dangerous rival that Christianity has ever had. For Hegelianism contains in a purified form, without mythology and without compromising historical associations, all that is true in the highest religion. The Hegelian comprehends, appreciates, and assigns its true place to Christianity among the manifestations of the human spirit, and, in so doing, sees through it and passes beyond it.

This essay forms a natural transition from McTaggart's books about Hegelianism to the present work, *Some Dogmas of Religion.* In many respects *Some Dogmas of Religion* is a model of popular philosophic writing. It presupposes no knowledge of philosophy; it is written with admirable clarity, and abounds with apt and amusing illustrations; and it deals with the problems which have interested almost all intelligent men in all ages. It has been out of print for some time, and second-hand copies of it have been difficult to find and expensive to buy. It therefore seemed highly desirable that a new edition should be printed, in order that students of philosophy and intelligent amateurs of the present generation might have the opportunity of procuring it for themselves at a reasonable price.

McTaggart defines a *dogma* as any proposition which has metaphysical significance, no matter whether it be accepted on metaphysical grounds or not. In the first chapter he argues that religion is impossible without dogmas, and defends this contention against apparent objections. In the second chapter he considers various grounds on which dogmas have been accepted. In this connexion he discusses (*a*) alleged immediate certainty, (*b*) general consent, (*c*) alleged miracles, (*d*) moral consequences, and (*e*) faith, as grounds for accepting religious dogmas. He concludes that none of these grounds is adequate, and that dogmas must be proved by ordinary reasoning from non-ethical premises if we are to have any right to believe them. There will still be plenty of room for the exercise of faith. For we shall need faith at many times to continue to believe the conclusions of our reasoning in the face of discouragement from within the apparent contradiction from without.

Perhaps the most interesting chapters in the book are those on *Human Immortality* and *Human Pre-existence.* McTaggart does not here attempt to *prove* human survival of bodily death. He held that positive arguments for immortality must come from metaphysics; and he claimed to supply such a proof, on Hegelian lines in the *Cosmology*, and in another and quite original way in the *Nature of Existence.* He took little interest in Psychical Research; holding that, even if the alleged results were certain and were incapable of a normal explanation, they would still be susceptible of so many alternative supernormal explanations as to add very little force to the probability of survival and none at all to that of immortality. What McTaggart claims to show here is simply that the antecedent objections to human survival, drawn from common sense and natural science, are quite baseless. In this connexion he takes an extremely Berkeleian view of matter, going so far as to say that the independent existence of matter is ' a bare possibility to which it would be foolish to attach the slightest importance '. It follows from McTaggart's arguments in his other works that the existence of each of us, *sub specie temporis*, will occupy the whole of time. He held it to be most likely that this existence will be split up into a series of many successive lives, each beginning with a birth and ending with a death. Here he takes this as an hypothesis; defends it against the more obvious difficulties; and claims that it would explain many well-known facts, such as love at first sight, and some men's innate capacity for activities which others acquire, if at all, late in life and with great pains. He tries to show that loss of memory of our previous lives would not make this kind of survival worthless, and would be, in some respects, a positive advantage.

In Chapter V McTaggart discusses the ancient problem of Free-Will and Determination. He begins by pointing out four important senses of " Freedom " in which it is compatible with complete Determinism. The rest of the chapter is devoted to the fifth meaning, viz., Indeterminism. He argues that the reality of this is not proved by the so-called " feeling of freedom ", nor by the fact that we are often unable to discover all the determininants of our decisions. Again, he contends that Determinism is compatible with the fact of moral responsibility and with the validity of our judgments of obligation. He then proceeds to attack Indeterminism directly. If it were true, he thinks, we should not be justified in making even probable conjectures as to what anyone would be likely to do in any circumstances. Moreover, we should never be justified in passing moral judgments on a man's *character* as distinct from his separate *actions*. The result is that no kind of punishment, except purely vindictive punishments which were precisely contemporary with the acts for which they were inflicted, could be justified.

McTaggart's discussion of this subject appears to me, I must confess, to be very thin and wire-drawn. All that he says is clear and acute, but one feels that the real question at issue slips through the meshes of his dialectic. Much the same criticism must be made on his treatment of Divine Omnipotence, which occupies Chapters VI and VII. He insists that "Omnipotence" must be understood to include the power of performing contradictions; if God be limited by the laws of logic, he cannot be omnipotent. Naturally McTaggart has little difficulty of making the doctrine of Divine Omnipotence, so interpreted, look extremely ridiculous. But the reader is left wondering whether it was worth while to lavish so much criticism and expend so much moral indignation on a doctrine which has never been held by any theologian or philosopher of repute. In Chapter VII McTaggart discusses the notions (i) of a creative but non-omnipotent God, and (ii) of a non-creative and non-omnipotent God.

McTaggart's conclusions in Chapter VII are roughly as follows. It would be impossible to ascribe perfect goodness to a being who had created the actual world. For the power of a creative being would have too few limitations to excuse him for creating a world with so much evil in it. On the other hand the moral character of a non-omnipotent and non-creative, but very wise and powerful, God could be defended. If matter really existed the traces of order which we find in the world would afford a fairly strong, though not absolutely conclusive, argument for the existence of such a being. But, if what appears to us as matter be really minds, and if these minds be so interconnected as to form a spiritual community, there is no need to postulate such an external cause of the order which we find in nature. The existence of such a God would still remain a possibility, and the only reason against believing in it is that there is no reason for doing so. McTaggart's atheism becomes still more definite in the *Nature of Existence*, where he shows that the structure of reality, as determined by him, is incompatible with the existence of either a creative or a controlling self, though it is compatible with the existence of a self which *appears* to control the rest of the universe.

There can be no doubt that McTaggart's greatest achievement is his last book, *The Nature of Existence*. It is the less necessary to give a detailed account of it as McTaggart himself has given an admirable synopsis in his contribution to *Contemporary British Philosophy*, vol. i. The work forms a complete deductive system of *a priori* metaphysics on the grand scale, and may quite fairly be compared with the *Enneads* of Plotinus, the *Ethics* of Spinoza, and the *Encyclopaedia* of Hegel. In English philosophical literature it occupies a unique position. One other Englishman, Professor Alexander, has indeed thought out and written down a highly comprehensive and original theory of the universe; but the distinguished author of *Space, Time, and Deity* would not count his work, nor wish it to be counted, as a deductive system with the smallest possible number of empirical premises.

McTaggart at one time had meant to write a new dialectic, and the original title of the book was *The Dialectic of Existence*. But, although he continued to hold that the dialectical method of argument is valid, he wisely decided in the end to use straightforward deduction in building up his own system. It will be worth while to indicate the logical peculiarities of McTaggart's general method, and the degree of certainty which he attached to his various conclusions. The premises of the first volume fall into three classes; viz., (i) axioms, i.e., propositions which are, and can be seen to be, intrinsically necessary; (ii) contingent propositions which are rendered completely certain by perception; and

(iii) a peculiar class of propositions, the description of which may be deferred for the moment. Only two premises of the second class are used, viz., that something exists, and that there is more than one substance. And the latter of these is not really needed, for it is entailed by the former together with one of the axioms. The argument now proceeds, using only premises of the first two classes, and therefore reaching conclusions which are absolutely certain if no mistake has been made, until it reaches the crucial point of the whole system. The crucial point is the following. McTaggart regards it as self-evident that every substance must consist of parts which are themselves substances. Now this axiom, when combined with certain propositions about substance which he has deduced from other axioms, threatens to lead to a complete contradiction. The deadlock can be avoided on one and only one condition. The proposition which asserts that this condition is fulfilled must therefore be accepted, though it is neither a self-evidently necessary proposition nor a contingent proposition which is guaranteed by perception. It is called the *Principle of Determining Correspondence*, and it is the only member of the third class of premises. The remaining conclusions of the first volume are certain, provided that no mistake has been made, except for the possibility that the Principle of Determining Correspondence may not be the only way of avoiding the conflict between the axiom of endless divisibility of substance and the deductions from the other axioms.

In the second volume the world as it appears to us here and now is viewed in the light of the conclusions of the first volume. The results are partly negative and partly positive. The negative conclusions are certain, for any apparent feature of the existent which would be incompatible with its nature, as determined in Volume I, must necessarily be delusive. Tried by these tests the characteristics of being spatial, being material, being a sensum, being a judgment, being a supposition, and many other apparent characteristics physical and psychical, are found wanting and are rejected as delusive. The delusiveness of temporal characteristics is supposed to be established independently by an argument of great ingenuity which McTaggart had published some years before in *Mind*. It will be seen that the negative aspects of McTaggart's system are much more startling than those of most idealists. On his view, not only do we radically misperceive all that we perceive by our senses, we also radically misperceive ourselves and our mental processes when we introspect. Nevertheless, McTaggart holds, and tries to prove, that, although introspection is thus largely misleading, it is an act of direct acquaintance with *oneself* and not merely with certain mental events or processes which belong to oneself.

The positive results of the second volume are admittedly only probable, though McTaggart thinks that their probability is very high indeed. The general line of argument is as follows. It has been proved in Volume I that the universe must consist of a certain set of substances called *Primary Parts*, each of which is divisible into parts within parts without end. These must be interrelated in certain complicated ways in order to answer the requirements of the Principle of Determining Correspondence. Does our everyday experience present us with any things that might reasonably be identified with these Primary Parts ? McTaggart's answer is that the required conditions could be fulfilled if each Primary Part were a mind whose whole content was its perceptions of itself, of certain other minds, of its own perceptions, and of their perceptions.

In addition it must be assumed that a perception of any part of a whole is *ipso facto* a part of a perception of that whole. A system composed of such minds would fulfil the necessary conditions, and we cannot imagine any other kind of system that would fulfil them. Now it must be admitted that our minds, as they appear to us in introspection, do not appear to have all these characteristics, and do appear to have some which are incompatible with these. But we already know that introspection must largely misrepresent the nature of our minds and their processes to us. So it is quite likely that each human mind, as it really is, is one of the Primary Parts of the universe. It is from this that McTaggart infers that each human mind is really eternal, and must appear, *sub specie temporis*, as persisting throughout the whole of time. And it is from the intimate cognitive relations which must subsist between the Primary Parts of the universe, if these be minds, that he infers that every mind, as it really is, must be in love with one or more others to a degree which we can at present only dimly imagine.

Love, according to McTaggart, is the fundamental emotion; and by 'love' he means, not philanthropy or benevolence, but that passionate personal affection which none of us in this life can feel towards more than a very few persons. No philosopher but Plato has treated love so seriously, has analysed it so carefully, or has written about it so eloquently as McTaggart. Yet there is a profound difference between the two philosophers on this point. For Plato the love of a man for his friend is only a stepping stone by which the soul rises to the contemplation and love of the Idea of the Good. For McTaggart it is the one supremely valuable thing in the universe; it cannot be a step towards something higher, for there is nothing above it.

Now, when McTaggart seeks to combine the positive and the negative parts of his doctrine, he is brought face to face with the ghost which haunts every system of Absolute Idealism. This is the seemingly hopeless conflict between the error which must exist if the negative results be accepted and the perfection which must exist if the positive results be accepted. Perhaps the finest part of the whole work is the transparent honesty with which McTaggart states and emphasizes this problem, and the heroic effort which he makes to solve it in detail.

Hegel brushes it aside with the magnificent epigram: '*Die Vollführung des unendlichen Zwecks ist so nur die Taüschung aufzuheben als ob er noch nicht vollführt sei*'; McTaggart accepted the spirit of this epigram and tried to show how it could be realized without contradiction. It is impossible here to do more than mention that, on McTaggart's view, all other misperception is bound up with the misperception of the world as being in time. His solution, if valid, would provide an answer to the two fundamental problems which all other systems of Absolute Idealism have shirked: 'How can a timeless and changeless reality appear to endure and to change?' and 'How can the perfect parts of a perfect whole misperceive it and themselves as imperfect?'

The reputation of books and their writers with posterity depends on so many unforeseeable conditions that no prudent person will risk a prophecy on such a subject. Deductive systems of speculative philosophy are at present out of fashion, and it may be that the human intellect has been so disheartened by past failures and is now so preoccupied with the methods and results of the natural sciences that it will never again take much interest in attempts to solve the riddles of the universe by deductive reasoning from *a priori* premises. But this at least may be said. The system expounded in the *Nature of Existence* is equal in scope and originality to any of the great historical systems of European philosophy, whilst in clearness of statement and cogency of argument it far surpasses them all. If subtle analysis, rigid reasoning, and constructive fertility, applied with tireless patience to the hardest and deepest problems of metaphysics, and expressed in language which always enlightens the intellect and sometimes touches the emotions, be a title to philosophical immortality, then McTaggart has fully earned his place among the immortals by his *Nature of Existence*.

It remains to say something of McTaggart as a

teacher and as a man. His teaching work in Trinity consisted mainly of lecturing. It has happily never been the custom of Cambridge to exhaust and sterilize its dons by sacrificing the best part of their lives to the drudgery of hearing and criticizing undergraduates' essays, and in McTaggart's time the duties of a college lecturer included even less of such work than they do at present. McTaggart was an admirable lecturer; he loved the work, and he gave many courses. His normal stint consisted of three courses of lectures for the Tripos, each of which went on throughout the three terms of the academic year. Each course consisted of two hours a week of actual lecturing, and a third hour of discussion. In addition he usually gave an advanced course of an hour a week, called *Problems of Philosophy.* In this he would generally take some important philosophical book that had lately appeared and would discuss it with the class. Moreover, for many years he gave a course of introductory lectures, one on each Friday evening of term, to members of the university and of the women's colleges who were not studying philosophy. It is a grave defect in the curriculum of Cambridge that the study of philosophy is confined to a few specialists, and that the vast majority of undergraduates go through their whole university career without suspecting the existence of such a subject. McTaggart's popular lectures were meant to do something towards meeting this defect. They were brilliantly successful, and it is quite certain that they implanted in a fair proportion of his listeners a lifelong interest in philosophy. So fond was McTaggart of lecturing that, even after he retired, he continued, by agreement with his successor, to deliver his courses on the *General History of Modern Philosophy* and the *Problems of Philosophy* as well as the popular lectures.

McTaggart was a highly peripatetic philosopher, and must have walked many miles in his lecture-room whilst conducting his pupils from Descartes to Hegel and from Pure Being to the Absolute Idea.

The smaller lecture-rooms at Trinity, now gay with green paint and brightened by the portraits of eminent Victorians which the fastidious taste of a later age has rejected from Hall, resembled in McTaggart's time the more neglected kind of family vault. Here he lectured to small but select classes, consuming at each lecture in successive sips a tumbler of cold water provided by the college. At intervals a representative of the College Office, known as a 'marker', would appear for a moment silently and suddenly at the door, armed with a list, and, after looking severely round at the audience and the lecturer, would as suddenly and silently vanish. It was never known what he suspected, or whether his suspicions were confirmed or allayed. These gloomy and even sinister surroundings were enlivened by McTaggart's verbal wit and the happy oddity of his illustrations. Phoenixes, dragons, griffins, rocs, and unicorns, indeed most of the fauna of heraldry and mythology, formed the staple subjects of his examples, and were imagined in situations in which one would have been greatly surprised to meet them.

McTaggart was better as a formal lecturer than as the conductor of a conversation-class, and he was better in lecturing on metaphysics than on the history of philosophy. In a conversation-class he was too apt to confute a questioner with a few pungent phrases and there leave the matter, instead of trying to draw him out and discover what, if anything, lay behind his question. Thus the conversation-classes were liable to dwindle into an uncomfortable silence after the first twenty minutes or so. Much the same criticism must be made on McTaggart's treatment of the great historical thinkers up to Hegel. Their fallacies and confusions were remorselessly exposed, as by an extremely able public prosecutor, and they left the witness-box with their reputations apparently ruined for ever. Yet the audience was left with the impression that they had hardly had a fair run for their money, and that, if they had been lucky enough to secure McTaggart as counsel for the defence, they might at worst have been dismissed with a caution. This impression was confirmed by the very different fate which befell Hegel when his turn came. In his case McTaggart lavished incredible patience and ingenuity to find a sensible meaning for the seemingly unintelligible and a plausible reconciliation for the seemingly inconsistent.

Though these were real defects, the undergraduates who attended McTaggart's lectures or wrote essays for him could not fail to be interested, instructed, and immensely impressed. Perhaps McTaggart never made a disciple, and certainly he never tried to. But on those undergraduates who worked with him he exercised the powerful formative influence of good example, the only kind of influence which can be exerted without impertinence and accepted without indignity. They learnt from a master of rigid reasoning and lucid writing how difficult it is to avoid, and how important it is to detect, logical fallacies and verbal ambiguities. They learnt how hard it is to *prove* or to *disprove* anything, by seeing that most of the arguments by which great philosophers have claimed to establish or refute propositions in fact do little more than slightly to raise or slightly to lower their probabilities. Insensibly their intellectual standards were exalted and refined, until slovenly thinking and loose rhetorical writing in themselves or in others began to evoke the same reaction of disgust as dirty finger-nails or bad table-manners or a Cockney accent. It must be added that the tendency to 'score off' a questioner, which was liable to manifest itself in the publicity of a conversation-class, was completely in abeyance when McTaggart dealt individually with his pupils in the privacy of his own rooms. Under the latter conditions, not only they, but many strangers who had no claim on his time or attention except an interest in the problems of philosophy, found him sympathetic helpful, and wonderfully patient.

McTaggart's character was original and very strongly marked. Perhaps his fundamental emotions were loyalty to his friends and devotion to certain societies of which he was a member. He could forgive any fault in a beloved individual except lukewarmness or opposition to the purposes of a beloved society. This made the war of 1914 to 1918 a particularly tragic event in McTaggart's life. He was passionately patriotic ; and he fully accepted at the time, and continued to accept to the day of his death, the view that the Allies were wholly right and the Central Powers wholly wrong. To some of his most intimate friends this view seemed both antecedently incredible and in conflict with known facts ; and they felt just as passionately that it was their duty, at a time when calm reason seemed likely to succumb to blind passion, to incur unpopularity by publicly stating and reiterating the other side of the case. Feelings were too deeply moved for either side to display that tact and forbearance which both would have shown under happier circumstances. The clash that ensued was a true tragedy in Hegel's sense, 'a conflict of right with right' ; and, in it, wounds were given and received which, in some cases never healed. It would be impertinent to pursue this matter further ; but this at least may be said. McTaggart's love of England was no arm-chair patriotism. Any one who knew him must acknowledge that he would willingly have died for his country; and he served it during the war in such ways as were open to a man of his age and physique, up to and beyond the limit of his powers.

The three societies to which McTaggart felt the strongest emotions of loyalty were Clifton, Trinity, and England. It would not be unfair to say that he regarded the Absolute as the heavenly pattern of which these were the least imperfect earthly copies. It was never his lot to take any public part in the affairs of England, but he was an assiduous and valuable member of the governing body of Clifton, and he played an active role on the College Council of

Trinity. The popular conception of a philosopher as a child in practical affairs has never gained much support from the facts of real life; the examples of Mill, Hume, Locke, Leibniz, and Plato are enough to refute it, and to them McTaggart must certainly be added. He was an admirable man of business, cool, cautious, and methodical, both in his own affairs and in those of the societies of which he was a member. Any one who had to make a difficult practical decision and needed advice, could hardly do better than to state his case to McTaggart and be guided by him.

McTaggart combined a number of opinions which, though logically consistent with each other, are seldom held by the same person. In the case of most of his contemporaries at Cambridge a knowledge of a small number of their principles or prejudices enabled one to infer all the rest with a fair degree of certainty. This was far from being so with McTaggart, who unwittingly exemplified Bergsonian principles by performing actions and expressing opinions which were incalculable before the event but rationally explicable after it. He added greatly to the gaiety of college meetings; for he was always liable either to use arguments which every one accepted to support conclusions which no one else had thought of, or to support conclusions that every one accepted by arguments which had occured to no one else.

As an illustration of an unusual combination of opinions one may mention the fact that he was an atheist, a firm believer in immortality, and a strong supporter of the Church of England against both popish and protestant dissent. Most of his views on church and state are explicable by the fact that he was in the main an admirable example of that most admirable, but now unhappily rare thing, an Erastian Whig. His defence of church establishment was stated in his early years in a famous speech at the Union, which caused acute embarrassment to most of its supporters; and this remained his view up to the end. An established church is desirable for two reasons. In the first place, it makes for freedom of thought *within* the church, for the limits of permissible theological divergence are ultimately settled by lay lawyers on purely secular grounds. And, secondly, it makes for freedom *outside* the church, for the jealousy which dissenting Christians feel towards the Establishment prevents them from uniting with it to persecute non-Christian opinions. McTaggart supported this deductive conclusion by examples drawn from the United States and the Colonies.

His Whiggism was shown again in his extreme constitutionalism. Antecedently it might have been supposed that he would have sympathized with the Fascist revolution in Italy. But actually he held that Fascism and Bolshevism are two sides of the same medal (a medal which, it would have been unkind to remind him, was struck by Hegel) and that he could not consistently bless the former whilst cursing, as he very heartily did, the latter. Again, he was an extremely strong free-trader; and this both caused him to vote Liberal in 1906 and enabled him to avoid doing so in 1910. For, soon after the Government of 1906 came into power, it introduced a patent bill in which it was enacted that any foreign firm which was granted an English patent must set up a factory in England. This was interpreted by McTaggart as a betrayal of the free-trade citadel; and, as all parties were now faithless to his Dulcinea, he was able to return with an easy conscience to the one which did not outrage all his other convictions and sentiments.

Perhaps the only political opinion of McTaggart's which is, at first sight, hard to reconcile with Whig principles is his belief in compulsory military service. This he had held strongly many years before the war, when it was highly unpopular with most Englishmen. But was not this really 'an appeal from the new to the old Whigs'? For did not the Whigs of Charles II's time object to mercenary standing armies, and extol in their place the old national militia?

Another apparent paradox in McTaggart's opinions was that he was as strongly 'liberal' in university politics as he was 'conservative' in national politics. He was, e.g., a strong feminist in the matter of the admission of women to full membership of the university. This paradox, however, depends largely on the usage of words. There is no essential connexion between liberalism and the view that men and women should be educated together, or between conservatism and the view that they should be educated separately. Nor is there any essential connexion between liberalism and the view that the colleges should be subordinated to the university, or between conservatism and the view that the university should be subordinated to the colleges. Yet those who hold the first alternative on these two subjects are called 'academic liberals', whilst those who hold the second are called 'academic conservatives'. There is thus no kind of inconsistency between academic liberalism and political conservatism, or between academic conservatism and political liberalism. If there were more men like McTaggart, who considered each question on its merits instead of dressing himself in a complete suit of ready-made opinions, such combinations would be much more frequent than they are, to the great benefit of both academic and national politics.

It remains to mention a few of McTaggart's more personal tastes and interests. He had a passion for ritual, which showed itself in his love of wearing his scarlet doctor's gown and taking part in university and college ceremonies. His knowledge of the history of university offices and rituals, of the minute details of procedure, and of the true order of the academic hierarchy, was extensive and accurate; and he was punctilious in insisting that no mistakes should be made in such matters. Perhaps this caused him to look with a slightly more lenient eye on popish than on protestant dissent; though it did not make him any less firm against the pretensions of the Bishop of Rome, or prevent him from referring to his church as 'the Roman schism'.

He loved good living, and he set an example to

other married fellows by the great part which he played in the social and corporate life of the college. He dined regularly in Hall; attended all college feasts; and was a faithful supporter of the old custom of drinking wine nightly in the Combination Room after dinner, a custom which has fallen into such decay in Trinity of late that McTaggart sometimes found himself on a week-night in the lonely, if splendid, situation of the Seraph Abdiel. Once a year he played at cards. The game, which was 'Beggar-my-Neighbour', used to be played after the Christmas Feast with another distinguished fellow of the College. McTaggart would start the game with sixpence in his pocket, and would play until he had lost it or until it was time to gather up his winnings and go home to bed; a system of limited liability which was highly characteristic of him. It was his custom after a feast to write down any story about a past or present member of the university which he had heard and had thought good. These stories, recorded each on a separate slip of paper, with the name of the teller, the date and occasion of the telling, and sometimes a few notes of his own, were kept in four file-boxes labelled 'College Stories'. He bequeathed them to an old friend; and we may perhaps venture to hope that, when a suitable time has gone by, they may be edited and printed.

McTaggart was an omnivorous reader of novels, good and bad. His memory for their plots and characters was extraordinary; he could, without apparent effort, give to an inquirer a full and accurate account of stories which he had read once years before. He was also devoted to those diaries, collections of letters, biographies, and memoirs which make the chief personalities of eighteenth-century England such living figures to ourselves. Few even of professional students of the eighteenth century can know their *Boswell*, their *Horace Walpole*, or their *Lord Hervey* better than McTaggart did. Certain Victorian poets had a great attraction for McTaggart; to judge from the frequency with which quotations from them occur in his works, his favourites were Browning and Swinburne. Such tastes and such knowledge made McTaggart a most valuable member of the library committee of the Union. His long and distinguished connexion with that society has been appropriately commemorated by setting apart a bookcase in the library, filling it with a collection of eighteenth-century memoirs bought by subscription, and affixing to it a brass memorial plate.

A biography, at best, is a series of photographs, taken from a limited number of positions, on a selectively sensitive plate, by a photographer whose presence affects the expression of the sitter in a characteristic way. There will certainly be omission and selection, and it is only too likely that there will be positive distortion. This sketch represents McTaggart as he appeared to one much younger than himself; whose relation to him was first that of pupil to teacher, and then, after a long interval and for too short a time, that of colleague. Those who knew him in his earlier years and in other relations would find much to add to this account, and perhaps something to alter in it. But no memoir of McTaggart which approximated to the truth could fail to convey the impression of a thinker of the very first rank, and of a rich, original, and lovable personality.

C. D. BROAD.

NOTE. This Introduction is based upon, and largely reproduces, the Obituary Notice of McTaggart which appeared in the Proceedings of the British Academy *for* 1927. *I have to thank the President and Council of the Academy for their kind permission to make use of this Notice for the present purpose.*

C. D. B.

SOME DOGMAS OF RELIGION

CHAPTER I

THE IMPORTANCE OF DOGMA

1. By metaphysics I mean the systematic study of the ultimate nature of reality, and by dogma I mean any proposition which has a metaphysical significance. This may seem at first sight a paradoxical definition. For dogmas are held, and disputed, by many people to whom metaphysics are absolutely unknown.

But we must remember that a proposition which has metaphysical significance may be held independently of metaphysical considerations. If a man asserts the existence of God because he accepts the argument from design, then his belief in God's existence rests on a metaphysical basis. If he asserts the existence of God because a priest has told him that God does exist, then his belief does not rest on a metaphysical basis, but it nevertheless has a metaphysical significance. For it decides, for him, a problem which is unquestionably of a metaphysical nature—one of those problems which must be dealt with in any systematic study of the ultimate nature of reality.

I believe that my definition of dogma is the one which accords best with the ordinary use of the word. Not all propositions about matters of fact are called dogmas. We do not give the name to the law of gravitation, nor to the statement that Waterloo was fought in 1815.[1] But all such statements as are

[1] The law of gravitation might be accepted by a Materialist or a Dualist as an expression of the ultimate nature of reality. In

found in the Christian creeds are called dogmas. And the name would be extended to statements of the same nature found in other creeds, and to the denials of these statements. 'Jesus is the Son of God' and 'Mohammed is the Prophet of God' are both dogmas. And so are 'there is a God' and 'there is no God'.

2. It may be objected that many creeds contain statements which would be called dogmas, but which are assertions of events as historical, and are not metaphysical at all. Such are, for example, the crucifixion and resurrection of Jesus, in the Christian creeds. Now it is quite true that, in asserting the death of Jesus, we are asserting a historical event, as much as if we were asserting the death of Bruno. But if it were regarded as *merely* a historical event, it would not be called a dogma. It has its place as a dogma in virtue of the belief that this death had some unique influence on the relation between God and man, and for any person who did not believe this there could be no reason for calling the assertion of the event a dogma. Any proposition as to the relation between God and man is clearly of metaphysical significance, and if it is asserted that the relation was in any way determined by a particular death, then the occurrence of that death has a metaphysical significance.

Again, a proposition is usually called a dogma irrespective of the reason for which it is believed. The assertion of God's existence is equally a dogma whether the believer has arrived at it by argument, or accepted it from tradition, or feels an instinctive and irresistible conviction to believe it.

that case it would be a metaphysical proposition, and might, I think, naturally be called a dogma. But the name would be refused to the law of gravitation as it is held by science, for that involves no metaphysical assertion and is accepted by Berkeleians and Hegelians as well as by Materialists and Dualists.

Now, since no proposition without metaphysical significance is called a dogma, and since so many which have that significance are commonly called by the name, it seems to me that it is desirable to give the name to all propositions with metaphysical significance. It will then, no doubt, include many propositions which are not usually called dogmas, since the word is generally used only in relation to religion, and many metaphysical propositions have but little bearing on religion. But it would be unsatisfactory to confine the use of the word to those metaphysical propositions which bear on religion, because the influence of metaphysical propositions on religion has many degrees of intensity, and it would be very difficult to draw the line between what was dogma and what was not.

3. I propose, therefore, to class as dogmas all propositions which have any metaphysical significance, and to define as religious dogmas those whose acceptance or rejection by any person would alter his religious position. Thus the existence of a personal God is a religious dogma, for the religion of a man who believes it cannot resemble very closely the religion of a man who disbelieves it. One may be as religious as the other, but it will be in a different form. On the other hand, the existence of matter is a dogma which does not seem to me to be religious. I do not see that the acceptance or rejection of it need involve any change in religious attitude.

How then shall we define religion? Religion is clearly a state of mind. It is also clear that it is not exclusively the acceptance of certain propositions as true. It seems to me that it may best be described as an emotion resting on a conviction of a harmony between ourselves and the universe at large.

Any definition less wide than this would be too narrow. The word religion is habitually used of the traditional national systems, such as those of the Hindoos, Greeks, and Romans; it is used of the revealed systems of religion[1]; and it is used of the attitude of various people who do not accept any of them. Plato, Spinoza, and Hegel would all, I suppose, be called religious men.

If the word is to be used in this way, it is clear that no one dogma can be regarded as essential to religion. For example, the cases of Buddhism and of Spinoza would prevent us from regarding belief in a personal God or in personal immortality as essential to it.

4. Our definition, on the other hand, is not too narrow, for it covers all the cases. In the case of the early traditional religions, indeed, the harmony is only rudimentary. In the early stages of these religions men had scarcely formed the conception of the universe as a whole, and did not therefore ask the question whether they were in harmony with it as a whole. But their religion was based on theories which enabled them to regard with more or less approval the part of the universe in which they were interested. The gods were regarded as having great power. They were also conceived as being, in the main, like men, as having the same ideals, sympathies, and standards as men. In so far as they differed from men they were held to be morally their superiors. (The actions reported of them would, indeed, have often been judged very wicked in men, but, when attributed to gods, they were not thought wicked. This distinction is often required in dealing with more developed religions.)

[1] For the sake of brevity, I shall use the term 'revealed religions' for all those systems which are held, by those who believe in them, to have been revealed.

On the whole, then, the dogmas of these creeds led to a belief that the world was to a large extent good, and better than it would have been judged to be by the same men if they had not held these dogmas. These religions, therefore, were accompanied by a conviction of a certain harmony between the individual and the universe.

We must also remember that it is just those religions in which the righteousness and power of the gods is only rudimentary, which put most weight on the possibility of propitiating the gods and influencing their decisions by prayers and offerings. And it is clear that the belief that we can induce the rulers of the universe to comply with our desires will produce a conviction of some harmony between ourselves and the universe—though perhaps the harmony would not be of the highest kind.

5. The position of magic, which appears to be the historical predecessor of the religions we have mentioned, seems different. Magic rests on the belief that it is possible by charms and rites both to compel men and non-human spirits to do my will in certain ways, and also to influence matter—either directly or through those spirits—so as to cause it to conform to my desires. The spirits affected by magic are not propitiated or persuaded—as in religion proper—but compelled by the efficacy of the magic.

Here there is no recognition of the government of the universe by beings better than ourselves—or at least not worse. We do not get that harmony between ourselves and the universe which comes from moral approval of the universe. But magic does assert a possible harmony—though of the lowest kind—between myself and the universe. For it asserts that the nature of the universe is such that I can—if I know the right trick—bend it more or less to my will. And thus I can bring the universe more or less into harmony with my desires.[1]

6. It might be objected that Buddhism does not assert any harmony between man and the universe, since it teaches that all existence is evil. But it teaches, also, that the constitution of the universe provides a way by which it is possible for each of us to escape from the tyranny of existence. With the wise and good man the universe is in harmony. For he strives towards the goal of Nirvana, and the universe is such that, if he is wise enough and good enough, he will attain it.

7. Our definition, then, is broad enough for whatever is usually called religion. But attempts are sometimes made to use the word in a much wider sense, and it will be well to examine three of the most important of these.

In the first place, it is suggested that religion should be defined as identical with morality. The best-known statement of this position is to be found in the Epistle of St. James (i. 27), 'Pure religion and undefiled before our God and Father is this, to visit the fatherless and widows in their affliction, and to keep himself unspotted from the world.'

This would, I think, be admitted not to be the most usual meaning of religion. It is generally advocated, indeed, as a change of meaning. It seems to me to be a bad definition, because, with two things and two words before us, it proposes to apply both words to one thing, and to leave the other thing nameless.

To do what I think right is obviously something very different from the possession of an emotion which arises from a conviction of my harmony with

[1] Cp. Hegel's *Philosophy of Religion* (Part II, Div. I, chap. i) and Mr. Frazer's *Golden Bough* (chap. i, p. 63, ed. 1900).

the universe. Nor are they always found together. Hume and Spinoza were both men who did what they thought right; but, while Spinoza was absolutely dominated by such an emotion, Hume, so far as we know, was absolutely devoid of it.

It is highly desirable that each of these separate things should have a separate name. Now the first has a name which is universally applied to it—morality. And if we take religion in the more usual sense, which distinguishes it from morality, then the second will also have a separate name. But if religion is to be taken as identical with morality, then the first will have two equivalent names, and the second will have none at all. This is surely wasteful.

8. The definition of religion as nothing but morality has had supporters worthy of much respect, but I think we can see that its value—for it undoubtedly had value—is due to a cause which is rapidly passing away. This cause is the belief, which has been very prevalent in the past, that it is a sin not to hold the true religion. (The phrase 'a true religion' is scarcely accurate, since religion is not a system of propositions but an emotion. But it is a usual and convenient phrase for the religion which normally comes from the acceptance of true dogmas, provided, of course, that the true dogmas are such as to permit a religion to be based on them.)

The extreme form of this belief—and it is not yet altogether extinct—is that any one who fails to attain the true religion before the death of his present body, will be tormented through unending time. This, however, is not so common as formerly. But the milder idea still lingers that it is in some degree sinful to fail in attaining the true religion. If this were true, we should escape serious difficulties if religion was identical with morality. It is, of course, sinful to be immoral. But it is absurd to represent as sinful all failures to understand the nature of the universe. Some such failures may be sinful, if they are due to indolence or to cowardice. But others clearly are not. They are due to intellectual errors. And to fail in matters of such difficulty—matters in which either Berkeley or Hume, either Aquinas or Scotus, must have failed—is little reproach to a man's intellect, and none to his virtue.

But the idea that religion is something, the failure to attain which is sinful, is dying out rapidly. To attain the true religion would be regarded by most people as good, and by many people as the highest good. But it would now be generally recognized—and certainly by all thinkers worthy of our serious consideration—that it is not a duty to attain the true religion, although, of course, it may be, and often is, a duty to seek it. And then there is no reason why we should not define religion to mean something different from morality, while, as I have pointed out, there are two reasons why we should do so—that it does less violence to the ordinary usage, and that it finds names for two things of great importance, instead of for only one of them.

9. The second proposed definition of religion which we must consider is not so wide as the first. Arnold speaks of religion as 'morality touched by emotion'. And the author of *Natural Religion* defines it as 'the influence which draws men's thoughts away from their personal interests, making them intensely aware of other existences, to which it binds them by strong ties, sometimes of admiration, sometimes of awe, sometimes of duty, sometimes of love'.[1]

[1] *Natural Religion*, Book II, chap. vi, p. 227 (ed. 1891).

This definition seems to me better than that which identifies religion with morality. It does not waste two names on one thing, since morality touched by emotion is something different from morality pure and simple. Nor does it disturb the ordinary application of the word so much, since it does not compel us to class all moral men as religious.

Still it does disturb the ordinary application of the word more than can be considered justifiable. Religion has always, I think, implied a belief in some fundamental harmony, some sort of reconciliation between the claims of our own nature and the facts of the universe. Now an enthusiasm about morality, or an enthusiasm about duty or love, does not by itself ensure harmony or reconciliation. Enthusiasm for any worthy ideal, whether fulfilled or unfulfilled, is doubtless good. But unless the ideal is fulfilled, or we believe it is going to be fulfilled, it does not bring peace but a sword. The more we long for an ideal, the less in harmony shall we be with a universe which refuses to realize it. And therefore we shall not be making the usual application of the word religion, if we apply it to cases of an enthusiasm for an ideal when belief in the realization of the ideal is absent.

This violation of usage may be productive of deception. For the usage is old and persistent, and with the word religion we have come to associate that particular happiness which comes from the belief that we are in harmony with the universe. And the association is not easily disturbed, even when a change in the meaning of the word has deprived it of all justification. I think that those people who use the word to mean nothing more than an enthusiasm for virtue, often unconsciously deceive themselves by transferring with the word the mystery and the restfulness which only clung about it in respect of its older meaning, and thus believe themselves to have kept what, in fact, they have lost.

10. A third definition of religion has been lately proposed by Mr. Lowes Dickinson.[1] According to his view, religion consists in the attitude of the spirit towards the general situation in which we find ourselves. So far I am able to agree with him. But he goes on to say that any attitude towards the universe is religious 'if it be greatly and imaginatively conceived'—even if it should be an attitude which includes condemnation and defiance of a universe recognized as evil.

For such a religion, dogma, in the sense in which I have used the word, would be necessary. We must know what the general situation is, before we can take up any attitude towards it. But, on this definition, religion can be based on *any* theory of the nature of the universe. All that is required is that we should take up a worthy and a dignified attitude towards the universe. And that is always possible, however bad or trivial the universe may be.

There is much to be said for this definition of religion, but on the whole it seems to me to be more convenient to keep to the common usage by which religion is conceived as something which brings with it rest and peace and happiness.[2] Now an attitude of defiance to a universe recognized as evil is worthy and dignified, but it is not restful, or peaceful, or felicific. And thus it might lead to confusion if such an attitude were called religion. The question, however, is of no importance for

[1] *Religion, a Criticism and a Forecast*, by G. Lowes Dickinson, chap. iii, p. 60.

[2] I cannot consider Buddhism as an exception to this, for the reasons given above (Section 6).

our present object, since the adoption of Mr. Dickinson's definition would leave dogma essential to religion—though not dogma of any particular nature.

11. If religion is to be defined as resting on a conviction of the harmony of ourselves with the universe, the question arises of how much harmony is necessary. If complete harmony were necessary, no one could be called religious except the few mystics who deny the existence of any evil, since any evil must involve some want of harmony. We must say, I think, that religion is a matter of degree. The more complete the harmony it asserts, the more completely religious will it be. Of course the more complete religion is not necessarily the more true, for it may assert a harmony which does not exist.

What then, we must now ask, is the minimum of harmony between ourselves and the universe that can be the basis of religion? Some minimum there must surely be. For the conviction that the universe was not quite as bad as it could possibly have been would involve a belief in some harmony between ourselves and the universe. But this is not sufficient for religion. It would be an inadequate foundation for a religion that every man is not always hungry. And yet this shows some harmony between ourselves and the universe.

It seems to me that the minimum harmony required to give us an emotion which could now be called religion, is that the universe should be judged to be good on the whole. That is to say, the harmony must be a harmony with what is judged by us to be the highest part of our own natures, and not with those of our desires which, even while we have them, we recognize as comparatively worthless or as wrong. And the harmony must be sufficiently complete to admit of the universe as a whole being approved rather than condemned.

I have said that this is necessary for an emotion which could *now* be called religion. In the more rudimentary stages of religion, no doubt, it is different. A god is worshipped if he is believed to make things rather better, or to abstain from making them worse, for the worshipper and his neighbours. No question is raised as to the universe as a whole, or as to the balance of good and bad. And in a still more rudimentary stage the question is only as to the satisfaction of the desires of the individual, regardless of their moral quality.

But religion has developed into a more exacting form. It was impossible, as the conception of an objective good developed, to find sufficient harmony with our nature in anything which we condemned as evil, even if it were personally convenient to ourselves. And when the universe came to be regarded as a whole—which was inevitable for monotheists—it was impossible to find sufficient harmony in anything less than the universe as a whole. When once the objective and the universal had been realized, no subjective or partial harmony could be adequate.

Thus the declaration of Mr. Kipling's dying girl, 'I bear witness that there is no God but thee, Beloved', is not religion. It is rather its explicit rejection in favour of something which is not religion—though it may well be infinitely better. But the belief that the love of man for man *is* God—which we find in some mystical philosophers, and possibly in the First Epistle of St. John—might be the basis of a religion, for it is an assertion about the ultimate nature of reality which might involve the consequence of our harmony with the universe.

12. If religion is to be defined in this way, or in any other way which bases it on a belief in fundamental harmony and goodness, I maintain that dogma is necessary to religion. Dogma is not religion, any more than the skeleton is the living body. But we can no more be religious without dogma than our bodies could live without their skeletons.

If we were to reject dogma, on what could we hope to base religion? It is said that we should still have science, on the one hand, and, on the other, virtue, with all the activities and pursuits the exercise of which are considered virtuous. Will either of these be sufficient to assure us that we are in a harmony with the universe sufficiently fundamental to form a basis for religion? Let us take science first.

13. If we assert that science is capable of assuring us of such a harmony, we assert that science can give us information of the ultimate nature of reality. For it is clear that science cannot assure us of our harmony with the universe unless it is able to tell us what is the nature of the universe. But if we assert this, then we have not got rid of dogma. The fundamental propositions of science have become metaphysical dogmas. In themselves they are not so, for they make no claim to express the ultimate nature of reality. This is shown by the fact that Materialists, Dualists, Berkeleians, and Hegelians, who differ so profoundly as to the ultimate nature of reality, all accept the same system of scientific propositions. But when these propositions are taken as the ultimate truth about reality, they are metaphysical.

'But', it may be replied, 'although these propositions may fall within the definition of dogma, they are free from the defects which have rendered us unwilling to declare dogma essential to religion. They have not the obscurity or the uncertainty of metaphysics. They are given us by science, and what science gives us is plain and certain.'

This, however, is a confusion. Science may give us these propositions as scientific truths, but it cannot assure us that they express the ultimate nature of reality, for that, as was said above, does not concern science at all. If they are taken as expressing that ultimate nature, then the statement that they do express it must either be proved, or simply assumed. To prove it we must go to metaphysics, for—to mention one point only—it is impossible to refute the alternative theories as to the nature of reality except by metaphysical arguments. And then our religion would rest, not on science, but on a metaphysical system of dogmas, which was what we had professed to avoid. But if we do not prove that science expresses the ultimate nature of reality, we have no right to believe that it does. For this is frequently denied, and it cannot be said to be a self-evident truth.

14. It is worth while, however, to consider another point. If the result of our metaphysical consideration was to convince us that the fundamental propositions of science express the ultimate nature of reality, they would be dogmas, but would they be such dogmas as would serve for a basis for religion? I do not think that they would be, because they would not give us any ground for believing that the universe was good.

A certain part of the universe is what is called, in ordinary language, matter. Now about this part of the universe science tells us that it is governed by certain laws which are of the type usually called mechanical. And there science leaves it. It does not inquire whether these laws are manifestations of deeper and more fundamental laws, or whether they are due to the will of a creative God. It does not deny that this is so; it does not assert it. It has nothing to do with the question.

But if the results of science are to be given metaphysical validity, then it would follow that these mechanical laws express the ultimate nature of that part of the universe of which science asserts them. For we are to have no metaphysics now but the results of science, and this is all that science tells us about them.

The behaviour of matter is of great importance for the question of the goodness of the universe. We may hold, indeed, that the only thing which can be intrinsically good or bad is conscious spirit, and that matter, which is unconscious, can only be good or bad as a means of producing good or bad results in spirits. But, in that part of the universe which we know empirically, matter is in close connexion with spirit—so close that the good or bad state of spirit must always largely depend on its relations with matter. Pain, for example, may not be the only evil, but it cannot be denied to be evil. And our relation to matter is capable of causing us great pain—sometimes almost continuous for a long period. And there is scarcely any quality, the possession of which has ever been held to be good for men, the development of which may not be prevented, or at least greatly thwarted, by the condition of the body or its environment. Science gives us no reason to suppose that this state of things will not be permanent.

Now have we any reason to believe that the action of matter, guided solely by mechanical laws, would be such as to make the universe good? It does not seem to me that we have, in the first place, the slightest right to believe this *a priori*. For there is nothing in the general nature of such mechanical laws which would tend to make them produce good more readily than evil, or would show that they would produce a universe good as a whole. It is entirely indifferent to them which they produce. It is, of course, possible that the action of those laws would produce such a universe. But it is no more probable than the contrary alternative, and the possibility must be at least probable before we can base a religion on it.

Revealed religions, as a rule, escape this difficulty by the hypothesis of a beneficent deity, who arranges and controls matter in such a way as to render it compatible with, and subservient to, the realization of goodness in the universe. Some systems of metaphysics escape it by maintaining that matter is essentially of the nature of spirit, and will be found in the long run harmonious to the demands of spirit. But science knows nothing of such theories as these, and if we are to make our metaphysics exclusively out of science, such theories are not available for us.

15. Let us pass from *a priori* to empirical considerations. There is no *a priori* reason why unloaded dice should turn up double sixes rather than any other number. And yet in a particular case it might be possible to know empirically that they had turned up double sixes. Is it possible to know empirically that the universe is good as a whole?

In the first place it does not seem possible to know empirically anything about the universe as a whole. All we can base such a judgement on is our very imperfect knowledge of what has happened on one planet for a few thousand years. To make an empirical inference from so little to so much would be as wild as to argue that all Chinese were evil because the first one we met turned out to be so.

And then, if we could legitimately make such an inference, would the inference be that the universe as a whole is good? Is that part of the universe which we know empirically, taken as a whole, good or bad? It certainly contains a great deal that is good. It also contains a great deal that is bad. There is much virtue and happiness. There is much sin and misery. Which overbalances the other it would be impossible to assert with any approach to accuracy. The judgement of the wisest man would be unduly affected by his own disposition, his own good fortune, and the character of that small part of the world of which he had personal experience. And we find that the judgements of wise men on this question differ as widely as possible.

Even if it were certain that the amount of good experienced by different people in the world empirically known to us was greater than the evil, would it follow that that world was to be considered as good on the whole, and to be approved rather than condemned? I do not think it would necessarily follow. For good and evil are very unequally distributed, and, whatever the aggregate of each may be, it cannot be denied that there are some people whose lives are much more evil than good. Now it seems to me that we must recognize each individual as an end in himself, and as having claims to possess the good—claims which cannot altogether be cancelled by any amount of good possessed by other people. A universe in which three people out of every five were in heaven and two in every five in hell might have a greater amount of virtue and happiness in it than of sin and misery. But I do not think we should be prepared to accept it as a good universe on that account.

If we take into account then, firstly, the great

amount of evil known to us, and, secondly, the great excess of evil over good in the lives of many people, as those lives are open to our empirical observation, we must, I think, come to the conclusion that, if the universe as a whole resembled what we can observe, we should have no adequate basis for a religion.

Some metaphysicians cut this knot by denying the reality of all evil, and by asserting that, in spite of appearance, the universe is completely good. Whether this is right or wrong, it is clear that it finds no support in science, and cannot form part of a metaphysical system consisting of transplanted scientific propositions.

16. There remains the view which, at any rate in the Western world, forms the most usual basis of religion—the view that things are improving, that the evil in the future will be less than the evil of the present, and (it is sometimes added) will eventually vanish altogether.

Now can science offer us this comfort? I do not see how it can. It cannot say that the individual will be happier in the future, for from the point of view of science there is not the slightest ground for supposing that we survive the deaths of our present bodies. And, if there were, it would be no ground for hoping that things would improve. The mere fact that life goes on is no reason for supposing that it improves. Some people are no better at sixty than at twenty. Some people are worse. Any confidence that the prolongation of life beyond death would involve improvement must be based on independent metaphysical considerations. It would remain utterly alien to science, even if science had admitted that life was prolonged after death at all.

So of the race. Even if science could give us

ground to believe that the human race would continue to exist indefinitely, there would be no guarantee that it would improve—indeed, no reason for supposing that it was more likely to improve than to deteriorate. Under certain circumstances races of living beings do degenerate, and these circumstances are just as likely to occur as more favourable ones.

But science gives us no ground to believe that the human race will continue to exist indefinitely. On the contrary, I imagine that it insists that the temperature compatible with human life is only a very transitory episode in the history of a planet. Neither of the individual nor of the race can it assert permanence. It reserves it for matter or for energy. And the permanence of these is scarcely adapted to afford us consolation. It is rather cold comfort—as Mill is reported to have replied to an enthusiastic Positivist—to look forward to our whole civilization being eventually transmuted into an infinitesimal augmentation of the temperature of space.

Nor could science comfort us by pointing out that each man may deliver himself from unhappiness by ceasing to exist. A metaphysic of scientific propositions would find no difficulty in believing that every man not only may, but does, cease to exist. And this, if life is evil, would doubtless be a consolation, for it would limit the amount of it which must be endured by each man, and thereby make it more tolerable. But while it would lessen the evil, the fact would still remain that the universe contains more evil than good, and we should not have an adequate basis for religion since such a universe would scarcely be called good as a whole. (See note, p. 37.)

17. It has sometimes been said that science, while it cannot give us so good a religion as can be given us by metaphysics or revelation, can, nevertheless, give us some sort of religion, which is better than none at all. The God revealed in science 'is also the God of Christians. That the God of Christians is something more does not affect this fact'.[1]

In the first place, science does not reveal any God at all. It is possible that the facts discovered by science may give us a legitimate ground for inferring the existence of a God. But the inference is not science. It is as much metaphysics as anything in Kant or Hegel.

Let us pass by this objection, however, and let us admit, for the purpose of the argument, that a God is revealed by science. Such a God, I suppose, is to be taken as the ultimate source of all the facts discovered by science. It has been occasionally maintained that God is only the part-cause of these facts, or only the cause of some of them. But any discrimination of this sort is obviously completely metaphysical. It involves some knowledge of God derived from other sources than the observations of scientific facts. If science can be said to tell us anything about God at all, it can only be as the being on whom all that is studied by science depends.

Now such a God as this cannot, I think, be fairly said to be the God of Christians. The God of Christians is held by them—rightly or wrongly—to embody the highest perfection which we can conceive. But a God of whom we only know that he caused those facts of which science tells us falls very short of such perfection. It may be said that, since the idea of a perfect God implies complete symmetry and order, and since science informs us of a certain incom-

[1] *Natural Religion*, Book I, chap. i, p. 22 (ed. 1891).

plete symmetry and order, the difference is from one point of view quantitative. But this difference may become qualitative in its effect upon religion. The difference between a greater and a lesser amount of food is quantitative, but it may involve a qualitative difference of life and death. So the difference between a being who fulfils our ideal of good and a being who falls short of it is from one point of view merely quantitative; but it may be all the difference between a God and a devil, and that, from the point of view of religion, may be considered qualitative.

18. It is clear that, so far as science can tell us, the good is often thwarted. In that case there are only two alternatives as to the God revealed in science. He may be utterly indifferent to good and evil. In that case he is not good. His control of the universe gives us no reason to suppose that the universe is good on the whole. Neither does he deserve the name of God—if that is to imply that he is a fit object of worship and reverence. For what quality would such a being have which would deserve worship? He would be, no doubt, stronger than we are. And if we suppose him to possess a lively, and not very delicate, sense of personal vanity, it might doubtless be prudent to worship him. But prudence seems the only merit that such worship would possess.

Or, on the other hand, the God of science may have regard for good and evil. In that case he ordained the evil, knowing that it was evil. And such a God as this has no limitations, which might have compelled him to ordain the evil as the only means to avoid worse evils. He was defined as the source of all that is known to science, so that he cannot be limited in any way known to science, and, as we have excluded all means of knowledge except science, we can have no reason to suppose him limited by anything else. We must suppose, therefore, that he put the evil there because he liked it. In which case the God of science seems to bear a close resemblance to the devil of theology.

He bears, indeed, a still closer relation to the God of some theological systems. But, as we shall see in Chapter VII, it is possible to construct a theology with a better God than this, while it seems impossible that the God of science should be better than this. Moreover, the God of theology is not the only alternative to the God of science, since it is quite possible to have a religion without a God at all.

19. We cannot, then, base religion on science. Can we base it on virtue? We have already seen reasons for deciding that neither virtue nor an enthusiasm for virtue *is* religion. But it remains possible that religion may be based on virtue. If a virtuous man could derive from his virtue, independently of anything else, a feeling of harmony with the universe as a whole, then virtue would be a sufficient basis for religion.

But can we get any such feeling from virtue alone? I think not. Morality, no doubt, still remains binding on us whether the universe is good or bad. The idea of the good is valid for me. If it is not valid for the universe, so much the worse for the universe. No doubt, too, however much we believed that the stars in their courses were fighting against us, we might feel not only enthusiasm but a certain amount of pleasure in carrying out the demands of our own consciences, and in striving to make the best of such a very bad business as the universe would then be. But it could not give us the sense of harmony with the universe. It sounds plausible to say that the possession of virtue ought to console us for everything, and that, therefore, we have only to be virtuous to feel in harmony with the universe, since with the virtuous man no element can disturb his happiness, or, consequently, affect the harmony. But we must remember that in proportion as we are devoted to virtue we care for its success, and must therefore be considerably affected by a world which denies success to it. A man who was so extremely virtuous that the defeat of virtue in all its endeavours was a matter of entire indifference to him, would scarcely be consistent. And, again, not only the virtuous man himself, but other people also, are subject to misfortune. A virtue which was so intense that it rendered us indifferent to the sufferings of others might be held to have passed into its opposite. The recognition of evil is not, as we have seen, incompatible with religion, but they can only be made compatible by convictions as to the predominance of good which would involve dogma.

The difficulty cannot be avoided by saying that these other people would have been happy if they had been virtuous. This, if it were true, would only deepen the tragedy, since it asserts that wherever we find the evil of misery we find also the evil of sin. Nor do we avoid it by saying that their wickedness is their own fault, even if that were true. For the difficulty is that there is evil in the universe, and that is not removed by any decision as to what being in the universe is responsible for the fact.

Again, how are we to deal with beings whose unhappiness cannot be removed by virtue because they are not capable of it—at least, not yet? Granted—and it is granting a good deal—that the contemplation of the moral imperative could solace a man in the spasms of hydrophobia, it would be unreasonable to expect such devotion to the ideal from a dog or a guinea-pig. And then how am I to prevent their pain from destroying the harmony?

Even if I were prepared to forgive the universe the evil which I myself suffer, that would not alter the fact that it was evil, and that the universe which inflicted it was likewise so far evil. And, even if I have the right to forgive the universe my own pain, it is clear that I have no right to forgive it the pain of others. Unless we have reason to believe that evil is outweighed by good we have no right to approve the universe. And we can have no reason for believing this which is not a dogma.

20. To pass from the general to the particular, it has sometimes been asserted that dogma is not essential to the Christian religion. This belief takes two forms. The first defines dogma in much the same way as we have defined it, and declares that nothing is essential to Christianity except its moral teaching. The second form, as we shall see later, uses dogma in a different sense.

Let us consider the first. The teachings of Jesus, and the teachings of the Christian Church, each contain precepts of morality. Why should we not assert that nothing else but this morality is of the essence of Christianity?

In the first place, we should have to assert that the vast majority of Christians—practically all of them—had been entirely deceived about what was essential to the religion in which they lived and died. We are not here compelled to decide whether the tenets of the founder of Christianity or of the fully developed Church are best entitled to be considered typical Christianity. For here they are agreed.

If we put no trust at all in the narrative of the Gospels—a scepticism which would be highly unreasonable — we should know nothing about the teaching of Jesus on any subject, morality included. But if we do put any trust whatever in that narrative, it is impossible to deny that Jesus held various dogmas to be true and important. His disposition does not seem to have been at all metaphysical, and the dogmas he taught were comparatively few and simple, and were advocated, as a rule, without any attempt at proof. But it can scarcely be denied that he believed in personal immortality. And it seems quite impossible to deny that he believed in a personal God, and that he believed that the relation of God to man could be suitably expressed by the metaphor of fatherhood. A man who held these dogmas, and who regarded them as important—and if these dogmas are true they must be important—was certainly not living without dogma.

It may be worth pointing out that the Sermon on the Mount, which is sometimes referred to as the ideal of undogmatic religion, in reality contains dogma in almost every line. 'Blessed are they that mourn: for they shall be comforted,' is not a moral precept at all. It commands nothing, and it forbids nothing. But it does make a statement about events, and one which cannot be verified by empirical experience, since many people mourn for years, and die uncomforted. The blessings on the merciful and the pure in heart may be held to be indirectly ethical, since they certainly seem to *imply* an injunction to be merciful and pure. But they also assert that the merciful shall obtain mercy, and that the pure in heart shall see God. These are not ethical injunctions, but statements asserting events. And they are not capable of empirical verification—indeed, in the sphere of our empirical observation they are not always true.

If these assertions about future events are to be verified without empirical observation, they can only be verified by deduction from the fundamental nature of reality. (Jesus, I suppose, derived them from his belief as to the nature of God.) In this case, they are dogmas.

21. But, it may be answered, Jesus may have believed dogmas, and yet not have believed them to be essential. But essential to what? There is certainly no reason to suppose that he believed that a man could not act morally, or please God, without holding these dogmas. Indeed it seems tolerably clear that he did not believe this. But the question is not whether he believed that holding these dogmas was essential to morality, or to God's favour, but whether he believed that they were an essential part of his own teaching. Will any one venture to suggest that Jesus would have regarded his teaching as not materially altered, if the belief in the existence and providence of God had been withdrawn from it?

And here, at least, Christianity has followed its founder. Dogma has not been, as it might be supposed some people believed, the monopoly of schoolmen. The simplest Christians have always believed that there is a God, that good is more pleasing to him than evil, that he watches and controls events. And all Christians have held some dogma on the subject of life after death—the great majority that such a life awaits every man, a few that it is conditional only. These are not all. Every Christian has always believed more dogmas than these, though all of them have not believed the same.

The importance of the dogma, again, has always

been at least as great as that of the moral teaching. The love of God and the hope of heaven are both based on dogma. And certainly morality has not been a more potent element in the religious lives of the majority of Christians than the love of God and the hope of heaven.

22. It is, of course, possible to say that Jesus and the Church were both mistaken as to the relative importance of their own beliefs. It is, indeed, almost impossible that they should have been deceived as to the relative importance of those beliefs for themselves. At any rate they were more likely to know than any one else can be. But it is possible to maintain that they were wrong as to the true relative importance of their beliefs, and that if they had seen more clearly they would have seen that the belief in God and immortality could not compare in importance with the moral precepts which we owe to Christianity.

If any one held this view, he could doubtless say that dogma was not essential to Christianity, provided he realizes that the discovery was first made in the nineteenth century, and has against it the almost unanimous opinion of Christians. But in that case Christianity will not be a religion. We saw reason before to confine the name of religion to cases which exhibited a conviction of harmony with the universe. And mere moral teaching can never, as we have seen, do this. It only tells us what the good is. It does not tell us how far the good is realized. And it is on this that our conviction of harmony with the universe depends.

It would, indeed, be absurd to adhere to a definition of religion which excluded Christianity, as Christianity is commonly understood. For when people speak of religion they most certainly mean to include Christianity. And any change in the definition which would alter the application of the word so materially would be intolerably inconvenient. But there is no reason why we should fix on a definition to include the proposed undogmatic Christianity. For this is something quite new, quite unlike Christianity as commonly understood, and quite unlike anything to which the name of religion has been generally given. We sin against no canon of definition, therefore, by saying that, if this is the true Christianity, then the true Christianity is not religion.

23. We pass to the second sense in which the undogmatic character of Christianity has been maintained. In this case a religious dogma is not defined, as we have defined it, as any metaphysical proposition which has influence on the character of religion. Dogma is sometimes defined as whatever propositions of this kind the definer dislikes. Or it is defined as being those propositions which are complicated, and can only be understood by trained theologians. Or it is defined as being those propositions on which Christians do not agree. And on such grounds we find the assertion made that Christianity does not depend upon dogma—not because a belief, for example, in God and in immortality are not considered necessary for Christianity, but because they are not considered dogmas.

The first definition of dogma, by which it is merely employed as a term of abuse for doctrines which are regarded as false, may be dismissed without much delay. Dogma has never meant this in the past, and it does not mean this now with most people. To use the word in this way creates great confusion, and has sometimes the further disadvantage of creating a false impression of impartiality. A man may be supposed to be asserting that certain teaching, for example, is impartial, when his real meaning is only that he does not consider it false.

Connected with this is the tendency to confine the use of the word to such propositions as are asserted without proof—a tendency probably due to the fact that the adjective dogmatic has frequently this meaning. But adjectives have often meanings which differ widely from those of the corresponding substantives. And it would be very inconvenient to call the same proposition a dogma, when no reasons are given for it, and undogmatic, if an attempt is made to prove it.

24. Let us take the second suggestion, that dogma should denote exclusively those propositions which are complicated and can only be understood by theologians. The objections to this view are two. In the first place, it has not been the most usual definition of the word in the past, and would exclude much that is commonly called dogma. In the second place, the propositions which it excludes and the propositions which it includes are like one another in such important characteristics that they ought to have some common name, and no other common name seems suitable.

On this view, the existence of God would not be a dogma, but the doctrine of the Trinity as expounded in the Athanasian Creed would be a collection of dogmas. The first of these is, at any rate, apparently simple, while the second has not even the appearance of simplicity. And almost every one can attach some meaning to the first, while the second would be absolutely unintelligible to many people. But the same differences exist between the multiplication table and an advanced treatise on mathematics, and yet both are said to consist of mathematical propositions. The assertion of God's existence and the Athanasian doctrine of the Trinity resemble one another in being assertions of a metaphysical nature, in having influence on the religion of those who hold them, and in being extremely controversial statements. It seems to me that these similarities render it desirable that they should have a common name.

But, even if we did define dogma like this, it would only be with important reservations that we could say that Christianity was undogmatic. In one sense it would doubtless be so. Many people who would be called Christians have either never heard of the complicated and technical dogmas, or have never attached the slightest meaning to the words they heard. It is clear, therefore, that these beliefs are not *psychologically* essential to Christianity. But it would be admitted on this theory that the belief in God's existence was essential to Christianity. Now some people would maintain, and some have attempted to prove, that the existence of God would involve a contradiction, unless the Athanasian theology were true. In this case, these dogmas would be *logically* essential to Christianity. In the same way, no one could maintain that Kant's theory of space was psychologically essential to a belief in the propositions of geometry, since it is notorious that many people accept the truth of geometry who have never heard of Kant's theory of space, or who have deliberately rejected it. But, if Kant is right, a belief in his theory of space would be logically essential to geometry, because, as he maintains, it is impossible that geometry should be true unless his theory of space were true also.

25. It remains to consider the view that dogma should be defined as that on which Christians do not agree. Here, once more, we must object that this is a departure from usage. Dogma has not meant this, and there is no reason why it should mean it now, unless to gratify the feelings of people who have a vague idea that it is liberal and tolerant to use dogma as a term of abuse. And then, why draw this precise line? If the existence of God is not a dogma, because all Christians believe it, why should we not say that transubstantiation is not a dogma, because all Romanists believe it? But if transubstantiation is a dogma, because some Anglicans do not believe it, why should we not say that the existence of God is a dogma, because there are Atheists who do not believe it?

If dogma were defined like this, would it be essential to Christianity? A dogma on which all Christians do not agree is clearly not psychologically essential to Christianity, since some Christians do not believe it. But, as in the last case, it may be logically essential to Christianity. For there may be a contradiction between asserting some of the admittedly essential doctrines (which on this view would not be called dogmas) and rejecting this dogma.

Even on the psychological question we must make a certain reservation. We often hear the argument that, since two men can both be Christians although they hold incompatible dogmas on a certain point, therefore the point is quite indifferent to Christianity, and a man may be a Christian without troubling himself about it all. The conclusion may be correct—and often is. But it does not follow from the premises, and may be false in cases where the premises are true. Because *A* can be either *B* or *C*, it does not follow that it can be neither. A human being need not be male, for it may be female, nor need it be female, for it may be male. But it would be a mistake to argue from this that it could be sexless. Some Christians say that man can be pleasing to God only by his works, some that he can be pleasing to God only by his faith, and some hold other views on the matter. None of these theories, then, can be psychologically essential to Christianity. But it does not follow that a man could be called a Christian, who had no belief as to the way in which man could please God.

26. Let us now return to the more general question. I have endeavoured to show that if religion and dogma are defined in a manner which accords with their general use, we must hold that, while dogma is by no means identical with religion, it is absolutely necessary to religion. This conclusion could be avoided by taking different definitions of religion and dogma. But the fact would still remain, that our beliefs on metaphysical subjects are of supreme importance for the determination of our attitude towards reality in general, and towards our own lives in particular, and are therefore, for many people, of supreme importance for their happiness.

It will depend on those beliefs, whether we shall consider the universe as determined by forces completely out of relation with the good, or whether, on the contrary, we may trust that the dearest ideals and aspirations of our own nature are realized, and far more than realized, in the ultimate reality. It will depend on them whether we can regard the troubles of the present, and the uncertainties of the future, with the feelings of a mouse towards a cat, or of a child towards its father. It will depend on them whether we look on our pleasures as episodes which will soon pass, or on our sorrows as delusions which will soon be dispelled. It will depend on them whether our lives seem to us worth living only as desperate efforts to make the best of an incurably bad business, or as the passage to a happiness that it has not entered into our hearts to conceive. It will depend on them whether we regard ourselves as temporary aggregations of atoms, or as God incarnate. These questions are not devoid of practical importance.

There are, indeed, people whom they do not interest, but they are in a minority. Experience shows us that such questions as these are of great interest to most people, nor is there any reason to suppose that the extent or the degree of that interest is lessening. The world of our empirical knowledge is no more capable of satisfying us than it used to be. It is probably less capable, for though it has doubtless improved, it has not kept pace with our increasing demands for improvement. And while we want more than we can find around us, questions of dogma will retain their influence on the happiness of mankind.

27. It is common to speak of metaphysical problems as abstract and unpractical. In reality, all other questions are abstract as compared with these, and most, as compared with these, are unpractical. Hence, indeed, arise many of the difficulties of metaphysics. If it progresses more slowly than science, it is often because science, by its comparative abstraction, gains in ease and simplicity what it loses in absolute truth. And often, again, it is because our dearest hopes hang on the answers to metaphysical questions, so that we are afraid to seek those answers, or to look them in the face when they present themselves, or to allow other people to face them.

28. The dependence of religion on dogma condemns religious questions to remain controversial and doubtful. If religion could be based on science matters would be different. In science we find a consensus of expert opinion, and we find progress. There is, of course, a margin of uncertainty in science. There are always questions which have been raised and not yet answered, or to which we find conflicting, and so uncertain, answers. But problem after problem is solved, and the solution becomes part of the common and undoubted property of mankind. The advance of science and the certainty of its results are beyond all doubt. What it all means is another matter, but we cannot deny that it is there to mean something.

With morality, again, the certainty, though not so striking as with science, is still very marked. It may be sometimes exaggerated. But if we compare the agreement of men's opinions on any metaphysical question—the existence of God, of matter, of immortality—with the agreement as to the general duty, and even the details, of honesty, of truthfulness, of courage, we shall find the balance overwhelmingly in favour of the latter. Indeed, the possibility of civilized life proves that the general agreement as to morality must be considerable.

Compare all this with dogma. If we take the religions which claim to be revealed, we do not find a single proposition laid down by any of them which is not challenged by others, nor does there appear any chance of discovering a common ground upon which it would be possible to settle the dispute. And if metaphysics is better off, it is still devoid of the agreement without which we can have no certainty. It advances, no doubt. But it only advances by changing the battle-ground, not by settling any problem finally. The questions evolve into different forms, but the answers are still various. We may hope that the long contest will eventually develop into a form where opposition will cease. But such a goal must at best be very distant, and many—though I cannot agree with them—fail to see any hope that it can ever be realized. For centuries to come we must resign ourselves to the admission that where we have dogma we shall have division.

29. Dispute without any confident hope of reconciliation is always bad—worst of all when, as must so often be the case in subjects bearing on religion, it implies a certain spiritual discord. If we could put dogma altogether on one side, or confine it to the studies and lecture-rooms of theologians and philosophers; if we could say that in spite of dogmatic divisions and doubts we could still have religious unity and certainty, still lack no element for a peaceful and happy life, then the world might surely count itself fortunate. But to do this is impossible, for it would ignore something essential to religion, and, in most cases, to a peaceful and happy life—the conviction of our own harmony with the universe.

Dogma means, now at any rate, division. But it may be doubted whether we shall get any unity worth preserving by the process immortalized by Mr. Saunders McKaye, which stripped mankind of their clothes, and then proclaimed them brothers 'on the one broad fundamental principle o' want o' breeks'.[1] It happens that the things about which we most disagree are the things about which we most want to know, and a unity which is attained by ignoring them is valueless.

It is not, of course, certain that dogma will deliver us from our troubles. We cannot set out on an inquiry and settle the answer beforehand. If we begin to inquire into what lies behind phenomena, the answer may be even more depressing than the superficial aspect of the phenomena themselves. But the only line of escape which is even possible lies in this direction. The phenomena of life, as we see them,

[1] Charles Kingsley, *Alton Locke*, chap. xxii.

can never give us the assurance of harmony that we want. To get this it is necessary to go behind experience, whether we take the path of revelation or of metaphysics.

It is here, as it seems to me, that the strength of the revealed religions of the world lies. If true, they would be adequate. They have arrived at the result that the nature of the universe is something with which it is possible that the wise and good man may find himself in harmony—usually, of course, by means of the dogma that the course of the universe is controlled by a benevolent God. They may be entirely unjustified in their conclusions. Their conceptions of divine benevolence may be of the most remarkable nature. But they change the whole aspect of heaven and earth for those who believe in them. The gifts they offer are worth taking—or at any rate seem so to those who are able to take them. And so, for all their faults, they possess considerable advantages over systems which have nothing to offer except rhetorical embellishments of ethical maxims.

30. The result is not entirely satisfactory. The only roads by which dogma has been reached in the past are revelation and metaphysics, and every year fewer people appear willing to accept any system of asserted revelation as valid without support from metaphysics. Now every one who studies metaphysics does not arrive at conclusions on which a religion can be based. And, even if they did, the study of metaphysics is only open to those who have a certain amount of natural and acquired fitness for it. The number of people who will be left between the rapidly diminishing help of revelation and the possibly increasing help of metaphysics seems likely to be unpleasantly large.

But it is useless not to face the facts. If the supply of bread runs short, we shall gain nothing by distributing stones. Such a course may even produce two positively evil results. It may persuade the ungrateful recipients, not only that there is a deficiency of food, but that there is no such thing as food at all. And it may prolong the scarcity, or even render it perpetual, by turning men's minds to quarries rather than to wheat-fields, as the source from which may arise some satisfaction for their desires.

Note to p. 19.—This position is different from the position of Buddhism. I conceive that Buddhism regards Nirvana, in spite of its negative nature, as true good and the only true good. But the view we are now discussing does not take annihilation as positively good, but only as the end of the series of good and bad events. It cannot compensate for the evil which has been suffered, but only prevents more from coming.

CHAPTER II

THE ESTABLISHMENT OF DOGMA

31. In this chapter I shall consider, in the first place, that belief which claims to dispense with argument altogether, and to rest itself on the immediate convictions of the believer. Secondly, I shall inquire into the validity of the argument that a dogma of religion is true because it is held by all, or by most, people, or because it is held by persons who can work miracles or predict the future. Thirdly, I shall inquire into the validity of the argument that a dogma of religion is true because its truth is of great importance for our happiness, or for the moral character of the universe. And finally, I shall consider the appeal which is often made to leave questions of religion to faith. I shall endeavour to show that none of these are valid, and that, if dogmas are to be established at all, they must be established by arguments, and by arguments different from those dealt with here.

32. It is not uncommon to hear the assertion that certain religious dogmas—the personality of God, for example, or the immortality of man, or the freedom of the will—do not require proof. 'I am certain of this', some one will say, 'without argument. My conviction does not rest on argument, and cannot be shaken by it. I decline to argue. I simply believe.' A belief which does not rest upon argument, in the case of any particular person, may be said to be held by such a person immediately, since argument is a process of mediation. The assertion here is, it will be noticed, not only that the belief does not rest upon arguments —i.e. that it is immediate—but also that it cannot be shaken by arguments.

Such a position is, no doubt, impregnable from outside. If a man's belief does not rest on reasons, and cannot be shaken by them, I may believe it to be mistaken, but I should be wasting time in attempting to argue against it.

If the person who holds a belief in this manner mentions the fact to me as a reason why I should not waste his time in trying to upset it, he is acting in a perfectly reasonable manner. And it is also strictly relevant to mention it if he is writing an autobiography —for it may be an important fact in his life. Also it is relevant as a contribution to statistics. It shows that one more person has this particular conviction in this particular way.

33. But it is not relevant if it is put forward for any other motive. Above all, it is absolutely irrelevant if it is put forward as a reason to induce other people to believe the same dogma. This is sometimes done. A man will assert his own immediate conviction of a dogma,[1] not as a reason for checking discussion, but as his contribution to the discussion. And here it seems certain that he is wrong.

What is the good of telling *B* that *A* has an immediate certainty of the truth of *X*? If *B* has a similar immediate certainty he believes *X* already, and must believe it, and, for him, *A*'s certainty is quite superfluous. If *B* has an immediate certainty of the falsity of *X*, or of the truth of something incompatible

[1] I am assuming for the present that an immediate conviction is also one which cannot be shaken by arguments. We shall see later on that this is not always the case.

with *X*, then he cannot believe *X*, and, for him, *A*'s certainty is quite useless. But supposing *B* has no immediate certainty on the matter at all, how will his knowledge of *A*'s immediate certainty help him? It cannot give him an immediate certainty, for, if he believes because *A* does, his belief rests on an argument, '*A* believes this, and therefore it is true,' and so is not immediate.

But can *A*'s immediate certainty be a valid ground for a reasoned certainty on *B*'s part? Why, because *A* does believe anything, ought *B* to believe it? That is ultimate for *A*, but it is not ultimate for *B*. Why should *B* accept this fact of *A*'s nature as decisive, or even in the least relevant, as to a truth which does not relate to *A*'s nature, but, for example, to the existence of a personal God?

34. An attempt has been made to show why *B* should do this — an attempt which seems to rest entirely on an analogy. The people who have not this immediate certainty are compared to the blind. A blind man has no means of perceiving a balloon which floats above him in the air. Yet he would be mistaken if he disbelieved the statement of his friends that the balloon was there. Similarly, we are told, if another man has an immediate conviction of a proposition, of whose truth I am not convinced at all, I ought to supply the deficiency in my nature by taking on trust from him what he perceives immediately.[1]

But an analogy is good enough to meet an analogy.

[1] The example I have given seems to me to do the argument more justice than the one usually taken, in which the blind man denies the existence of colour. For most people, whether blind or not, believe that colour does not exist except in the sensations of those who see. If a blind man denied the existence of colour in this sense, he would not be analogous to a person who denied the truth of the belief of others, but to a person who denied that the others had that belief.

A man in delirium frequently believes that he sees assassins lurking in a corner, or rats leaping on his bed. He is as firmly convinced that he sees them as I am that I see the balloon above me. His physicians do not see them. Would they do well to believe that they were there, but that some limitation of their own faculties prevented their seeing them? They do not believe this. They do not send for the police to arrest the assassins, or for a terrier to catch the rats. And it would be generally admitted that they are right.

Now which is the more correct analogy here? When some people have an immediate conviction of the truth of some particular dogma, and others have not, are these others in the position of the blind man or of the physician? Such cases, it seems to me, are settled, outside the sphere of religious dogma, in one of two ways. Sometimes they are settled roughly by counting heads. The blind are fewer in number than those who can see. But only one man can see the assassins or the rats. Any one else who enters the room cannot see them.

If we were to decide on this plan there would be little reason for any one else to believe a dogma because of *A*'s immediate certainty of it. People who have, or believe themselves to have, the immediate certainty of a religious dogma are always comparatively rare—much rarer than the people who believe in the dogma. Let us take, as an example, the existence of God. A great majority of the inhabitants of the United Kingdom accept this dogma. But I should say that by far the greater number of them believe in it for some reason, good or bad,—the authority of the Church, the statement of the Bible, the argument from design, or the like. The number of those who hold it because of an immediate certainty would be but small.

Moreover, the people who have such immediate convictions agree very little among themselves. Some, for example, have immediate convictions on the subjects of God, immortality, and free will. Others have them on the subject of God alone, or of free will alone, or of immortality alone. Others have them in different combinations, and others on different subjects altogether. If the sight-perceptions of mankind varied as much as this, the blind would rightly decline to put much faith in them.

35. But the test of counting heads, though sometimes the only possible test, is crude and unsatisfactory. We have generally better reasons. A blind man has good reasons for believing that other people have sources of knowledge which he has not. They tell him, for example, that a table is six feet in front of him. He cannot perceive this at the time, but by walking forward he can test it by touch, and he finds it correct. When this has happened several times, the hypothesis that other men have a trustworthy sense, which he has not, becomes far more consistent with his own experience than the hypothesis that they are all labouring under a delusion. When the delirious man, on the other hand, asserts that a rat has come up through a solid floor, or that he is menaced by a man who has long been dead, or who is breathing flame, the hypothesis that he sees something, to which other people are blind, would conflict with the general fabric of experience far more than the hypothesis that he is mistaken.

It is in this way that we ought to test the immediate convictions on religious dogma which we do not happen to share, before we decide whether to accept them as the basis for a reasoned, non-immediate, belief on our own behalf. But to do this is to inquire whether the existence of the object of the immediate belief harmonizes better with our experience than the non-existence of it. And when we make this the test, we have really given up all reliance on *A*'s immediate conviction, and are endeavouring to support our belief on the direct evidence for the truth of the proposition. *A*'s conviction, at most, *suggests* the dogma to us, if we had not heard of it before; the ground of our belief in the dogma is no longer *A*'s belief in it.

In the case of the blind man, the matter would be different. The perceptions of sight of those who surround him are very numerous, and when he has tested them a certain number of times he can believe in the rest without testing them. In these subsequent cases, therefore, his belief *is* based on the perceptions of others. But no man professes to have a very large number of immediate convictions on religious dogmas. It would thus be impossible to argue here that a man's immediate convictions had been proved right on so many points that they might be trusted on the rest. They can only be trusted by us in the cases in which they can be proved. And then *our* belief rests entirely on the proof, and his immediate conviction only furnishes the suggestion for us, and not the reason for our belief.

36. Thus, even granting that *A* has an immediate conviction of the truth of some religious dogma, it is quite irrelevant to me, though decisive for him. But it is by no means certain that *A* has an immediate conviction when he thinks he has. In many cases—though certainly not in all—it seems very probable that he has not. A man may make mistakes in judging and classifying what takes place in his own mind, just as much as he may make mistakes about other things.

For example, a man may be confused as to what it is of which he is immediately certain. He may think that his immediate certainty is of the existence of a personal God, when, in his case, it may be only that the ultimate reality is spiritual. That an ultimate spiritual reality must necessarily be a personal God may be a proposition which he believes on account of reasons—or which, perhaps, when clearly stated, he is not prepared to accept at all.

Or, again, closer analysis may convince him that the proposition, of which he supposed himself to have an immediate certainty, is really dependent for him on other propositions. If it can be proved to him that he was not justified in basing it on those other propositions—either because they are false, or because it does not properly follow from them—he will abandon the result which he had previously thought beyond the reach of argument.

So far we have assumed that a belief which is immediate—that is, which does not rest on arguments—cannot be shaken by them. But an immediate belief may rest on prejudices or tradition. (Of course, if tradition is explicitly accepted as likely to lead to truth, then it is a reason for belief, whether it is a good reason or not, and the conclusion is not immediate. But when a man believes a tradition merely because it has never occurred to him to question it, then the tradition is not a reason for belief, though it is a cause.) Now a belief of this sort, although it does not rest on arguments, may be shaken by them. For it may be shown that it is caused by prejudice or tradition, and this demonstration—though it refutes no arguments for the belief, since there were none to refute—may cause the believer to change his opinion.

The result at which I arrive is that the statement,

that any man has an immediate conviction on a matter of religious dogma is one which he ought not to expect to have any relevance for others, and which he ought only to make, even for his own guidance, after careful tests have convinced him, in the first place, of what his belief really is, and in the second place, that it is not based on arguments. Even then, he ought not to consider the matter closed, unless equally careful tests have also convinced him that his immediate conviction is not to be shaken by arguments. The impotency of argument on matters of religious dogma is always to be regretted. For it is notorious that people do differ on these subjects, and, where argument is impotent, nothing can be done to promote an agreement. Where nothing can be done, the evil must, of course, be recognized. But we are bound in each case to make ourselves quite sure that the evil cannot be removed.

37. It is certain, no doubt, that, if we are to have any knowledge at all, we must have some immediate convictions, and that if we are to have any true knowledge at all, some of our immediate convictions must be true. For nothing can be proved unless we start from something already known, and, if we could know nothing unless it were proved, we could never start at all.

But it would not follow from this that every man must have immediate convictions on matters of religious dogma, or that he must have true immediate convictions on that subject. For it is possible to have knowledge without having immediate convictions as to religious dogmas, although it is not possible to have knowledge without immediate convictions of some sort.

Again, there is nothing to be regretted in the immediacy of our convictions as to the validity of a syllogism in Barbara, or as to the Law of Contradiction. We cannot doubt them, and we cannot prove them. But the inability to prove them is not a disaster here, because nobody denies them. Where we cannot argue, we can do nothing to remove differences of opinion. But there is no harm in this, where there are no differences of opinion to remove. With religious dogma it is different. For every religious dogma of the truth of which any man has an immediate conviction, is believed by many men to be false.

38. We must now consider the second branch of our subject—the arguments which urge that a religious dogma is to be believed by me, because it is held by certain other people.

It has been attempted from time to time to rest the truth of dogmas on the fact that every one believed them. But it is clear, that, if an argument is wanted at all, this argument cannot be true. If no one doubts a proposition, it is superfluous to spend time in proving it. If any one doubts it, then it cannot be truthfully supported by the assertion that every one believes it. Moreover, the assertion is notoriously false. It is impossible to produce any religious dogma which no one has doubted, or even any religious dogma which no one has definitely disbelieved. The view that all persons who profess to disbelieve in certain dogmas are only lying for the sake of notoriety has fortunately only historical interest, since it finds no place in the controversies of the present time.

39. Again, we are invited to believe a dogma because the belief in it, though not universal, is very general. We are sometimes told, indeed, that the belief is universal, except in the case of those people whose minds have become so deeply sophisticated, either by their own action or the influence of others, that they are unable any longer to see the truth which is normally perceptible to every one.

This argument, however, involves a vicious circle. The fact that a position has been reached by a gradual abandonment of primitive ideas and beliefs, effected by a process of self-culture and education, does not necessarily condemn it. Indeed, all advances in science and morality are made in this way. The apparent force of the argument lies in the word 'sophistication'. And here the circle comes in. For how are we to distinguish sophistication from healthy development, except from the one leading to the false and the other to the true? And, as the question to be proved is just whether the conclusions to which the process leads are true or false, to call the process sophistication begs the question while professing to prove it.

It might perhaps be possible to avoid the circle by determining a development as sophistical on account of its *moral* characteristics, and inviting us, when this has been done, to distrust the intellectual result produced by it. But it would not, I think, be now seriously maintained that any religious dogma was certain to all men, except to those who had disqualified themselves by a life of exceptional wickedness.

40. Or, again, the appeal to the general opinion may not criticize the intrinsic trustworthiness of the opinions of the minority, but may confine itself to pointing out that they *are* the minority, and that the opinion of the majority, therefore, is to be preferred.

This ground of belief does not seem very strong. For it has often been acknowledged, by general consent, that the majority has been wrong, for long periods, and on important questions, and that the minority has been right. If we take the opinion of the majority merely because it is their opinion, we adopt a principle which would have led us wrong in very many cases in the past. Why should we trust it for the present or the future? If, on the other hand, we endeavour to recommend this particular opinion of the majority as being from its nature more likely to be right than the opinion of the minority, we have passed away from the argument from majorities, since any intrinsic reasons for the truth of the dogma would be of the same weight if they had as yet only convinced a single person.

Moreover, even if the argument from the opinion of the majority were legitimate, is there any case where we could safely apply it? If it were to have any weight at all, it would surely be only in cases where there is a decisive majority. But on what religious dogmas is there such a majority? If we take into account the whole world (and I do not see that we have any right to exclude any part of it when we are counting heads) it would probably be difficult to tell on which side the majority was as to such questions as the existence of God or human immortality. And if we try (a task almost, if not quite, impossible) to weigh opinions as well as to count them, we find that on these subjects the opinions of wise men show no more agreement than those of men in general. An appearance of a decisive majority for some particular dogma may be gained, no doubt, by first excluding certain nations on the ground of their asserted inferiority, and then insisting that the opinion of every man within the circle of more favoured nations is to be counted as of equal value. But such a course seems to be indefensibly inconsistent.

41. There remains the argument that certain dogmas should be accepted because they have been held by men, or beings incarnate in human bodies, who have worked miracles, including the miracle of predicting the future.

A miracle is an event which we cannot explain by any natural law known to us, and which is therefore attributed, by the believers in its miraculous character, either to a special divine interference with the course of nature, or to the action of some law, differing in its nature from those which explain non-miraculous events. It is then argued that the occurrence of such events at the will of, or in connexion with, a particular being, is evidence, either that that being is himself divine, or that he enjoys special divine favour, and, in either case, that his teaching on matters of religious dogma is trustworthy.

The evidence for the existence of miracles is an inquiry beyond our purpose. But we may remark in passing that, as Hume has pointed out [1], if miracles are to be accepted as evidence of the truth of a religion, then whatever evidence there is for the miracles of one religion is evidence *against* the truth of all incompatible religions. There is perhaps no reason, if there are miracles at all, why they should not occur in connexion with several incompatible systems. There might be reasons why a God should work miracles in connexion with a false religion. Or again the miracles of all the systems except one's own might be ascribed, as they used to be ascribed, to devils. But then miracles would prove nothing about the truth of a religion. If, on the other hand, they can prove anything about it, then none but a true religion can have miracles connected with it. Of two religions with incompatible dogmas, one, at least, must be false, and

[1] *Enquiry concerning Human Understanding*, Sect. 10 (p. 99, ed. Green and Grose).

therefore only one, at most, can have miracles connected with it. Thus neither religion can be proved true, without disproving the existence of the miracles of the other religion. And in so far as these latter are at all probable, they render the truth of the first religion improbable.

42. Supposing that miracles were proved to exist, and to exist in connexion with one religion only, should we be entitled to believe that religion to be true? It seems to me, to begin with, that the existence of the miracle would not prove that it was due to the action of God—meaning by God a supreme being. The amount of power required for any miracle, however startling, can never be proved to be more than finite. And in that case it is always possible that it should have been performed by some being whose power, while much greater than human power, might be far below the power of a supreme being.

If then a miracle were due to the action of such a super-human but non-divine being, would it give any reason to suppose the religion to be true? I see no reason to believe that a being who can raise the dead, or prophesy the future, or assist a man to do these things, would be a specially trustworthy guide on matters of religious dogma. The power of influencing the course of events, and the power of apprehending religious truth, are not always closely connected. Napoleon greatly excelled the average English clergyman in the first, but it would be a rash inference that he excelled him in the second.

But even if it were certain that a non-divine miracle-worker was our superior generally, as well as in the power of working miracles, it would not follow that we should go right if we trusted him on religious dogmas. Men would often go wrong by following the teaching of their spiritual superiors. Buddha and St. Paul were both the spiritual superiors of the average monk, Buddhist or Romanist. But it is clear that on certain points either a monk who followed Buddha or a monk who followed St. Paul would have gone wrong, since either Buddha or St. Paul must be wrong where they differ.

Waiving this difficulty, and assuming that the miracle could prove the special interference of the supreme being, so that the religion connected with it could be accepted as his revelation, should we then be safe in accepting it as true? We should not be justified, I submit, unless we had previously proved that the supreme being was good. For we have no reason to suppose that he will tell us the truth except that it would not be a good act to deceive us. If he is indifferent to the good, or if he is positively malignant, he may well tell us lies, either from caprice or in order to gratify his malignancy.

It is obviously impossible to trust to the revelation to tell us that he is good, since we have no reason to trust the revelation at all unless we know that he is good. This goodness must be proved independently. And thus one of the most important of dogmas cannot be proved by a miracle-based revelation.

43. If, however, this dogma has been independently proved, are we then entitled to accept the divine revelation as true? Even then I do not think that we can do this. A God—that is, a good supreme being—will doubtless regard deceit as an evil. But there is, beyond doubt, much evil in the universe, and, if we are satisfied that there is a God, we must regard that evil as in some way compatible with his goodness. And then why not that further evil of a misleading divine revelation? If, for example, we attribute the existence of evil to God's limited power, and say that cancer and plague exist because they are the best that God can do for us under the circumstances, how can we be sure that the best thing he can do for us under the circumstances is not to deceive us about religious dogma? How can we be sure, for example, if God tells us we are immortal, that it is not a deceit—bad in itself, but good as the means of avoiding some greater evil? If it were the best thing he could do for us, there would be nothing extraordinary in his working miracles to do it.

44. The third branch of our subject is the attempt to prove dogmas by what may be called a *reductio ad horrendum.* Unless a certain dogma is true, it may be said, the universe would be intolerably bad—either intolerably miserable or intolerably wicked—and therefore the doctrine must be true.

It may be remarked, to begin with, that it is not so easy to establish the premise of this argument as is sometimes supposed. When we are told that the universe would be intolerably bad unless *A* were true, we must remember that all dogmas involve complex ideas, and that it may be part only of *A* which is essential to avoid the evil. If it is asserted, for example, that the universe would be intolerable if human actions were completely determined, analysis may reveal that what is meant is only that it would be intolerable if they were completely determined from outside.

Again, tastes differ, and tastes change. A Viking or a Maori warrior might well find that the prospect of an immortality without fighting made the universe intolerable. And he might well be supported by the public opinion of his own society. But the life of the modern Christian—and many of these are Scandinavians, and a few are Maoris—is not rendered miserable by his conviction of the peacefulness of heaven. Examples like these should make us careful before we assert that the universe would be proved worthless if some dogma were proved false.

But there are cases, no doubt, where the premise would be true. We can easily imagine dogmas—or even recall them in history—which it would be scarcely possible to reconcile with any judgement, from any standpoint, except that the universe was very bad. Of the dogmas logically contradictory to these, therefore, we may assert, with scarcely a trace of doubt, that unless *they* are true the universe is very evil.

45. But what of that? What reason have we, at this point, to assert that the universe is *not* very evil? I say 'at this point', because, when we have investigated the fundamental nature of reality, we may find reasons to believe that, in point of fact, the universe is not very evil. But till we have investigated the more important dogmas of religion we have not investigated the fundamental nature of reality, especially as it relates to good and evil. It is only by the determination of such questions as the existence of God, the immortality of man, the purposiveness of things, and the like, that we can determine whether the universe is of a nature which, in point of fact, is not very evil. To use the principle that it cannot be very evil, in order to determine these very problems, would be to beg the question, unless we are in a position to lay down, before we know what the nature of the universe is, that at any rate it cannot be very evil.

This is what the argument before us does. It takes the statement that the universe cannot be very evil as a truth evident in itself—evident before we know what the nature of the world in other respects is—and makes it the basis of further investigation. With what right? If it were very evil, the fact would be very much to be regretted. If its evil were due to the uncontrolled action of any conscious being, that being would be very much to be blamed. But have we any reason to believe that it is not very evil? Reality and goodness are, at any rate *prima facie*, separable. Whenever I admit that I have faults, I admit that something is real which is more or less bad. What argument can be brought forward—none, I think, ever has been brought forward—to show that reality and *extreme* badness are not ultimately compatible?

46. It may be said that, although this line of argument is not permissible in establishing whatever dogmas are taken as fundamental, it may be used in certain cases, when the more fundamental dogmas have been established, to prove further dogmatic propositions. If, for example, it were first proved in some other manner that the universe is entirely dependent on the will of a benevolent God, might we not therefore conclude that the universe is not very bad, and that therefore, for example, we must be immortal, because, if we were not immortal, the universe would be very bad?

I do not, however, think that this is valid. For it must be remembered that any argument which would prove that there was no evil in the universe would be at once condemned by the incompatibility of its conclusion with notorious facts. There is evil in the universe. The slightest pang of toothache, the slightest envious thought, proves that beyond all doubt. It is, therefore, clear that the principle which determines the universe does not exclude all evil from it. And, since this is so, how can we venture to put any limits to the amount of evil which it will admit into the universe? Desirable as it would be to do this, I do not see how it could possibly be done. I do not mean that it is impossible to determine the nature of the universe to such an extent as to be able to assert that, as a matter of fact, in spite of the evil in it, it is more good than evil. But I maintain that this can only be done by first finding out what the nature of the universe is, and by discovering in this manner that it is, in fact, more good than evil. We cannot argue, before we know the characteristics of the universe, that it cannot have a particular characteristic, because it would be very evil, while the universe, or its creator, is perfectly good. For if such an argument could prove anything, it would prove that no evil exists at all. And an argument which proves that is reduced to an absurdity.

The objections I have put forward above depend upon the assertion that it is beyond all doubt that there is real evil in the universe. They would be removed, therefore, if we accepted the view, held by some metaphysicians, that it is impossible that any part of reality should be evil, and that there is no real evil in the universe at all [1]. But, should this view be accepted, while it would destroy my objections, it would destroy no less the arguments to which they were objections. The considerations which induced those metaphysicians to assert that there was no real evil in what appears to us as toothache and envy, would also—since they are always of a quite general nature—induce them to assert that there was no real evil in the consequences which would follow from the falsity of the dogma to be proved. And thus the whole argument for the truth of the dogma would

[1] Cp. Section 171.

vanish, since it rested exclusively on the evil results that would follow from the falsity of the dogma.

47. But, it may be said, why should we not argue as much from our desires and aspirations as from anything else? Are they not as real as anything else in the world? And are not those desires and aspirations, which are directed to the establishment of perfection, either in ourselves or in the world at large, as good as anything in the world? Are we not as much entitled to argue from their existence and their goodness as from any other fact?

This is a consideration which is often urged. So far as the frequent exhortation to trust the heart rather than the head means anything, it appears to mean this. But the position rests on a misunderstanding of a nature so elementary that it could scarcely have escaped detection if the writers who used it had not been blinded by the supposed attractiveness of the conclusion. For the question is not whether we can deduce anything from the existence and goodness of our desires and aspirations. No person in his senses ever denied that we could. The question is what we can deduce. And, especially, can we deduce from their existence or goodness the conclusion that they will be eventually gratified?

Our desires and aspirations are real. From this, of course, we can argue that whatever is inconsistent with their reality must be false. But in what way is the failure of a desire to be gratified inconsistent with its reality? I can see no contradiction whatever in the statement that a desire is real, but remains ungratified. The statement is often true. Many people had a real desire that the Pretender should be victorious in 1745, but they were disappointed.

Our desires, indeed, on such subjects as the existence

of God, or of immortality, are of very different importance from the desire for a political revolution. But they are, as desires, no more real. The reality of a desire relates to its existence as a psychical fact, and from this point of view all desires are on a level. If the reality of any desire is compatible with its nonfulfilment, then we can never argue from the reality of any desire to its fulfilment. If we wish to make a distinction between the desire for heaven and the desire for the restoration of the Stuarts, we can only do so on account of the greater importance of the *object* of the former. And if, on account of this greater importance, we argue that the desire for heaven cannot remain unfulfilled, although the other has remained unfulfilled, we have abandoned the argument from the reality of the desire, and gone back to the argument—already considered—from the amount of evil which the falsity of the dogma would imply.

It should also be noticed that, if the reality of a desire ensured its eventual gratification, then, even if we limited ourselves to those desires which bear on religious dogmas, we should be involved in contradictions. Some men desire that an omnipotent God should exist. Others feel that, in a universe which contains evil, the existence of an omnipotent God would be the culminating evil. Some men passionately desire immortality, others the loss of their personal identity. Each desire is as real as the desire for the contrary result. In this, of course, there is no contradiction. There is no difficulty in believing that *A* desires that there should be a God, and *B* that there should not be a God. But if a desire involves its fulfilment there would be a hopeless contradiction. For it is impossible that God should both be and not be.

This last difficulty is generally concealed from view by a distortion of the evidence, which is certainly in most cases unconscious, but is none the less illegitimate. The man who argues from the reality of desires to the truth of dogmas often, in the first place, ignores the races to which he does not belong. In the next place, he leaves out of account those people of his own race whose desires are different from his own. This latter elimination is the more practicable since such arguments as these are generally put forward in favour of the orthodox ideas of a particular time and place, and therefore there is only a minority to ignore. And in this way he comes to assert that 'the human heart imperatively demands' something or the other, when all that he is entitled to say is that he desires it himself, and that the majority of his race agree with him.

48. Similar considerations apply to the argument that because our desires and aspirations are of high moral value we are entitled to believe that they will be fulfilled. There are two different positions which it is possible to confuse here. One is that the objects of the desires would, if attained, have high moral value. The other is that the desires themselves have high moral value. The argument based on the first of these we have already considered. It is a variety of the argument that certain things must exist, because their non-existence would be so bad, which was discussed above.

But the other remains to be considered. And the fact on which it is based is no doubt often true. The desires and aspirations of men for the truth of various dogmas may have very high moral values. And it must be noticed that they may have that value in cases where the objects of the desires are devoid of it. One man thinks that it is right that a sinner who dies impenitent should be tormented unendingly. Another thinks that it is not right that any one, under any conditions, should be tormented unendingly. One of them must be wrong as to what would be, under certain conditions, a good state of things. But the desire of each that what he thinks good may be realized may have high moral value.

Again, if the highest good for man be an eternity of conscious worship, then it must be a mistake to hold that the highest good for man is to be merged into an impersonal Absolute. But the desire of one man, who holds the first to be best, to gain heaven, and the desire of another man, who holds the second to be best, to gain personal annihilation, may both have high moral value, since each is a desire for what is conceived to be the highest good.

But, admitting the goodness of these desires, what right have we to conclude that they will be fulfilled? Is there any incompatibility between the goodness of a desire and its failure? My desire to be learned may be good, though obstacles may keep me ignorant. My desire to save a drowning man may be good, though he may sink before I can reach him. That a good desire is unfulfilled is an argument of more or less weight against the goodness of the universe in general, but not against the goodness of the desire. Why should desires for the truth of dogmas be different from the rest? And if every good desire was necessarily to be fulfilled, an absurdity would arise, since desires for quite incompatible things may, as we have seen, both be morally valuable.

At any rate, it may be said, any dogma which would paralyse our activity cannot be true. What is meant is not that the truth of the dogma would prevent any one from acting, but that the *belief* in the truth of the dogma would prevent the believer from acting. Now this is no reason for doubting the truth of the belief. It may be a great calamity that people should find their power of action paralysed. But great calamities sometimes happen. And besides, what would be evil in this case would not be the truth of the dogma, but the belief in its truth. So that, even if such an argument was legitimate at all, it could only tell us that people would not believe the dogma. It could not tell us that the dogma was false.

49. And is there any dogma the belief in whose truth would paralyse action? Is there, to begin with, any dogma the belief in which would make action absurd? It is sometimes said that a belief in materialism would make action absurd. If materialism is true, then each man ends at the death of his body, and the human race will almost certainly be frozen out of existence some day. No good result that we can achieve will have any chance of permanence. And this, it is said, will render all action—or at any rate all moral action—absurd.

But why should it do so? It would be absurd to act, no doubt, if action made no difference in any result which was of value. But neither materialism nor any other dogma, which has ever been maintained, could lead to this conclusion. We may not survive the death of our bodies, and the race may be destined to endure for only a few brief millions of years. But, meanwhile, the race has not yet ceased to exist, and here we are, particular individuals. And, while we are here, whatever the future may be, it is better that we should be full than hungry, better that we should work than steal, better that we should read Robert Browning than that we should read Robert Montgomery. It is worth while to bring about these things for ourselves and others, and since that is so, action is not absurd. Even if every man were destined to an unending hell at the end of his present life, it would still be better for that present life to be of one sort rather than another sort.

It may be said, however, that, although there are no dogmas belief in which would make action logically absurd, yet there might be some dogmas belief in which would make action psychologically impossible. Some dogmas might represent the world as inevitably so bad that we should cease, in our despondency, to do what was in our power to make it better, or even to care for those improvements in our own condition for which only selfish motives would be required. It is possible that belief in some dogmas might have this result, though, as I pointed out above, that could not have any bearing on the question of their truth. If a man did firmly believe that he himself, and every one he knew, were going to hell when they died, he might be paralysed with despair. Even this is not certain. But what does seem quite certain is that men are not paralysed in action merely because they do not believe in the eventual and permanent triumph of the good. If they were, it would imply that they thought more about the far distant future, and less about the present and near future than is reasonable. For we have seen that such paralysis, even if it did occur, would not be reasonable. Now it is surely notorious that the average man is so far from thinking more than is reasonable about the distant future that he habitually thinks less than is reasonable about it. All study of economic facts proclaims this. And in religious matters it has been the constant theme of preachers since preaching began. Many men who firmly believe that death will be for them the beginning of intense and unending happiness are profoundly depressed at the thought that death is inevitable. Many men have committed sins in the firm belief that, should they die while committing them, they would go to hell. A member of a race which discounts such expectations at such a rate will scarcely be deterred from action by the conviction that for himself and his friends it will be all the same in a hundred years, and for the world in general it will be all the same in some thousands of centuries.

50. There is one more form which the argument from consequences takes. Practice, we are told, is supreme over theory. All thought is action, and all action is directed towards an end. And, therefore, practical considerations are the supreme test of truth. And, therefore, if we want a particular conclusion to be true or false, or at least if we want it very intensely, we are entitled, and indeed bound, to assume it to be true or false accordingly.

To discuss the truth of the view that practice is supreme over theory would take us too far away from our subject. I will only remark that, so far as I know, all attempts to prove this have consisted of demonstrations that all theory depends upon practice. Admitting this to be true, from one point of view, it seems to me no less true that from another point of view all practice depends upon theory, and that the true conclusion is that the two are reciprocally necessary to each other, and that priority or supremacy can be ascribed to neither.

But it is not necessary to determine this point, for, however it is determined, the argument fails. Let us take a case of theory which depends on practice, and let us ignore the question whether that practice does not in its turn depend upon theory. If a man studies medicine, with a view to acting as a physician, his knowledge is conditioned by practice. A knowledge of medicine is not acquired without strenuous exertion. And the exertion has an end—to acquire money, or to acquire fame, or to cure his patients. Let us take the last. Then his possession of knowledge is dependent on his will to cure the patients who consult him. But for his resolve to be able to do this he would not have acquired the knowledge at all. But if he were to allow himself to make practice the criterion of his knowledge, and, because he desired to cure every patient, to believe that he would succeed in doing so, his belief would be generally admitted to be indefensible.

Now I cannot see any difference between this conduct and that to which the advocates of the supremacy of practice invite us. No one would consider dogma unless he had some end in view. That end may be to know the truth for its own sake. But it may be, and no doubt very often is, the hope of discovering that the universe is good. But it is one thing to investigate the nature of the universe in the hope that we may find that it is good, and quite another to declare that we shall find this result, because we hope to find it.

51. We have now, I think, examined the principal forms in which the argument from consequences presents itself. It only remains to apply to it the test which it is so anxious should be applied to everything. What would be the consequences of the validity of this argument?

The question has sufficient practical importance to justify the inquiry. The good or evil consequences which would result from the truth of a proposition, which so many people hold to be true, can never lack interest. But it also has some bearing on the truth of the argument. The argument is that whatever would be very bad cannot be true. If it should turn out that the argument's own truth would have destructive effects on morality, then its supporters may, of course, deny that it is very bad to exercise destructive effects on morality. But this they are scarcely likely to do. Or else they must admit that, if the argument is true, it proves that it cannot be true, since it belongs itself to the class of very bad things of which it denies the truth. And this would be fatal to the truth of the argument.

'What would be very bad cannot be true.' This seems to many people—and naturally enough at first sight—rather an inspiring and elevating assertion. What is more flattering to morality, which deals with the good, than to make goodness the test of reality? But the consequences of the proposition are far reaching. If that which is very bad is not true, it follows—it is valid even by formal logic—that what is true cannot be very bad.

Extreme badness excludes truth, we are told. So long as anything seems certainly bad, and is not certainly true, this appears to be advantageous for goodness. But supposing some day the truth should be revealed without possibility of doubt—and supposing it should turn out to be what we had previously thought very bad? Then we shall be bound to believe that it is not very bad—not because our opinions on the badness have changed, but because the existence of the thing proves that we were mistaken.

It sounds favourable to morality to assert that Tertullian's hell, and the pleasure which the inhabitants of heaven take in witnessing it, are impossible because they are hideous. And at present, whatever the effect on morality, it is a comforting belief. But supposing we should wake some day to find ourselves in that hell, or in a heaven where the blessed were enjoying the sight of it. Then, if the argument from consequences is valid, we should have to believe that neither the existence of such a hell nor of such a heaven was morally revolting. And such a reversal of our moral judgements could scarcely, I think, be represented as favourable to morality.

52. Even without any such demonstration of such a truth, what would be the effect on morality? It would still be true, if the argument from consequences were correct, that if anything were real, it could not be very bad. That is to say, our moral judgements have no independence. There are things which cannot be very bad, because they possess the non-moral quality of being real.

Surely this destroys the very essence of morality. Morality passes judgement on whatever is real. It pronounces it to be good or bad. And it seems to me that it is the very essence of morality to hold that in this judgement it is independent—that it is able to say of reality that it is bad because it has the quality x, and because x, however fundamental to reality, is bad, or again to say of reality that it is bad because it has not the quality y, and because y, however alien to reality, is essential to goodness.

It is absurd to ask whether reality or goodness be the more fundamental. Each is supreme in its own sphere, and the spheres are so different that they cannot come into conflict. What is real is real, however bad it is. What is not real is not real, however good it would have been. On the other hand, what is good is good, however unreal it is. What is bad is bad, however real it is. And so it is our duty to be humble in judging of reality, and imperious in judging of goodness. For what is real is real, however we may condemn it. But, on the other hand, what we condemn—if we condemn rightly—is bad, even if it were the essence of all reality.

The moral evil of the argument from consequences seems to me to be that it makes us imperious in the wrong place, where our imperiousness is arrogance, and, by an inevitable consequence, makes us humble in the wrong place, where our humility is mean and servile. When the reality of a thing is uncertain, the argument encourages us to suppose that our approval of a thing can determine its reality. And when this unhallowed link has once been established, retribution overtakes us. For when the reality is independently certain, we have to admit that the reality of a thing should determine our approval of that thing. I find it difficult to imagine a more degraded position.

53. It remains to speak of the appeal, sometimes made, to leave dogmatic questions to faith. In so far as this means faith in a proposition, it presents nothing new. If the faith is asserted to be based on reason, then the question will arise whether the reasons are valid, and it becomes a question of argument. If the faith dispenses with reason, we have again the appeal to immediate conviction.

We are sometimes invited to have faith on account of the very limited amount of our knowledge, and the possible errors in it. The argument is not, I think, one which gains any importance by being advocated by thinkers of repute, but it is sufficiently popular to deserve some consideration.

The fact on which it is based is unquestionably true. We know very little, compared to what there is to be known; and what we take for knowledge is frequently error. If this were assigned as a reason for not being certain as to the truth of our conclusions—and especially of our conclusions on obscure and disputed subjects—the argument would be unquestionably legitimate. And if it were given as a reason for complete scepticism, the conclusion, though exaggerated, would not be very surprising. But it is somewhat remarkable that our want of knowledge on any subject, should be put forward as a reason for coming to a particular conclusion on that subject.

Yet this is often done. If it is suggested that there is no evidence that the universe is working towards a good end, the doubter is reminded of the limitations of his intellect, and on account of this is exhorted to banish his doubts from his mind, and to believe firmly that the universe is directed towards a good end. And stronger instances can be found. An apologist may admit, for example, that for our intellects the three facts of the omnipotence of a personal God, the benevolence of a personal God, and the existence of evil, are not to be reconciled. But we are once more reminded of the feebleness of our intellects. And we are invited to assert, not only that our conclusions may be wrong, not only that the three elements may possibly be reconciled, but that they are reconciled. There is evil, and there is an omnipotent and benevolent God.

54. This line of argument has two weaknesses. The first is that it will prove everything—including mutually incompatible propositions—equally well. It will prove as easily that the universe is tending towards a bad end as that it is tending towards a good one. There may be as little evidence for the pessimistic view as for the optimistic. But if our intellects are so feeble that the absence of sufficient evidence in our minds is no objection to a conclusion in the one case, then a similar absence can be no objection to a conclusion in the other. Nor can we fall back on the assertion that there is *less* evidence for the pessimistic view than for the optimistic, and that, therefore, we should adopt the latter. For if our intellects are too feeble for their conclusions to be trusted, our distrust must apply equally to their conclusion on the relative weight of the evidence in the two cases.

The other objection to the argument is that it implies that, if we cannot trust our conclusion that *A* is false, we have no alternative but to conclude that *A* is true. But there is a third alternative to being confident of the truth or confident of the falsity of *A*. It is to abstain from judging about *A* at all. And it is this which would seem to be the more reasonable alternative, supposing our intellects are as weak as they are asserted to be. If I have only taken a hasty view by twilight of my neighbour's garden, it would be rash of me to place much trust in my failure to see any lilies in it. But it would be even more rash if I proceeded from the untrustworthiness of my negative conclusion to a confident assertion that there *were* lilies in it, and that there were exactly seventeen of them.

Even in this case, however, I should not have to ignore an *a priori* conviction of the impossibility of lilies. But the argument from the feebleness of our intellects is often used as a reason why we should believe a state of things to exist which our intellects pronounce to be self-contradictory. I might as well call on you and myself to believe that in some remote corner of the universe the Law of Diminishing Returns devours purple quadratic equations. It seems to us, certainly, that a quadratic equation cannot have colour, or be eaten. But then, how inadequate are our merely human powers to limit the resources of the infinite!

55. But there is another form of the appeal to faith which requires more serious consideration. We are invited to have faith, not in the truth of a proposition, but in the goodness of a person. A man trusts his friends, or his political leader. He believes them to have good motives for actions whose motives he is unable to detect. He often believes them to have good motives in cases where, but for his personal faith in them, the circumstances would strongly suggest that they were actuated by bad motives. Subsequent events often—though not always—prove that he was right. Can we not, we are asked, trust God as we trust our friends?

In the first place it must be remarked that this form of faith can only have a very limited application in the establishment of dogma. It assumes, to begin with, that the dogma of the existence of a personal God has been already established. For the appeal to trust God as we trust men loses all plausibility if God is not a person. If the ultimate reality of the universe were an aggregate of atoms, or a chaos of sensations, or a substance devoid of will, intellect, and purpose, it would be futile to trust it.

Then our faith in a man does not enable us to predict his actions—which, indeed, are often determined, as in the case of a statesman, by considerations which are inaccessible to us. All that it does is to render us confident that they will be wise and virtuous. And a corresponding faith in God will not enable us to determine whether we are immortal, whether our wills are undetermined, or similar questions of dogma. It will only give us light on one particular dogma—that the world is wisely and righteously ordered.

And even here it will not by itself enable us to say that the world *is* wisely and righteously ordered. For my faith in a man only enables me to be confident that his ends will be well chosen and pursued. They may not be attained, for that may be prevented by forces beyond his own control. All that such faith then can teach us of God is that his end is the good ordering of the universe. If we are to be certain that his end will be attained, we must, in some other manner, have established the dogma that God is either omnipotent, or at any rate so powerful as to be free from the risk of eventual defeat.

56. But, even with these limitations, should we be entitled to trust God as we might trust a man whose designs we could not follow? I do not think that we should. Of course, if we have convinced ourselves by direct argument that God is working towards the good and is strong enough to realize it, then we should be sure of his intentions and his success in cases where we could not divine his purpose or directly perceive his success. But this would not be the faith of which we speak. It would be demonstration. If God's nature is proved to be such that he always wills the good, then in any particular case it is clear that he does will it. The faith in God which we are now discussing is a substitute for demonstration, not an instance of it.

We do not put faith in all men, but only in some of them. Why is this? I take it that our faith is an induction from experience. If a man has always acted honourably, and now acts in a way which, viewed in itself, would seem to us dishonourable, we think it more probable that our judgement on the character of this action is mistaken, than that our mass of previous judgements on his former conduct should be mistaken, or that his character should have suffered a sudden change for the worse. We say, therefore, that we are confident that circumstances, at present unknown to us, prevent the action from being dishonourable.

Sometimes, indeed, we have faith in a man of whom we know nothing. But, after all, we know that he is a man. And our faith in this case is based on the experience of the past which tells us that men have never, or very rarely, been known to commit the particular crime or to omit the particular duty in respect of which we have faith in the man before us.

Faith in man, then, rests on an induction—an induction from the previously observed conduct of the man in question, or of men in general. Can such an induction be legitimately made in the case of God, supposing his existence as a person to be already proved? I do not think it can be. For consider how enormous is the scope of the conclusion of the inference as compared with the scope of the observations on which it can be based. What are the limits of our knowledge of what are, on this theory, God's acts? We know a very few of those which have happened on one planet for a few thousand years, together with a few isolated facts about events beyond this planet. On the strength of these we are invited to believe in a uniform law applying to all his actions for the whole universe. We know that the universe is much larger than our sphere of observation. It is perhaps even infinitely larger. Surely to conclude from so little to so much would be ineffably rash. Judas, according to the old legend, once gave a cloak to a leper. If any man who had observed this had argued that the whole of the life of Judas was one continuous succession of virtuous deeds, his conclusion would be admitted to be unfounded. Yet that action would have borne a larger proportion to the whole life of Judas, than those of God's actions which we directly know can be supposed to bear to the whole of his actions.

57. This objection would, I think, be fatal even if every one of the divine actions which we directly know was one which suggested a good purpose. But it is universally admitted that this is not the case, and that many of those facts of the universe which we directly know do not suggest a good design as their most obvious explanation. I will not inquire whether the facts known to us show more good than evil. It is certain that the two are so nearly balanced, that both the evil and the good have been considered, by different observers, to be the greater. Such a mixed experience as this is possibly not incompatible with the existence of a God who is working for the good and who is strong enough to succeed. But it does not form an adequate proof of his existence.

It is clear that we cannot put faith in God without reference to our knowledge of his actions, although we can, in certain cases, do this with man. We trust them from our experience of other men. But if there is a God, he is probably not one of a class of Gods, and, if he were, we should know no more of them than of him. It is true that a personal God would be included with men in the class of persons, but the difference between God and man would be far too great to justify any inference from the conduct of the one to the conduct of the other.

58. There are, of course, cases in which faith does not depend on induction—or indeed on any basis of reason at all. If *A* loves *B*, it is frequently the case, though by no means always, that he will decline to adopt any theory of *B*'s action which involves blame to *B*, even if the facts are such that he would have adopted the theory without hesitation in the case of any person whom he did not love. It has been suggested that this is the right analogy for our faith in God. If we love him, it is said, we shall have faith in his working for good, and that faith will be justifiable.

If this is even psychologically possible, it is clear that it must be possible to love God before deciding whether he is good or not—perhaps a better expression would be, to love a being otherwise answering to the description of God, before deciding whether he possesses the remaining divine quality of goodness. For, if a belief in the goodness has to precede the love, it is clear that the love cannot be the ground of the belief in goodness.

It is, fortunately, possible to love men regardless of their wickedness. Could it be so with God? Could we love an otherwise divine being who was wicked? If he were conceived as omnipotent, or as only self-limited, I should imagine it to be impossible—though it is difficult to be certain. But if he were conceived as a finite being of limited power, working in a world of which he was not the ultimate creator, then I can see no difficulty in a man loving him, irrespective of his goodness or wickedness, as a man might be loved.

This conception of God is not, of course, a very common one. But for those who hold it the position which we are discussing is, no doubt, psychologically possible. They can love God, having satisfied themselves of his existence, with a love as ultimate and super-moral as that of friend for friend. And then, no doubt, they may be led on from this to assume his goodness when there is no evidence, or insufficient evidence, for it.

Such a position is possible, then, but is it justifiable? The analogy, at any rate, is not encouraging. For, after all, the object of any belief is to gain the truth. A belief which does not do this stands condemned. Now it is notorious that the faith in a person which is based on love for him frequently does lead to a false belief, and not to a true one. If a man's mother is convinced of his innocence when a jury is convinced of his guilt, experience shows that the jury is much more likely to be right than the mother.

Nor is faith in the goodness of the beloved essential to love, as has sometimes been maintained. It is fortunate that it is not. For there are cases where the blindest faith in a man's goodness must give way before the demonstration that he is bad. And, if faith in goodness were essential to love, then love would have to cease when this happened. But it need not cease then, and it often does not. We are better than Tennyson—or at least Guinevere interpreted by Tennyson—made us out to be. We need not love the highest when we see it. And we can love the lowest when we see it—when the lowest happens to be the person we love.

59. The conclusion I submit is that on matters of dogma we cannot dispense with proof, and we cannot prove anything by considering the people who believe it, or the disastrous consequences which would follow from its falsity. We must prove our dogmas more directly, if we are to continue to believe them. This will leave all questions of dogma more or less problematic, and many quite unanswered. And this is doubtless unpleasant. But unpleasant things are sometimes true.

Is there then no moral element involved in belief in religious dogma? I believe that to acquire true belief in religious dogma does require moral qualities—in almost every case—in the seeker. But they are required, not to show us what the truth is—for that purpose they seem to me as useless to the metaphysician as to the accountant—but to prevent our turning away from the truth. In the first place, a man will scarcely arrive at truth in these questions without courage. For he must seek before he can find, and at the beginning of his search he cannot tell what he will find.

And he will also need—unless he is almost incredibly fortunate—a certain form of faith. He will need the power to trust the conclusions which his reason has deliberately adopted, even when circumstances make such a belief especially difficult or painful. There are leaden days when even the most convinced idealist seems to *feel* that his body and his furniture are as real as himself, and members of a far more powerful reality. There are times when the denial of immortality seems, to the firmest disbeliever in immortality, a denial which he has scarcely strength to make.

But, whatever is true, it is quite certain that truth is not affected by incidents like these. If all reality has been proved to be spiritual, it cannot have ceased to be spiritual because to-day I am ill or overworked. If I had no reason to believe in immortality yesterday, when other people's friends were dead, I have no greater reason to believe in it because to-day my friend has died.

If we want to know the truth, then, we must have faith in the conclusions of our reason, even when they seem—as they often will seem—too good or too bad to be true. Such faith has a better claim to abide with hope and love than the faith which consists in believing without reasons for belief. It is this faith, surely, which is sought in the prayer, 'Suffer us not for any pains of death to fall from thee.' And for those who do not pray, there remains the resolve that, so far as their strength may prevail, neither the pains of death nor the pains of life shall drive them to any comfort in that which they hold to be false, or drive them from any comfort in that which they hold to be true.

CHAPTER III

HUMAN IMMORTALITY

60. I do not propose to offer here any arguments in support of the positive assertion that men are immortal. I believe that such arguments exist, and that, in spite of the difficulty and obscurity of the subject, they are of sufficient strength to justify a belief in our immortality.[1] But to expound these arguments would require an elaborate and lengthy treatise of technical metaphysics, for they could only be proved by a demonstration of some idealist theory of the fundamental nature of reality. My present design is merely to consider some arguments against immortality which have been based on certain facts of ordinary observation, and on certain results of physical science. I shall endeavour to show that those arguments are invalid, and that the presumption against immortality, which they have produced in many people, should be discarded.

It is better to speak of the immortality of the self, or of men, than of the immortality of the soul. The latter phrase suggests untenable views. For, in speaking of the identity of a man during different periods of his bodily life, we do not usually say that he is the same soul, but the same self, or the same man. And to use a different word when we are discussing the prolongation of that identity after death, calls up the

[1] Cp. my *Studies in Hegelian Cosmology*, chap. ii.

idea of an identity less perfect than that which lasts through a bodily life. The form in which the question is put thus implies that the answer is to be in some degree negative—that a man is not *as much* himself after death as he is before it, even if something escapes from complete destruction.

Moreover, it is customary, unfortunately, to say that a man *has* a soul, not that he *is* one. Now if our question is put in the form 'Has man an immortal soul?' an affirmative answer would be absurd. So far as it would mean anything it would mean that the man himself was the body, or something which died with the body—at any rate was not immortal—and that something, not himself, which he owned during life, was set free at his death to continue existing on its own account. For these reasons it seems better not to speak of the soul, and to put our question in the form 'Are men immortal?'

61. What reasons are there for supposing that our existence is only temporary? I see around me bodies which behave so like my own, that I conclude that they are related to other conscious selves in the same way that my body is related to myself. But from time to time these bodies are observed to cease to behave in this way, and to become motionless, unless moved from outside. Shortly after this the body dissolves into its constituent parts. Its form and identity as a body are completely destroyed. The experience of the past leads me to the conclusion that the same thing will happen in the future to every human body now existing, including my own.

How does this affect the question of my existence? It is clear that if I am a mere effect of my body—a form of its activity—I shall cease when the body ceases. And it is also clear that, if I could not exist without this particular body, then the destruction of the body will be a sign that I have ceased to exist.

But, besides death, there is another characteristic of nature which tends to make us doubt our immortality. Of all the things around us, from a pebble to a solar system, science tells us that they are transitory. Each of them arose out of something else, each of them will pass away into something else. What is a man that he should be exempt from this universal law?

Thus we have three questions to consider: (1) Is my self an activity of my body? (2) Is my present body an essential condition of the existence of my self? (3) Is there any reason to suppose that my self does not share the transitory character which I recognize in all the material objects around me?

62. With regard to the first of these questions, it is certain, to begin with, that my body influences my self much and continuously. A large part of my mental life is made up of sensations. Sensations are continually produced in connexion with changes in the sense-organs of my body, and, so far as we know, they are never produced in any other way. And the course of my thoughts and emotions can be profoundly affected by the state of my body. If my body gets no food for twenty-four hours, they will be affected one way. If I introduce whisky or opium into it, they will be affected another way. If my body is very fatigued, the ordinary current of my mental life will be entirely suspended in profound sleep, or completely broken by dreams. If any of these processes is carried far enough, my body dies, and I cease to have any relation to it for the future, which is certainly an important event for me, whether I survive it or not.

It is equally certain that the mind acts on the body.

My limbs, on many occasions, move according to my will. And the normal behaviour of the body can be altered by the mind, as much as the normal behaviour of the mind can be altered by the body. Grief, or fear, or anger, can produce bodily illness, and even death.

Now each of these groups of events—the effects of body on mind and of mind on body—could be explained on the hypothesis that the self and the body were two separate realities, neither of which was the mere product of the other, though each affected the other, and caused changes in it. And it might be thought that this would be the most natural conclusion to adopt, since the action appears to be reciprocal—mind acting on body as much as body acts on mind.

63. There is always, however, a very strong tendency to adopt the view that the self is a mere activity of the body—or at any rate to hold that the only escape from this view lies in accepting some form of revealed religion which denies it. The cause of this tendency is, in the first place, the incomplete nature of the explanation which would be furnished by the recognition of the self and its body as independent realities.[1] All ultimate explanation endeavours to reduce the universe to a unity. The self is spirit, the body is matter. Spirit and matter, taken as independent realities, are very heterogeneous to one another. It is evident that a theory which makes either spirit or matter to be the sole reality in the universe, introduces a greater degree of unity than a theory which makes them to be equally real.

[1] By independent I do not here mean isolated, or unconnected realities, but such as stand on an equal footing, so that though each is connected with the other, neither is subordinate to the other.

Monism then, whether it be materialism or idealism, is more attractive to the majority of inquirers than dualism is. We must now consider the various causes which tend to make a materialistic monism more plausible than an idealistic monism, and which impel us to the conclusion that matter is the only reality, while human spirit is nothing more than one of the activities which characterize matter when it is in the special form of a human body. (It is immaterial for our present purpose whether the adherents of this view suppose matter to exist as a substance, to which these activities belong, or whether they say that the activities *are* the matter. The difference is insignificant, although the second alternative is sometimes put forward as a great improvement on the first. The essential point is that the spiritual is in either case reduced to a temporary form of an activity whose fundamental nature is non-spiritual.)

64. One of these causes is the fact, so continually pressed upon the notice of every man, that the nature of matter is almost entirely independent of his will. I cannot create matter, and there are narrow limits to the extent to which I can alter it. I cannot make into bread the stone which I see and touch. However passionately I may desire that it should be bread, however serious the consequences to myself and others of its remaining a stone, a stone it remains. By a transition which is natural though illegitimate we tend to believe that whatever is so independent of our will must be independent of us altogether.

To some extent, indeed, the will can affect matter. But the amount of its effects is comparatively insignificant. All the exertions of human beings can only affect the surface of the earth, and that very slightly. On the other hand, matter seems far more powerful in its influence on spirit. The diminution of the temperature of a single planet is an absurdly trivial episode in astronomy. But, if the planet were our earth, it would put an end to the only conditions under which, as far as our observation goes, it is possible for spirit to exist. Since spirit, then, appears so much weaker than matter when they are taken separately, is it strange that, when an attempt is made to reduce the one to the other, it is spirit that is called on to give way?

In matter, too, we can observe a unity and a persistence which *may* belong to spirit but does not obviously belong to it. Spirit we only know in the form of separate individuals, set in the midst of matter, only by means of which they are able to communicate with one another. No human spirit has ever, as far as we know, been open to observation for much more than a hundred years, and the lower animals only slightly exceed this limit. Matter forms one vast system, which history informs us has existed for thousands of years, while science extends the period to millions.

And, again, the amount of knowledge which science gives us about matter is far greater than the amount which it gives us about spirit. On the one side is the whole vast extent of the physical sciences. On the other side we have only psychology—and not the whole of psychology. For the psycho-physical side of that science deals as much with matter as it does with spirit.

All this increases the apparent importance of matter, and seems to render it more probable that matter, rather than spirit, is the sole reality. Spirit, then, would be the way in which matter behaves under certain circumstances. And in support of this it may be said that

p. 82 (line 15). For " only by means of ", *read* " which forms the only means by "

the activity of matter does take different forms. The same energy, science informs us, which sometimes shows itself as heat, shows itself at other times as motion, or, again, as electricity. And this same energy, it is asserted by the materialist, is transformed under other circumstances—when it is found in a human body—into thought, will, and emotion. Certainly, he admits, thought, will, and emotion are not very like heat, motion, and electricity. But then heat, motion, and electricity are not very like one another. And, if they can all be reduced to this common unity, why should not the forms of consciousness share the same fate?

65. These conclusions depend, it will be seen, on the proposition that matter can exist independently of spirit. For if this were not so, it would obviously be absurd to explain away the separate reality of spirit by making it one of the temporary forms which the activity of matter takes. Deeper inquiry will, I think, show us that matter cannot be independent of spirit, that, on the contrary, matter is only an appearance to the mind which observes it, and cannot, therefore, exist independently of spirit. If this is the case we cannot be entitled to consider the self as the activity of its body.

Of what nature is the matter supposed to be which, it is asserted, can exist independently of spirit? It is not conceived as having all the qualities which, in ordinary language, we ascribe to matter. We say of an orange that it is soft, yellow, sweet, and odorous. But these qualities are not held to belong to the orange when it is not being observed. In strictness they are not held to be qualities of the orange at all, but effects excited in the observer by qualities of the orange. The orange is no more yellow when no one

p. 83. (lines 20 to 23). For "matter cannot be independent .... independently of spirit," *read* "there is no reason to believe that matter does exist."

sees it than it is desired when no one knows of its existence.

But the object is conceived as having other qualities which really do belong to it, and give it that nature which it has independently of observation, and if no one observes it. Its size, its shape, its position in space, its motion, and its impenetrability are of this nature. It is these qualities, or others of the same nature, which have the power, under certain circumstances, of exciting in the observer the sensations of softness, yellowness, and the like.

The qualities which are held really to belong to the matter are often called its primary qualities. The others are called its secondary qualities, though, on this theory, it is scarcely correct to call them qualities of the object at all.

Matter, then, is held to be extended, to have position, and to be capable of motion independently of observation. It is also impenetrable—that is, no two pieces of matter can occupy the same position in space. But it has no colour, it is neither hard nor soft, it has no taste, no smell, and no sound.

This is matter as it is conceived in physical science. It may be said also to be the ordinary conception, for although we speak of an orange as yellow, yet the idea that it is not yellow in the dark is generally known and generally accepted.

66. What reason can be given for a belief in the existence of matter? I conceive that such a belief can only be defended on the ground that it is a legitimate inference from our sensations.

This view has been contested, but I believe that the objection to it rests on a misunderstanding. It has been said, and with perfect truth, that my belief in the existence of matter does not *arise* as an inference from my sensations. I do not first become aware of my sensations and then infer the existence of an orange. On the contrary, I am aware of the existence of the orange first. If I am studying psychology or am doubtful of the validity of my knowledge I may then consider the sensations of sight, touch, and so on, connected with my knowledge of the object. But in most cases I never do consider the sensations at all. And there are young children who are quite aware of the existence of a material world, but who have never realized that they have sensations.

These facts are sufficient to refute the view, which has sometimes been held, that our belief in a material world *arises* as an inference from our sensations. But they are quite irrelevant to the question now before us—whether our belief in a material world must not be *justified*, if it is to be justified at all, as an inference from our sensations. And when such facts are used, as not infrequently happens, as bearing on this question, it involves a very serious confusion.

The belief in a material world requires justification. It is natural, in the sense that every one who has not reflected on the subject holds the belief as a matter of course, together with many of those who have reflected on it. But it is not inevitable. It is possible to disbelieve it. Many philosophers have done so. And there is, at any rate, nothing obviously self-contradictory in its denial. Berkeley's theory on the subject —to take only one out of many theories which deny the existence of matter—whether true or false, is not self-contradictory.

Since disbelief in the existence of matter is neither impossible nor contradictory, the question becomes inevitable—what is the justification of the belief? And it becomes more pressing, because in many cases

p. 85. (line 30) For " is not self-contradictory ", *read* " is not obviously self-contradictory."

our judgements as to the existence of matter are admitted to be wrong. In the first place, the quite unreflective consciousness has no more doubt that the world of matter is coloured than it has that the world of matter is extended. But either this or the more reflective judgements of science and the modern world must be wrong here, since they disagree. Again, if a man, who sees a cloak hanging up by moonlight, believes that he sees before him the body of a dead friend, it is obvious that he has completely mistaken the character of the matter before him. And if our judgements as to what the external object is are so often wrong, we have little justification for assuming without inquiry that our judgement that there is an external object is ever right.

There is a stronger case than this. For in dreams we do not only make wrong judgements as to the nature of matter, but as to the existence of matter. If a believer in the existence of matter dreams that he sees a roc's egg, he no more doubts, during his dream, that the roc's egg exists as independent matter, than he doubts, during waking life, that his table exists as independent matter. And yet, on waking, he will admit that in his dream he was neither observing a roc's egg nor any other really existing matter which he mistook for a roc's egg. Not only was his dream-belief 'this is a roc's egg' mistaken, but his dream-belief 'this is independently existing matter', was also mistaken. And if this is mistaken, it is mere credulity to trust his belief in the table's existence without examination. For that belief is no stronger and no more evident than the other had been previously.

67. On what can we base a justification of the belief in the independent existence of matter? Nothing is available except the sensations. They are there, and they are certain. We never believe that we are observing matter unless we experience sensations more or less analogous to the qualities we believe to exist in the matter. We may not be conscious of the sensations as such at all. Indeed, as was said above, in the majority of cases we never are conscious of them. But whenever we look for them, on such occasions, we find them. And the sensations are certain. I may be wrong in believing that matter exists independently of me. But the suggestion that I am wrong in believing I have a sensation is absurd. The belief is not sufficiently separable from the sensation for the possibility of error. I may, of course, be wrong in believing that I had a sensation in the past, for memory may deceive me. And I may be wrong in the general terms which I apply to a sensation, when I attempt to classify it, and to describe it to others. But my knowledge that I am having the sensation which I am having is one of those ultimate certainties which it is impossible either to prove or to deny.

And we find that although the sensations are generally ignored, as sensations, when the correctness of the judgement about the matter is not doubted, yet, as soon as I myself, or other people, entertain a doubt of the correctness of the judgement, the situation is changed. If it is suggested that what I believe to be an experience of matter of a certain sort is really a dream or a delusion, I fall back on the sensations which I have experienced, and consider whether they can be accounted for on any other hypothesis than that of the existence of the matter in question. If they cannot, I consider that I was right in my judgement that the matter did exist.

And we must act in the same way if a doubt arises, not merely of the correctness of our judgements that this or that matter exists, but of the correctness of all judgements that matter of any sort exists. The fact which it is impossible to deny is that we have the sensations. Are we entitled to conclude from this that the material world really exists, and that the natural judgement that it does exist—which is not, however, as we have seen, an inevitable or universal judgement—is correct?

68. It is evident that the sensations are not themselves the matter in question. A sensation is not matter, and it cannot exist apart from the self to whom it belongs. It can have no independent existence. But the sensations, since they begin to exist, must have causes.[1] Now it cannot be said to be obviously impossible that all the causes of my sensations should lie within my own nature. It is certain that they do not lie within that part of my own nature of which I am conscious, for I am not conscious of producing my sensations. But it might be said, as Leibniz has said, that all my sensations arise out of the depths of my own unconscious nature, and that when a self has once come into existence it is as independent of outside influences in its sensations as a clock, when once wound up, is in striking. But there are difficulties in the way of this view into which we have no time to enter, and I do not wish to lay any weight on the possibility of its truth. I am prepared to admit—what seems to me by far the more probable view—that all my sensations have causes which are not myself nor anything in myself. Such causes must in each case be merely part-causes. I am unquestionably

[1] This step might not be accepted by any one who denied the universal validity of causality. A thinker however who denied the universal validity of causality could not, as far as I can see, have the least justification for a belief in the existence of matter.

one of the causes of my own sensations, for, if I did not exist, my sensations also would not exist.

It may thus be admitted that my sensations make it, at any rate, highly probable that some reality exists, which is not myself or anything within myself, but exists independently of me. But we have not got to matter. A reality which exists independently of me need not be matter—it might, for example, be another spirit. We do not call anything matter unless it possesses the primary qualities of matter given above. These qualities correspond to certain sensations, or elements in sensations, and the presence of the sensation in me is held to prove the existence of the corresponding quality in the material object.

69. But is this legitimate? The independent reality has been admitted to be the part-cause of the sensations, but that does not prove that it is like them. Causes do not necessarily resemble their effects. Happiness in *A* does not resemble the misery which it may cause to the envious *B*. An angry man does not resemble a slammed door. A ray of sunshine does not resemble a faded water-colour.

70. And, on this very theory, the external causes of all mental events do not resemble those events. When I see a sphere of red-hot iron I have sensations of form, sensations of colour, and (if I am near enough) a feeling of pain. Now the ordinary theory of matter makes the matter the cause of the sensations of colour and of the feeling of pain, as much as of the sensations of form. Yet it denies that the matter is red or painful. Here, therefore, is an external cause of mental events which does not resemble them. It is therefore impossible to fall back on the principle, that the external cause of mental events always resembles them. And what other principle have we to justify us in ascribing the primary qualities to the external causes of the sensations?[1]

The distinction between the primary and secondary qualities renders the theory of the existence of matter less tenable than it would otherwise be. In the first place, there is the inconsistency, which we have just noticed, of asserting that we can argue from some of our sensations to a resemblance in their causes, and not from others. If our perception of the secondary qualities varies from time to time, and from individual to individual, so also does our perception of the primary qualities. If our perception of the primary qualities exhibits a certain uniformity from time to time, and from individual to individual, so also does our perception of the secondary qualities.

And, in the second place, matter, while extended and impenetrable, is destitute both of colour and of hardness, since these are secondary qualities. Now the sensations of extension and impenetrability only come to us by sight and touch. When they come by sight, they are invariably conjoined with sensations of colour; when they come by touch, they are invariably conjoined with sensations of hardness. We cannot even imagine to ourselves a sensation which gives extension without giving either colour or hardness.

Thus the theory which makes the external causes of our sensations material, reaches a climax of incon-

[1] It must be noticed that the resemblance which the theory attributes to the sensations and their external causes is very limited. The causes are not sensations, nor are their qualities sensations. All that can be said is that, in some way not too easy to define, certain predicates of the causes resemble the content of some of the sensations which are the effects of those causes. But it is not necessary for my argument to follow out the ambiguities and difficulties which follow from this elaborate combination of similarity and difference between sensations and matter.

sistency. Its one defence was the principle that the causes of the sensations must resemble the sensations they cause. But now it turns out that what the causes are to resemble is a mere abstraction from our sensations—a naked extension, which is so far from being a sensation which we experience, that we cannot even imagine what such a sensation would be like.

71. Is it possible to avoid this inconsistency by dropping the distinction between primary and secondary qualities? Shall we say that matter has not only shape, size, position, motion, and impenetrability, but also colour, hardness, smell, and taste? This view certainly avoids some of the objections to the more ordinary theory. It does not make an arbitrary and gratuitous difference in the treatment of two sets of qualities. And it gives matter a nature not utterly unlike our experience, and not utterly unimaginable by us.

But on the other hand the theory would no longer have the support of physical science. For that science treats matter as devoid of the secondary qualities, and it endeavours to show that the primary qualities of matter, under certain circumstances, excite in us the sensations of the secondary qualities.

Of course the independent existence and ultimate nature of matter is a question for metaphysics and not for science. And therefore a metaphysical theory that matter possesses the secondary qualities as well as the primary cannot be upset by the fact that science, working from its own more superficial point of view, finds it convenient to treat matter as possessing only the primary qualities. If science keeps to its own sphere, it cannot clash with any metaphysical theory. If attempts are made to treat its results as if they were metaphysical truths, they have no claim to validity in this sphere, and a metaphysical theory is none the worse for being incompatible with these misapplications.

But the theory that matter exists depended very largely for its plausibility on the illegitimate support which it obtained by taking science as if it were metaphysics; and if it loses this support, as it must in the suggested new form, it loses, indeed, no real strength, but much of what caused people to believe it. As has been already said, the fact that physical science treats matter as independent of spirit, and that physical science forms a vast system, coherent, accepted, and, from its own standpoint, irrefutable, has done much to strengthen the belief that matter, at least, must be real, and that, if one of the two must be explained away by the other, it is spirit which must go, and matter which must stay. The inference is quite illegitimate, since nothing in physical science touches, or can touch, the question of the independent existence of matter. But it is an inference which is frequently made. And when the theory of the independent existence of matter defines the nature of that matter in a manner completely different from the definitions of physical science, it will no longer be able to gain apparent support in this way.

72. Nor does the amended theory, while less inconsistent than the original form, altogether avoid inconsistency. The red-hot sphere of iron is now admitted not only to be a sphere, independent of any observer, but to be red, independent of any observer. But the pain still remains. It is not asserted that the iron is painful, although it causes me pain. Now the pain is a result produced in the observer which is quite as real as the sensations of form and colour, and quite as independent of the observer's will. It is likewise just as uniform. The iron will not give me the sensations except under certain conditions. (I shall not see it to be red, for example, if I am blind, or have my eyes shut.) And, under certain conditions, quite as definite, it will inevitably give me the feeling of pain. Yet nothing resembling the mental effect is attributed to the cause in this case. Why should a difference be made between this case and the others?

And, even if we limit ourselves to sensations, the amended theory does not escape inconsistency. For, even if the secondary qualities are predicated of matter, it remains impossible to assert that matter is like the sensations which it causes. These sensations change for me from moment to moment. If I look at a thing under one set of conditions, as to light and shade, I get one sensation of colour from it; if I change the conditions next minute I get quite a different sensation. And if two men look at it simultaneously under the different conditions of light and shade they will have, simultaneously, the two different sensations of colour which I had successively. Now it is impossible to suppose that the object has at once two different colours. And if it has only one, then that colour must differ, at least, from one of the two sensations experienced by the two observers, since these sensations differ from one another.

The same is the case with the other secondary qualities. And it is also the case with the primary qualities. Two men who look at a cube from different positions simultaneously have two quite different sensations of its shape—not merely numerically different, but sensations which do not resemble one another. Yet an object cannot have two shapes at once, and each of these men would, under normal circumstances, agree about the shape of the object, although they started from non-resembling sensations. It is clear, therefore, that the shape attributed to the object cannot resemble the sensations of shape which it causes, since they do not resemble one another.

73. Now if it is once admitted that the qualities attributed to the external object do not resemble the qualities of the sensations it causes, we have no reason to attribute those qualities to it at all. The only reason we had for supposing the causes of our sensations to have these qualities was the supposed resemblance of the qualities to the sensations. But now it becomes clear that the qualities attributed to the causes, although partially resembling the sensations, do not resemble them completely. It follows that a cause of a sensation may lack some of the qualities of the sensation it causes. And in that case there seems no reason for denying the possibility of its being quite different, and having none of the qualities in question.

It may be replied, no doubt, that it is nevertheless possible that the causes of the sensations do possess qualities partially resembling the sensations. The causes exist, and must have some qualities. And it may be these qualities which they have, and so they may be entitled to the name of matter. But such a possibility would be far too vague to give any support to the theory that matter exists. They may possess these qualities, for there is no reason why a cause should not resemble its effect in certain respects. But there is no reason to believe that they do possess them, or that their possession of them is in the slightest degree probable. A man who boils a lobster red may have a red face—there is nothing to prevent it. But his action in causing the redness of the lobster gives us no reason to suppose that his face is red.[1]

The result is that matter is in the same position as the Gorgons or the Harpies. Its existence is a bare possibility to which it would be foolish to attach the least importance, since there is nothing to make it at all preferable to any other hypothesis, however wild.

74. If we ask, then, of what reality the vast mass of knowledge holds true which science and everyday life give us about matter, we must reply that it holds true of various sensations which occur to various men, and of the laws according to which these sensations are connected, so that from the presence of certain sensations in me I can infer that, under certain conditions, I shall or shall not experience certain other sensations, and can also infer that, under certain conditions, other men will or will not experience certain sensations.

It will be objected that this is not what common experience and science profess to do. When we say that this bottle contains champagne, and this vinegar, we are not talking about our sensations. And physical science deals with such things as planets, acids, and nerves, none of which are sensations.

It is quite true that it is usual to express the conclusions of common experience and of science in terms which assume the independent existence of matter. Most people in the past have believed that matter

[1] The statement that the bare possibility of the external causes being material still remains open must be taken as referring only to the arguments in this chapter. I believe that further consideration should convince us, for reasons closely analogous to those of Hegel and Lotze, that all substance must possess certain characteristics which are essential to the nature of spirit, and incompatible with the nature of matter. If this view is right—a question beyond the purpose of this book to investigate—the existence of matter would be positively disproved.

p. 95. (footnote, line 4) For "closely analogous", *read* "somewhat analogous".

does exist independently; our language has been moulded by this belief, and now it is easier and shorter to express our conclusions in this way. Besides this, most people at present do hold the metaphysical opinion that matter exists independently, and tend to express themselves accordingly.

But the conclusions remain just as true, if we take the view that matter does not exist. Something has been changed, no doubt, but what has been changed is no part either of common experience or science, but a theory of metaphysics which forms no part of either. And so we sacrifice neither the experience of everyday life nor the results of science by denying the existence of matter. We only sacrifice a theory of metaphysics which we have already seen cannot be justified.

I say, in ordinary language, that this is champagne and this is vinegar. Supposing that there is neither champagne nor vinegar as matter existing independently of observation, but that it remains true that a certain group of sensations of sight and smell is a trustworthy indication that I can secure a certain taste by performing certain actions, and that another group of sensations of sight and smell is a trustworthy indication that I can secure a different taste by performing similar actions. Does not this leave a perfectly definite and coherent meaning to the experience of everyday life, which fits every detail of that experience as well as the more common theory does, and only differs from it on a question of metaphysics?

75. It is the same with science. Every observation made by science, every uniformity which is established, every statement as to the past or the future which it asserted, would still have its meaning. The observations would inform us of what had been experienced, the uniformities would tell us the connexions of various experiences, the statements as to the past and future would tell us what has been or will be experienced, or would be so if the necessary conditions were present. What more does science tell us, or what more could it desire to tell us? If the language in which scientific results are generally expressed does seem to tell us more, and to imply the independent existence of matter, that is not science, but metaphysics—the unconscious and uncritical metaphysics of ordinary language — and its rejection does not involve the rejection or the distrust of a single result of science.

Science requires, no doubt, that experience should exhibit certain uniformities, so that a certain experience can safely be taken as an indication of what other experiences will follow it under certain conditions. But this proves nothing as to the independent existence of matter. If the external causes of my sensations, and I myself, have a constant nature, the sensations which are their joint result will exhibit uniformities. And a non-material cause can have a constant nature just as easily as a material cause could have.

Science also requires that experience should have a community of nature between different persons, so that it shall be possible for us to infer from any experience what the experience of another person would be under conditions more or less similar. This, again, can be explained as easily without matter as with it. If my nature and that of other persons were not more or less the same, our experience would not be similar, whatever the nature of its external cause. But if our natures resemble one another, then it is obvious that the action on us of the same external cause would produce results which resembled one another.

76. The denial of matter, it must also be noticed, does not lead us towards solipsism—that is to say, to the denial by each individual of all reality except himself. The arguments which prove that my sensations must have causes which are not myself, nor in myself, but are some other reality, lose none of their force if we decide that these causes are not of a material nature. And the other arguments against solipsism—the consideration of which is apart from our present object—are just as strong on the hypothesis that matter does not exist.

It might be supposed that the theory I have been advocating was a form of agnosticism. Agnosticism holds that we can know nothing but phenomena. Beneath these phenomena lies a reality on which they are based, but of this reality, agnosticism declares, we can know nothing. If we only know of the external causes of our sensations that they do cause the sensations, have we not in effect taken up the agnostic theory that the reality on which phenomena depend is unknowable?

But this is not the case. Agnosticism says that we can know nothing whatever of the reality behind the phenomena. And, in saying this, it contradicts itself. For it asserts that such a reality exists, and that it stands in certain relations to the phenomena. Thus we do know something about it, and it is therefore not the case that we can know nothing about it.

But the theory which I have put forward does not say that we can know nothing about the causes of sensations. It only says that we do not know that they are like the sensation they cause. Even if this should destroy all knowledge of them except of the fact that they were causes, it would not be a general assertion of the impossibility of any knowledge of them, and so there would be no inconsistency in saying that we knew they were causes. To know *m* of anything is inconsistent with being unable to know anything of it, but it is quite consistent with knowing nothing about it except *m*.

Nor does it follow that we know nothing else about the causes of our sensations if we cannot conclude that they resemble the sensations. It might be possible, as various philosophers have maintained, to determine the qualities which must belong to every substance in virtue of its being a substance. And it might turn out that this could give us a considerable knowledge of the nature of these substances. We might, for example, be led to the conclusion that all substance was spirit. But we cannot here do more than point out the possibility of such a result.

77. And we have thus, I think, proved our original contention that the self cannot be one of the activities of its own body. If the self were, as such a theory would require it to be, merely a way in which matter behaved under certain circumstances, it would be possible to explain the self satisfactorily in terms of matter. And it would be possible that a state of things should exist in which those circumstances, which determine the activity of matter to take the form of spirit, occurred nowhere in the universe, which would then be a universe of matter without any consciousness. But so far is this from being the case that we can, as we now see, only explain matter in terms of a conscious self, and to talk of matter existing without consciousness is absurd. Matter is so far from being the sole reality, of which the self is only an

p. 99. (line 7) For " anything of it ", *read* " anything about it ".
p. 99. (third and fourth from bottom) For " we can, as we nowsee, only explain matter in terms of a conscious self ", *read* " we have, as we now see, no reason to believe that matter exists at all ".

activity, that, taken by itself, it is not a reality at all. The only things which have, in any sense, the qualities attributed to matter, are the sensations experienced by selves. In place of an independent reality we find events in men's minds which are real, indeed, but not an independent reality. Matter is simply our illegitimate inference from these events.

This may be put in another way. If my self is one of the activities of my body, then, since my body is only events in the life of some conscious being, my self must also be events in the life of some conscious being. It is clearly absurd to suppose that I am an activity of my body, as my body is known to myself, for then I should be events in my own life. But it is equally impossible that my self should be one of the activities of its own body as perceived by some other self. In that case the self *A* would be events in the life of another self *B*. But how about *B*? By the same rule it also will have to be events in the life of another self. If this self is *A*, the absurdity will recur in an aggravated form. For then *A* would be the events which happened in a self which was itself events in *A*. But if we say that *B* is events in the life of a third self *C*, the same question will arise about *C*, and so on without end. If every self is only events in the life of some other self, no self is explicable until we have reached the end of an infinite series—that is, no self is explicable at all. And so we are brought back to the conclusion that the self cannot be an activity of its body.

I may be thought to have dwelt unnecessarily on this point. Surely, it may be said, it is obvious that the theory that the self is an activity of the body must fall with the theory of the independent existence of matter. Surely no one would maintain that the body

p. 100. (line 9) " since my body ", *read* " since what appears as my body".

only existed for spirit, and, at the same time, that spirit was an activity of body. Yet this has been done. Men of ability have maintained that what I call matter is nothing but my thoughts and sensations, and, at the same time, that my thoughts and sensations are nothing but an activity of my brain—which, being matter, will itself be thoughts and sensations!

78. The bearing of this discussion on the question of our immortality is that it disproves a hypothesis which would render immortality incredible. If the self was an activity of the body, it would be impossible that it should continue to exist when the body had ceased to exist. We might as well suppose, in that case, that the digestion survived the body as that the self did. But the body, as we have now seen, only exists for the selves which observe it, and we cannot, therefore, reduce any self to be an activity of its own body.

It has been admitted, indeed, that there is reality external to myself—the reality which includes the external part-causes of my sensations—although we are not justified in regarding that reality as material. And nothing that we have said excludes the possibility that my self may be a product or activity of some other reality, and one which is destined to cease to exist when some change takes place in its cause.

But while this view has not been refuted, there is not any reason, that I can see, why it should be held to be true, or even probable. There is no reason why we should regard our selves as the product or activity of any other reality whatever, and there is no reason why, if we did regard them as such products or activities, we should consider them likely to cease.[1]

[1] It is commonly held that human selves are not products of non-divine realities, but that they are all produced by God. I have

If the external reality had been independently existing matter, it would have been different. In that case there would have been, as we saw above, a strong tendency to regard matter as the only ultimate reality, and the self as an activity of its body. The tendency would not be due to a logical necessity, since the facts, as we have seen, would not be inconsistent with the hypothesis that spirit and matter were independent, though connected, realities. But the tendency would be very strong, owing to our desire to find as much unity as possible in the universe. If the self is an independent reality, it is a non-material reality. And, granted the independent existence of matter, more unity would be gained by denying the independent reality of spirit. But without independently existing matter the case is changed. No increased unity is gained by making the self a mere activity of something else, unless that something else is already known to exist and to be of a non-spiritual nature. Independently existing matter would, of course, be of a non-spiritual nature. But, when we have rejected this, I have no reason to believe that the reality outside myself is non-spiritual, and so I should gain no increased unity for the universe by denying the independent reality of my self.

And, again, if the self is an activity of its body, it must be a temporary activity, since the body is only a temporary combination of matter. But if the self were an activity of some non-material reality outside itself, there would be nothing to disprove the permanence of the state of things which produces the

given in Chapter VI the reasons why this view does not seem to me to be necessary. But, supposing that they are produced in this way, we should have no ground for supposing that their divine production involved their subsequent destruction, though it is not, of course, incompatible with such destruction.

self—though, of course, there would equally be nothing which proves that permanence.

79. We must now pass on to our second question. My self cannot be a form of the activity of my body. But it is still possible that the nature of my self makes the possession of my present body essential to it. Granted that the body could not exist except for knowledge, it may be that the knowledge of my body, by myself or other selves, is a necessary condition of the existence of my self. In that case it would be an inevitable inference that when my body dissolves, and ceases to be known as a body at all, my self must have ceased also. If *A*, whenever it exists, is necessarily accompanied by *B*, then the cessation of *B* is a sure sign of the cessation of *A*.

What evidence is there in favour of such a view? In the first place, while we have plenty of experience of selves who possess bodies, we have no indubitable experience of selves who exist without bodies, or after their bodies have ceased to exist. Besides this, the existence of a self seems to involve the experience of sensations. Without them, the self would have no material for thought, will, or feeling, and it is only in these that the self exists. Now there seems good reason to suppose that sensations never occur in our minds at present without some corresponding modifications of the body. This is certainly the case with normal sensations. And, even if the evidence for clairvoyance and thought-transference were beyond dispute, it could never prove the possibility of sensation without bodily accompaniments. For it could not exclude—indeed, it seems rather to suggest—the existence of bodily accompaniments of an obscure and unusual kind.

p. 103. (lines 6-9) For " the possession of my present body. . . .by myself or other selves, is " *read* " the perception of my present body, by myself or other selves, a necessary condition . . . "

80. But, after all, these considerations would, at the most, go to show that *some* body was necessary to my self, and not that its present body was necessary. Have we, after the results already reached, any reason to suppose that the death of the body must indicate anything more than that the self had transferred its manifestations to a new body, and had, therefore, passed from the knowledge of the survivors, who had only known it through the old body? The apparent improbability of this lies, I think, simply in our instinctive recurrence to the theory that the self is an activity of the body. In that case, no doubt, it would be impossible that it should be successively connected with two bodies. But that theory we have seen to be untenable. The most that a body can be is an essential accompaniment of the self. And then the supposition that the self has another body would fit the facts quite as well as the supposition that the self has ceased to exist.

There seems no reason why such a change should not be instantaneous. But even if it were not so, no additional difficulty would be created. If a body is essential to the action of a self, the self would be in a state of suspended animation in the interval between its possession of its two bodies—a state which we might almost call one of temporary non-existence. But this is nothing more than what happens, as far as we can observe, in every case of dreamless sleep. During such a sleep the self, so far as we know, is unconscious—as unconscious as it could be without a body. Yet this does not prevent its being the same man who went to sleep and who woke up again. Why should the difficulty be greater in a change of bodies?

81. And then, have we any reason, after all, to

suppose that a body is essential to a self? It seems to me that the facts only support a very different proposition—namely, that, *while a self has a body*, that body is essentially connected with the self's mental life.

For example, no self can be conceived as conscious unless it has sufficient data for its mental activity. This material is only given, as far as our observations can go, in the form of sensations, and sensations again, as far as our observations can go, seem invariably connected with changes in a body. But it does not follow, because a self which has a body cannot get its data except in connexion with that body, that it would be impossible for a self without a body to get data in some other way. It may be just the existence of the body which makes these other ways impossible at present. If a man is shut up in a house, the transparency of the windows is an essential condition of his seeing the sky. But it would not be prudent to infer that, if he walked out of the house, he could not see the sky because there was no longer any glass through which he might see it.

With regard to the connexion of the brain with thought, the chief evidence for it appears to be that diseases or mutilations of the brain affect the course of thought. But this does not prove that, even while a man has a brain, his thoughts are directly connected with it. Many things are capable of disturbing thought, which are not essential to its existence. For example, a sufficiently severe attack of toothache may render all consecutive abstract thought impossible. But if the tooth was extracted, I should still be able to think. And, in the same way, the fact that an abnormal state of the brain may affect our thoughts does not prove that the normal states of the brain are necessary for thought.

Even if the brain is essential to thought while we have bodies, it would not follow that when we ceased to have brains we could not think without them. The same argument applies here as with the organs of sense. It might be that the present inability of the self to think except in connexion with the body was a limitation which was imposed by the presence of the body, and which vanished with it.

82. We have now considered the two arguments against the immortality of the self which spring from the death of the body. But we have said nothing as to the bearing on this question of stories as to the ghosts of the dead. Such stories, however numerous and well authenticated, could never give us any positive evidence that the self was undying. At the most they could prove that it survived its body for a few centuries. But indirectly the evidence could be of considerable importance. For it might possibly prove that the self survived the death of its body. Now the death of its body is by far the strongest reason that we have for doubting the self's immortality. And if the appearances of ghosts could prove that this reason had no weight, they would have removed the greatest difficulty in the way of the belief.

Much of the evidence offered on this subject is doubtless utterly untrustworthy. But there is a good deal which investigation has failed to break down. And there is much to be said in support of the view that, after all deductions have been made for fraud, error, and coincidence, there is still a sufficient residuum to justify the belief that such apparitions are in some cases caused by the dead man whose body they represent.

But the mere proof that there was this causal connexion between the dead man and the apparition would not suffice to prove that the dead man had survived his death. A chain of effects may exist long after its original cause is destroyed. Chatham may be one of the chief causes of the pride which England excites in an Englishman to-day, but this proves nothing as to Chatham's present existence. And, as far as I know all stories of apparitions would be equally well explained by the theory that a man might, before his death, initiate a chain of circumstances which would cause his apparition to appear, after his death, under certain conditions, to men still alive. In this case, nothing would be proved about his existence after death.

This may appear improbable. But, on the other hand, any attempt to prove empirically that man could survive death would have to struggle with such an enormous mass of negative evidence that its antecedent improbability would also not be small. Investigation may give us more evidence, and evidence incompatible with any theory except that of survival. But at present it seems to me that we have much more chance of proving our immortality by metaphysics than by psychical research.

83. We now come to the third question. Is there any reason to suppose that my self does not share the transitory character which I recognize in all the material objects around me?

What exactly is this transitory character? When science says that a material object—a planet, or a human body—ceases to exist, what does it mean? It does not mean that anything is annihilated. It means that units, which were combined in a certain way, are now combined otherwise. The form has changed. But everything which was there before is there now.

We need not inquire whether this distinction between an unchanging matter and a changing form can have more than a rough approximate correctness. It is sufficient to note that the analogy of science—whatever weight may be attached to it—does not give us reason to suppose anything to be transitory except combinations.[1]

84. Is the self a combination? It certainly resembles a combination in one respect, for it is differentiated and contains a plurality. We can have different sensations at the same moment, and sensations, thoughts, and desires can exist simultaneously. But it does not follow from this that a self is a combination. For if a whole is a combination it is built up of parts which could exist without being combined in that way, while the combination could not exist without them. If the bricks of a wall, for instance, were destroyed, the wall would be destroyed too. But the wall might be destroyed by being taken to pieces, and the bricks would remain unchanged.

Do the parts of the self stand in this relation to it? Could my thoughts, my volitions, my emotions, exist isolated, or in new combinations, when my self had ceased to exist? It seems clear to me—the point is too ultimate for discussion—that they cannot. It is inconceivable that a thought, a sensation, a volition, or an emotion should exist outside of a self. And it is inconceivable that the same thought, sensation, volition, or emotion which was once part of my mind could ever be part of somebody else's. The self, we

[1] I do not mean to imply that science necessarily accepts any units as indivisible and imperishable. My point is that it tells us that whatever does perish does so only by the separation of the parts of which it is composed. Those parts may themselves be combinations. Thus it is possible that they may perish, and so on *ad infinitum*. But nothing perishes but combinations.

must say, is complex, but not a compound. It has parts, but it is not built up out of them. For, while it depends on them, they depend just as much on it.

The self, therefore, cannot cease by the separation of its parts. For its parts only exist as united in it, and therefore could not separate from it. If it did cease to exist, it could only be by annihilation. It is not only that the form would have changed, but that the form and content alike would have perished.

Now there is no analogy in science to suggest the probability of this. For science treats nothing as perishable except combinations. This, indeed, does not give us any safe analogy for the persistence of the self. In the first place, there is reason to doubt the absolute validity of the distinction between content and form, which science finds it convenient to make. And, in the second place, the difference between a self and matter is too great for an analogy from one to the other to be very conclusive. But at any rate science gives no analogy against us.

85. All this still leaves us very far from a positive assertion of immortality. Even though the death of the body is no argument for the destruction of the self, and the self cannot be decomposed into its parts, it is still possible that the self should not be immortal. And this view has been held in many systems of idealism. It may be maintained, for example, that finite individuals only exist to carry out some divine purpose, and that it is possible that an individual may cease to be necessary for such a purpose, and so cease to exist. This was Lotze's view. Or again, it may be maintained that there is something contradictory in the idea of a self, which prevents us from regarding it as an adequate expression of reality, and that therefore there is no reason to suppose that any particular self shares the eternity which is characteristic of true reality.

To meet such doubts as these it would be necessary to construct a complete metaphysical system. We should have to determine what was the general nature of all reality, and whether that nature involved the existence of finite selves. And if in this way we reached the conclusion that the existence of finite selves was eternally necessary, the question would arise whether each self was eternal, or whether, on the other hand, there was an unending succession of transitory selves. And, if the former alternative were accepted, we should have to consider the relation between eternity and immortality. All that I have endeavoured to do here has been to show that the more obvious arguments against immortality—those which have most weight with most people—have no validity.

In spite of all arguments, however, the idea that the self cannot be immortal continually returns to us. Reflection may drive it away, but in unreflective moments it besets us again. We seem so small, and the transitory seems so great. It is always hard—there are times when it seems impossible—to believe that each of us can be a permanent element in a universe in which nations and planets are but momentary shapes.

And the belief in immortality seems all the more incredible when we consider many of the believers. Many people believe in it because they wish it to be true, their desires blinding their judgements. Many believe in it on the authority of some religion claiming to be revealed—most of which must, on any hypothesis, be untrustworthy. It is illogical to conclude that a belief cannot be true because it has generally been believed for mistaken reasons, but it is difficult, in practice, to keep our distrust from spreading from the reasons to the belief. Yet I think that reasons for the belief in immortality may be found of such strength that they should prevail over all difficulties.

CHAPTER IV

HUMAN PRE-EXISTENCE

86. In this chapter I wish to point out some reasons for thinking that, if men are immortal, it is more probable that the beginning of the present life, in which each of us finds himself now, was not the beginning of his whole existence, but that he lived before it, as he will live after it. I wish, then, to consider the explanation which this theory, if true, would afford of some of the facts of our experience, and to consider what would be the practical value of such immortality as it can offer us.

The present attitude of most western thinkers to the doctrine of pre-existence is curious. Of the many who regard our life after the death of our bodies as certain or probable, scarcely one regards our life before the birth of those bodies as a possibility which deserves discussion.[1] And yet it was taught by Buddha and by Plato, and it is usually associated with the belief in immortality in the far east. Why should men who are so anxious to-day to prove that we shall live after this life is ended regard the hypothesis that we have already survived the end of a life as one which is beneath consideration?

The explanation of this, I suppose, is that in modern western thought the great support of the belief in immortality has been the Christian religion. Under

[1] Lotze, for example, treats it as a serious objection to a particular argument for immortality, that it would lead to the 'strange and improbable' conclusion of pre-existence. *Metaphysic*, Section 245.

p. 112. (line 6) For " I wish, then ", *read* " I wish, secondly " these circumstances a form of the belief which was never supported by that religion was not likely to be considered of any importance. And, for some reason, Christians have almost unanimously rejected those theories which placed pre-existence by the side of immortality, although there seems nothing in pre-existence incompatible with any of the dogmas which are generally accepted as fundamental to Christianity.

87. The most effective way of proving that the doctrine of pre-existence is bound up with the doctrine of immortality would be to prove directly that the nature of man was such that it involved a life both before and after the present life. But, as I said at the beginning of the last chapter, such a demonstration, if it is possible at all, as I believe it to be, would be far beyond the scope of this book, since it would involve a determination of some of the most fundamental characteristics of reality.

I must content myself with stating in a more general manner my grounds for believing that any evidence which will prove immortality will also prove pre-existence. There are two ways in which a proof of immortality may be attempted. The first is the directly metaphysical way. We may attempt to show that the nature of man is such that he cannot cease to exist while the universe continues to exist; or that his nature is eternal, and that an eternal nature cannot have an end in time; or pursue some similar line of argument.

In this case it seems to me that, if we succeed in proving immortality, it will be by means of considerations which would also prove pre-existence. I do not see how existence in future time could be shown to be necessary in the case of any being whose existence in past time is admitted not to be necessary. If the universe got on without me a hundred years ago, what reason could be given for denying that it might get on without me a hundred years hence? Or if it is consistent with my eternal nature that its temporal manifestation should begin at some point in time, could we find any reason for supposing that the cessation of that manifestation at some point in time would be inconsistent with that nature? I do not see of what kind such a reason could be, nor do I know of any attempt that has been made to establish one.

88. There is another way in which attempts have been made to prove immortality. This consists in demonstrating that the universe is the work of a benevolent creator, or has a purpose harmonious with our ideals of morality, and then arguing that the absence of immortality would be inconsistent with the benevolence of such a creator, or with such a moral purpose. Arguments of this type could prove immortality more readily than they could prove pre-existence. No wrong can be done to the non-existent, and it could hardly be made a reproach to the goodness of the universe that it had waited a long time before it produced a particular person. But, once produced, any person has certain moral claims, and if it could be shown that his annihilation was inconsistent with those claims, we could argue from the goodness of the universe to the impossibility of his annihilation.

Can we, however, validly conclude from the goodness of the universe to the impossibility of a particular evil? It cannot be denied that some evil does exist. The ultimate nature of reality, then, is not incompatible with the existence of some evil. And when this is once admitted, can we hope for an *a priori* proof that any particular evil is too bad to be consistent with the nature of the universe? It seems to me that we cannot, and that we must therefore reject all arguments which attempt to prove that a thing is unreal because it would be evil.

We may call arguments of this sort ethical, since they involve the conception of the good. Modern demonstrations of immortality have almost always been of this character, and not purely metaphysical, and this explains why it has often been held in modern times that immortality was proved, although pre-existence has almost always been disbelieved. Even the arguments of the eighteenth century, which were attacked by Kant, had an ethical element in them. Their supporters endeavoured, indeed, to prove by purely metaphysical considerations that the nature of man's spirit was such that it could not be destroyed in the ordinary course of nature. But they held that each man had been created by an act of the divine will, and they admitted that a similar act could destroy him. In order to show that God never would will to destroy a man whom he had once created, they either fell back on the asserted evidence of revelation, or contended that such destruction would be inconsistent with what we knew of God's moral character, in which case their argument had passed over into the ethical class.

If, as I have maintained, ethical arguments of this sort are invalid, we are forced back on the purely metaphysical arguments, and here we seem unable to treat the past and the future differently. My conclusion is, then, that any demonstration of immortality is likely to show that each of us exists through all time—past and future—whether time is held to be finite or infinite.

89. We must now inquire what consequences would follow from the truth of pre-existence and immortality. Each man would have at least three lives, his present life, one before it, and one after it. It seems more probable, however, that this would not be all, and that his existence before and after his present life would in each case be divided into many lives, each bounded by birth and death. This doctrine of a plurality of future lives and of past lives may be conveniently referred to as the doctrine of plurality of lives.[1]

90. There is much to be said for the view that a plurality of lives would be the most probable alternative, even on a theory of immortality which did not include pre-existence. We do not know what is the cause which produces the limitation of our present lives by birth and death, but some cause there must be, and a cause which produces so important an effect is one which plays a great part in our existence, as long as it continues to act.

If we accept immortality and reject a plurality of lives—and this is the most common opinion, though plurality of lives is accepted more frequently than pre-existence—we must hold that the causes, whatever they are, which operate on each of us so as to cause his death once, will never operate again on any of us through all future time. This is, of course, not impossible. The true nature of death may be such that there is no need, and no possibility, of its repetition. But I do not see that we have any reason to believe this to be even probable.

[1] In one sense, of course, a belief in pre-existence and immortality is itself a belief in a plurality of lives, since it is a belief in three at least. But it will, I think, be more convenient to reserve the name for the belief mentioned above—that for each of us existence on either side of the present life would be divided into more lives than one.

p. 116. (fifth line of footnote) For " either side ", *read* " one or both sides".

It is quite clear that a life which stretched on unendingly without death would in many respects be enormously different from our present lives. An attempt to imagine how our present lives would be transformed if neither we ourselves, nor our fellow men, had in future any chance of death, will make this evident. A believer in immortality who denies, or regards as improbable, the doctrine of the plurality of lives, must assert, or regard as probable, that the death which ends his present life for each of us will change profoundly and permanently the conditions of all future life. And for this there seems no justification.

If we are immortal, the value of our existence either remains permanently at about its present level, or rises or falls after death. In the first case, we should have no reason to suppose that it was so changed that death would not recur. As I have said, it is not impossible that it should be so. But when anything has a particular characteristic, the presumption is that, if that thing continues to exist, its characteristic will not suddenly vary. The presumption is certainly not strong, and it can give us no firm belief. But it is, I think, sufficient to render it rather more probable that the characteristic of periodic mortality will not be left behind at the end of our present lives.

91. I do not think that this would be very generally denied. The denial of the plurality of lives is generally based on the belief that our lives do not remain at the same level after death. It is not because men have died once that it is held that they cannot die again. It is because it is believed that after death they are in heaven or hell, the one much above the level of earthly life, the other much below it. It is contended that the change effected in this manner renders further deaths improbable. This is especially maintained with regard to heaven.

It might be admitted that a state of absolute perfection would render further death improbable. But even the best men are not, when they die, in such a state of intellectual and moral perfection as would fit them to enter heaven immediately, if heaven is taken as a state of absolute perfection which renders all further improvement unnecessary and impossible. This is generally recognized, and one of two alternatives is commonly adopted to meet it. The first is that some tremendous improvement—an improvement out of all proportion to any which can ever be observed in life—takes place at the moment of death, at any rate in the case of those who die under certain conditions. For this, so far as I know, there are no arguments. The other and more probable alternative is that the process of gradual improvement can go on in each of us after the death of our present bodies.

But if our existence immediately after our present life is imperfect, and a state of improvement and advance, it has not yet reached that absolute perfection which might make future deaths improbable. And it seems to me that the natural inference from this view —though it is not drawn by the majority of those who hold it—is that this life will be followed by others like it, each separated from its predecessor and successor by death and re-birth. For otherwise we should be limited to the hypothesis that a process of development, begun in a single life bounded by death, would be continued as an indefinitely long life not divided by birth and death at all. And to suppose, without any reason, such a change from the order of our present experience seems unjustifiable.

Should any persons be destined to attain a state of great and permanent degradation, there would be still less reason for supposing that this would exclude all death from their future existence. Death may possibly be incompatible with absolute perfection, but it has no characteristic which can be suggested as incompatible with the extreme of human degradation. In addition to this we may urge, as in the case of heaven, that it is unreasonable to suppose an extreme change at the moment of death, and that, even if the completed degradation was likely to exclude death, there could be no reason for supposing that the process towards it would do so from the first.

92. Again, processes begun in this life are sometimes finished in it, and sometimes left incomplete. We continually find that death leaves a fault without a retribution, a retribution without a repentance, a preparation without an achievement, while in other cases, where the life has lasted longer, a similar process is complete between birth and death. If men survive death, we must expect that these processes, when not worked out before death, will be worked out in a future life. And if the content of our existence after death has so much similarity, in essential features, with the content of our present lives, the presumption is increased that they have not changed so far as to have shaken off the necessity of periodical death.[1]

93. There seems, therefore, good reason for regarding plurality of lives as the least improbable alternative, even if we accept immortality without accepting pre-existence. But if pre-existence is also accepted, the case for a plurality of lives becomes stronger. For then the death which alters my present life is no longer an unique event in my existence. One life, if no more,

[1] On this subject we may refer to Browning's *Evelyn Hope.*

came to an end for me before my present life could begin. Thus any theory would be false which should try to reject the plurality of lives on the ground that it was probable that death could only occur once in a man's existence. And the plurality of lives could only be regarded as improbable, if there was reason to suppose that an event, which happened twice in a man's existence, would never happen a third time. Now while it might be contended—though, as I have said, I do not think it could be rightly contended—that there were features about death which made it probable it would only occur once in a man's existence, it is difficult to see the slightest ground for the suggestion that there is anything about death which should make it improbable that it should occur three times, although it was known that it occurred twice. We can only accept immortality and pre-existence, while rejecting the plurality of lives, if we hold that the causes which break off a life by a death, after remaining dormant from the beginning of our existence, act twice within an interval of from five minutes to about a hundred years, and then never act again through all future time.

The result seems to be that, even granting that pre-existence is certain, there can be no absolute demonstration of plurality of lives, but that the plurality of lives is the more probable supposition in any case, and is still more probable on the hypothesis of pre-existence.

94. There are various features of our present life which can be explained more satisfactorily on the theory of pre-existence than on any other. I do not, however, wish to suggest that the ease of explaining them on this hypothesis, or the difficulty of explaining them without it, is so great as to form any proof of the doctrine of pre-existence. That doctrine, I believe, can only be proved by metaphysical arguments of the type mentioned at the beginning of this chapter.

The most important of these features is to be found in personal relations. Two people who have seen but little of each other are often drawn together by a force equal to that which is generated in other cases by years of mutual trust and mutual assistance.

The significance of this fact has been, I think, very much underrated.[1] It is generally explained, when any attempt at explanation is made, by the capriciousness of sexual desire. This explanation is inadequate, because the fact to be explained is found with as great proportional frequency in friendships which have no connexion with sexual desire.

On the theory of pre-existence such relations would naturally be explained by the friendships of past lives. The love which comes at first sight, and the love which grows up through many years in this life, would be referred to similar causes, whose similarity would account for the similarity of the effects. Each would have arisen through long intimacy, and the only difference between them would be that in one case the intimacy had been suspended by death and re-birth.

95. Again, as a man grows up certain tendencies and qualities make themselves manifest in him. They cannot be entirely due to his environment, for they

[1] The same may be said of all facts connected with the love of one particular human being for another. Philosophy and theology, when they profess to take men's love seriously, generally confine it either to a love for God, or to a passion for mankind as a whole. It is rarely that the writings of a philosopher or a theologian find anything in a young man's love for his sweetheart except a mixture of sexual desire and folly, or anything in a young man's love for his comrade except folly pure and simple. Hegel is, I think, to be regarded as an exception. Possibly, also, the writer of the first epistle of St. John.

are often very different in people whose environment has been very similar. We call these the man's natural character, and assume that he came into life with it. Such tendencies and qualities, since they are not due to anything which happens after birth may be called innate, as far as the present life is concerned.

Now when we look at the natural characters of men, we find that in many cases they possess qualities strongly resembling those which, as we learn by direct experience, can be produced in the course of a single life. One man seems to start with an impotence to resist some particular temptation which exactly resembles the impotence which has been produced in another man by continual yielding to the same temptation. One man, again, has through life a calm and serene virtue which another gains only by years of strenuous effort. Others again have innate powers of judging character, or of acting with decision in emergencies, which give them, while yet inexperienced, advantages to which less fortunate men attain, if they attain to them at all, only by the experience of years. Here then we have characteristics which are born with us, and which closely resemble characteristics which, in other cases, we know to be due to the condensed results of experience. If we hold the doctrine of pre-existence, we shall naturally explain these also as being the condensed results of experience—in this case, of experience in an earlier life.

96. But, it may be said, can we not explain these features of our life quite as well by means of the theory of heredity, without accepting pre-existence? In the case of personal relations, I do not see that heredity would help us at all. I have admitted that it is not impossible to explain the facts otherwise than by pre-existence. The attraction may be simply due to something in the character of each of the two persons, though in many cases we cannot see what that something could be. In this case it is possible that the element in question has been produced by heredity. But there is nothing in heredity which should make it likely that it should produce this result rather than another, and so the abstract possibility that the attraction is due to some undetected element in the two characters is not increased by the suggestion that the characters were produced by heredity. On the theory of pre-existence, however, we can regard the effects as produced by a cause which would be likely to produce this result rather than another—that is, by relations formed in an earlier life.

Heredity, however, can produce a more satisfactory explanation of innate aptitudes. My ancestors cannot—if pre-existence is false—have loved my friend, and therefore there is nothing in the fact that I inherit from them that explains my loving him at first sight. But my ancestors may have yielded to certain sins, or resisted them, or practised certain activities, and then, supposing that I can inherit the results which they have acquired,[1] there would be a reason why I should have an innate strength or weakness in certain directions, which closely resembled similar characteristics which other men have acquired by their own action in the course of their present lives.

We must, however, remember that such innate dispositions often occur in cases where nothing of the sort can be traced among the ancestors—even if, as sometimes happens, the ancestors themselves can be traced for many generations back. It is possible, no doubt, that the acquirement of some more remote

[1] The possibility of this, however, is, to say the least, highly uncertain.

ancestor may have remained dormant through the intervening generations and have now re-appeared, but the explanation is naturally much less probable than it is in the cases where the ancestral acquirement is known to have existed.

But, as I have said, while I regard the explanation of these facts by pre-existence as better than any which can be offered without it, I do not regard the superiority of the explanation as sufficient to give by itself any appreciable probability to pre-existence, which, if established at all, must be established by more directly metaphysical arguments.

97. Whether acquired qualities can be inherited or not, there is no doubt that there is a certain tendency for men—not merely their bodies, but themselves—to resemble their ancestors. And it may be thought that this would be an objection to our theory of pre-existence. If a man's character is determined by his previous lives, how can it be also determined by the character of the ancestors by whose bodies his body was generated?

There is, however, no real difficulty here. We may have reason to believe that a man's character resembles to some extent that of his ancestors, but it would be impossible to demonstrate, and there is no reason to believe, that there are no elements in it which could not be derived from that source. On the other hand, the doctrine of pre-existence does not compel us to deny all influence on a man's character of the characters of his ancestors. The character which a man has at any time is modified by any circumstances which happen to him at that time, and may well be modified by the fact that his re-birth is in a body descended from ancestors of a particular character.

98. Thus the two ways in which the character in

this life is said to be determined need not be inconsistent, since they can both co-operate in the determination, the tendencies inherited with the body modifying the character as it was left at the end of the previous life. But there is no impossibility in supposing that the characteristics in which we resemble the ancestors of our bodies, may be to some degree characteristics due to our previous lives. In walking through the streets of London, it is extremely rare to meet a man whose hat shows no sort of adaptation to his head. Hats in general fit their wearers with far greater accuracy than they would if each man's hat were assigned to him by lot. And yet there is very seldom any causal connexion between the shape of the head and the shape of the hat. A man's head is never made to fit his hat, and, in the great majority of cases, his hat is not made to fit his head. The adaptation comes about by each man selecting, from hats made without any special reference to his particular head, the hat which will suit his particular head best.

This may help us to see that it would be possible to hold that a man whose nature had certain characteristics when he was about to be re-born, would be re-born in a body descended from ancestors of a similar character. His character when re-born would, in this case, be decided, as far as the points in question went, by his character in his previous life, and not by the character of the ancestors of his new body. But it would be the character of the ancestors of the new body, and its similarity to his character, which determined the fact that he was re-born in that body rather than another. The shape of the head—to go back to our analogy—does not determine the shape of the hat, but it does determine the selection of this particular hat for this particular head.

But how, it may be asked, would each person, in this case, be brought into connexion with the new body that is most appropriate to him? I do not see any difficulty here. We know that various substances which have chemical affinities for one another will meet and combine, separating themselves, to do so, from other substances with which they have been previously in connexion. And we do not find anything so strange or paradoxical in this result as to make us unwilling to recognize its truth. There seems to me to be nothing more strange or paradoxical in the suggestion that each person enters into connexion with the body which is most fitted to be connected with him.

99. And, if there were any difficulty in this supposition, it is a difficulty which would be just as serious for the theory adopted by most believers in immortality who reject pre-existence. If no man existed before the formation of his present body, the question still arises—how did he become connected with a body such that his character resembles the characters of the ancestors of that body? The question would not arise if we supposed that the whole character of the self was simply produced by the body. But this is not the ordinary view. Indeed, it would be difficult to hold this without also holding that the self, as well as its character, was produced by the body. And such a view as this would be all but incompatible—if not quite incompatible—with the belief in immortality.

Again, the question of how the connexion is determined, might be considered to have been answered if it were held that the parents created the new person at the time that they generated the body. I will not discuss the difficulties which, as it seems to me, are involved in this view, since I am dealing with the consequences of pre-existence, and not with the theories which deny it. It is sufficient to remark here that this is not the view most generally adopted. The common belief is that the person is created, not by the parents of his body, but directly by the supreme power of the universe.

And then the question still remains—how does this person get into connexion with the appropriate body, since they come into existence independently? It seems that there are only two alternatives. It may be said that the connexion is due to a special act of divine providence in each case. But, if it is legitimate to invoke such a special act at all, it is surely just as legitimate to invoke it to make a connexion for a previously existing person as for a newly created person. Or else it may be said that the appropriate connexion is brought about by some general law. And there can be no greater difficulty in supposing such a law to act on persons who had previously existed than in supposing it to act on persons newly created. The difficulty, therefore, if there is one, is no greater for those who accept pre-existence than for those who deny it.

100. Is the truth of pre-existence desirable? How much would an immortality be worth to us which was coupled with pre-existence? The most serious objection relates to memory. We do not now remember anything of any previous life. If, nevertheless, we have lived previously, and have forgotten it, there seems no reason to expect that we shall remember our present life during subsequent lives. Now an existence that is cut up into separate lives, in none of which memory extends to a previous life, may be thought to have no practical value. We might as well be mortal, it has been said, as be immortal without a memory beyond the present life. The question becomes more serious if not only pre-existence, but also the plurality of lives is true. For then it might reasonably be feared that we might lose memory, not only twice in our existence, but an indefinitely large number of times.

Sometimes, indeed, it has been asserted that such a state would not be immortality at all. Without memory of my present life, it is said, my future life would not be mine. If memory ceases at the death of my body, I cease with it, and I am not immortal.

If each life had no continuity with its successors, and no effect on them, then indeed there might be little meaning in calling them lives of the same person. But we cannot suppose that this could be the case. If the same self passes through lives, any change which happens to it at any time must affect its state in the time immediately subsequent, and, through this, in all future time. Death and re-birth, no doubt, are of sufficient importance to modify a character considerably, but they could only act on what was already present, and the nature with which each individual starts in any life would be moulded by his experiences and actions in the past. And this is sufficient to make the identity between the different lives real.

101. It has also been objected that the re-birth of a person without a memory of his previous life, would be exactly equivalent to the annihilation of that person and the creation of a new person of exactly similar character. (By this it is not meant that the new person would be exactly similar to the old one at the moment of the latter's annihilation, but that he would be exactly similar to what the old person would have been if he had undergone the process of re-birth.) Now, it is argued, I should not regard myself as immortal if I knew that I was to be annihilated at

p. 128. (line 15) For " through lives ", *read* " through various lives ".

death, even if I knew that an exactly similar person would then be created. And therefore, it is concluded, re-birth without memory cannot be considered as real immortality of the self.

But the objection supposes an impossibility. There could not be another self which would have a character exactly similar to what mine would have been under the same circumstances. The self is not a 'thing in itself', whose nature is independent of its qualities. The self is a substance with attributes, and it has no nature except to express itself in its attributes. If the character of the new self, under certain circumstances, were exactly similar to my character under the same circumstances, its attributes would be exactly similar to my attributes. Then the substance also would be the same, and I should not be annihilated at all.[1] But if there were a new self, then the difference between the selves must be expressed by some difference in the attributes. Then the new self would not be of exactly similar character to what I should have been under the same circumstances, and therefore the creation of a new self would *not* be exactly equivalent to my rebirth. Thus exact similarity of attributes is always sufficient to prove personal identity, not because it would be sufficient if the substance were different, but because it proves that the substance is the same.

[1] It will be seen that I am assuming here that there cannot be two different substances with exactly similar attributes. It does not lie within the scope of this book to discuss this principle, commonly known as the Identity of Indiscernibles. It is sufficient for our present purpose to remark that the principle is accepted by most philosophers of the present day. And those who deny it, and assert that things which are exactly similar may yet be numerically different, would not hold that the annihilation of one thing and the creation of another could be exactly equivalent to the continuance of the first, even though the second was exactly similar to the first. For, although exactly similar, they would be numerically different.

102. We may say then that, in spite of the loss of memory, it is the same person who lives in the successive lives. But has such immortality as this any value for the person who is immortal?

I do not propose to discuss whether any immortality has any value. Some people maintain that all human existence is evil, however favourable the conditions. Others regard existence as of such value that they would be prepared to choose hell rather than annihilation. Among those who differ less violently, some regard the life of the average man on earth at present as of positive value, while others will only regard it as valuable if it is the necessary preparation for a better life which is to follow. Such differences as to the value of life must obviously produce great differences as to the value of its unending prolongation. All that I shall maintain here is that the loss of memory need not render immortality valueless if it would not have been valueless without the loss of memory.

If existence beyond the present life is not expected to improve, and yet immortality is regarded as valuable, it must be because a life no better than this is looked on as possessing value. Now it is certain that in this life we remember no previous lives, whether it be because we have forgotten them, or because there have been none to remember. And if this life has value without any memory beyond itself, why should not future lives have value without memory beyond themselves? In that case a man will be better off for his immortality, since it will give him an unlimited amount of valuable existence, instead of a limited amount. And a man who believed that he had this immortality would have a more desirable expectation of the future than if he did not believe it. If, indeed, a man should say that he takes no more interest in his own fate, after memory of his present life had gone, than he would take in the fate of some unknown person, I do not see how he could be shown to be in the wrong. But I do not believe that most men would agree with him, and to most men, therefore, the prospect of a continuance of valuable existence, even with the periodical loss of memory, would still seem to be desirable.

103. But immortality is not only, or chiefly, desire because it will give us more life like our present life. Its attraction is chiefly for those people who believe that the future life will be, at any rate for many of us, a great improvement on the present. Heaven is longed for, not merely because it will be unending, but because it will be heaven.

Now it might be said that our chief ground for hoping for a progressive improvement after death would be destroyed if memory periodically ceased. Death, it might be argued, would not only remove us from the field of our activity, but would deprive us of all memory of what we had done, and therefore whatever was gained in one life would be lost at death. We could no more hope for a permanent improvement than a man on the treadmill can hope to end higher than he started.

We are not discussing the chance of future progress, but only the relative chance of such progress if memory ceases at death. We must ask, therefore, what elements of value are carried on by memory from the present to the future. And then we must consider whether they can be carried on without memory.

I think I shall be in agreement with most people when I say that memory is chiefly of value in our lives in three ways. In the first place, it may make us wiser. The events which we have seen, and the conclusions at which we have arrived, may be preserved in memory, and so add to our present knowledge. In the second place, it may make us more virtuous. The memory of a temptation, whether it has been resisted or successful, may under various circumstances help us in resisting present temptation. In the third place, it may tell us that people with whom we are now related are the people whom we have loved in the past, and this may enter as an element into our present love of them.

The value of memory, then, is that by its means the past may serve the wisdom, the virtue, and the love of the present. If the past could help the present in a like manner without the aid of memory, the absence of memory need not destroy the chance of an improvement spreading over many lives.

104. Let us consider wisdom first. Can we be wiser by reason of something which we have forgotten? Unquestionably we can. Wisdom is not merely, or chiefly, amassed facts, or even recorded judgements. It depends primarily on a mind qualified to deal with facts, and to form judgements. Now the acquisition of knowledge and experience, if wisely conducted, may strengthen the mind. Of that we have sufficient evidence in this life. And so a man who dies after acquiring knowledge—and all men acquire some—might enter his new life, deprived indeed of his knowledge, but not deprived of the increased strength and delicacy of mind which he had gained in acquiring the knowledge. And, if so, he will be wiser in the second life because of what has happened in the first.

Of course he loses something in losing the actual knowledge. But it is sufficient if he does not lose all. Most progress is like the advance of a tide, whose waves advance and retreat, but do not retreat as far as they advanced. And is not even this loss really a gain? For the mere accumulation of knowledge, if memory never ceased, would soon become overwhelming, and worse than useless. What better fate could we wish for than to leave such accumulations behind us, preserving their greatest value in the mental faculties which have been strengthened by their acquisition.

105. With virtue the point is perhaps clearer. For the memory of moral experiences is of no value to virtue except in so far as it helps to form the moral character, and, if this is done, the loss of the memory would be no loss to virtue. Now we cannot doubt that a character may remain determined by an event which has been forgotten. I have forgotten the greater number of the good and evil acts which I have done in my present life. And yet each must have left a trace on my character. And so a man may carry over into his next life the dispositions and tendencies which he has gained by the moral contests of this life, and the value of those experiences will not have been destroyed by the death which has destroyed the memory of them.

106. There remains love. The problem here is more important, if, as I believe, it is in love, and in nothing else, that we find not only the supreme value of life, but also the supreme reality of life, and, indeed, of the universe. The gain which the memory of the past gives us here is that the memory of past love for any person can strengthen our present love of him. And this is what must be preserved, if the value of past love is not to be lost. The knowledge we acquire, and the efforts which we make, are directed to ends not themselves. But love has no end but itself. If it has gone, it helps us little that we keep anything it has brought us.

But past hours of love are past, whether we remember them or not. Yet we do not count their value to be lost, since their remembrance makes love in the present stronger and deeper. Now we know that present love can also be stronger and deeper because of past love which we have forgotten. Much has been forgotten in any friendship which has lasted for several years within the limits of a single life—many confidences, many services, many hours of happiness and sorrow. But they have not passed away without leaving their mark on the present. They contribute, though they are forgotten, to the present love which is not forgotten. In the same way, if the whole memory of the love of a life is swept away at death, its value is not lost if the same love is stronger in a new life because of what passed before.

Thus what is won in one life may be preserved in another, if the people who love in the first life love the same people in the second, and if their love is greater in the second because it was there in the first. Have we any ground to hope that these two conditions will be fulfilled?

107. Let us take the first. We shall, if my theory is right, have many lives—perhaps many millions of lives, and perhaps an infinite number. Now if the fact that I loved a person in this life gave me no reason to suppose that I should love him in any other, then the whole value of love would be as much confined to a single life as if there were no immortality. And in that case it might perhaps be said that the value of life was equally confined, and that immortality, though real, was worthless.

The chance of a love recurring in any future life,

p. 134. (lines 5-6) after " lost " and before " since ", *insert* " when they are remembered ".

(line 27) " . . . . *and perhaps an infinite number.*" McT. adds a footnote to this in margin—" I do not hold this now."

must depend primarily on the conditions which determine where and how the lovers are born in the future life. For if memory does not survive death, it will be impossible for love to occur in any life in which people do not meet. If the conditions which determine the circumstances of our birth, and through them our juxtapositions throughout life, were themselves determined by chance, or by some merely mechanical external necessity, the probability of meeting our friends in another life would be too small to be regarded.

108. This is a consideration of great importance, but it does not affect the question of the comparative value of immortality with or without loss of memory. Let us take the more ordinary view according to which our existence after this life will be one and unbroken, with a possibility of remembering in it, not only the events which occur in it, but also the events of this life. If the course of that future life is determined by chance, or by mechanical necessity, there will be no reason for hoping that we shall meet beyond death the people whom we have loved in this life. Nor would there be any reason for hoping that the love thus denied fruition would be able to remain unextinguished through unlimited ages of separation and new activities. Once admit events to be determined in this way, and there is no comfort to be gathered from immortality, whether with or without memory, either for love or for any of our other interests.

If immortality is to give us an assurance or a hope of progressive improvement, it can only be if we have reason to believe that the interests of spirit are so predominant a force in the universe that they will find, in the long run, satisfaction in the universe. And, in this case, the constitution of the universe would be such that, whether with or without memory, love would have its way. I will not here inquire whether the ultimate significance of spirit is anything except love. But it will scarcely be denied—least of all by those who feel the difficulties which I am now considering—that the significance of love for spirit is very great. And, if this is so, then the emotional relations which exist between people must be highly significant of their real positions towards one another in the scheme of the universe.

In other words, people who are joined by love cannot be dependent for their proximity to each other—and consequently for the possibility of their love—on some chance or mechanical arrangement whose recurrence we could have no reason to expect. Their love is not the effect of proximity, but its cause. For their love is the expression of the ultimate fact that each of them is more closely connected with the other than he is with people in general. And proximity in a particular life, like everything else, is the effect—or, rather, the manifestation under particular circumstances—of those relations which make up the eternal nature of the universe.

If, therefore, love has joined two people in this life, we have, on the assumption we have been discussing, good reason for believing that their existences are bound up with one another, not for one life only, but for ever. This would not involve their meeting in every life, any more than it would involve their meeting every day of each life. Love can survive occasional absences, and is often even stronger for them. And the universe is on a large scale, which might require long absences. What we are entitled to believe is that, while time remains, their eternal nearness must continually find its expression in proximity in temporal life.

109. As for the second condition; if friends are not to be separated, then certainly the value of love in one life need not perish because there is no memory of it in the next. If by means of it we make our relations stronger and finer, then they will be stronger and finer at the next meeting. What more do we want? The past is not preserved separately in memory, but it exists, concentrated and united, in the present. Death is thus the most perfect example of the 'collapse into immediacy'—that mysterious phrase of Hegel's—where all that was before a mass of hard-earned acquisitions has been merged in the unity of a developed character. If we still think that the past is lost, let us ask ourselves, as I suggested before, whether we regard as lost all those incidents in a friendship which, even before death, are forgotten.

110. I do not deny that in each particular life the prospect of the loss of memory at the end of it will appear to some extent a loss and a breach of continuity. In losing memory we lose that in which we have found great value. Arguments may convince us—as I have said, I think that they ought to convince us—that we do not lose all the value, or any of the highest value, but only the comparatively worthless form, a form which the lapse of years would change to a positive evil. But no doubt we shall always have a tendency to shrink from the loss of memory. Yet I believe that, as we come to understand life better, we shall shrink from such a loss less and less.

We may, I think, fairly conclude that the value of immortality would not be lessened much, if at all, by pre-existence. For the loss of memory which pre-existence renders probable, seems to me the only ground on which it has been held to diminish the value of immortality.

111. Pre-existence, indeed, as we have seen, renders more probable a plurality of future lives. And the prospect of a great number of lives—perhaps an infinite number, though this is not a necessary part of the theory—gives us the prospect of many dangers, many conflicts, many griefs, in an indefinitely long future. Death is not a haven of rest. It is a starting-point for fresh labours. But if the trials are great, so is the recompense. We miss much here by our own folly, much by unfavourable circumstances. Above all we miss much, because so many good things are incompatible. We cannot spend our youth both in the study and in the saddle. We cannot gain the benefit both of unbroken health and of bodily weakness, both of riches and of poverty, both of comradeship and of isolation, both of defiance and of obedience. We cannot learn the lessons alike of Galahad and of Tristram and of Caradoc. And yet they are all so good to learn. Would it not be worth much to be able to hope that what we missed in one life might come to us in another? And would it not be worth much to be able to hope that we might have a chance to succeed hereafter in the tasks which we failed in here?

It may be that the change, the struggle, and the recurrence of death, are endless, or, again, it may be that the process will eventually destroy itself,[1] and merge in a perfection which transcends all time and change. Such an end may come, perhaps, but at any rate it cannot be near.

But though the way is long, and perhaps endless, it can be no more wearisome than a single life. For with death we leave behind us memory, and old age, and fatigue. And surely death acquires a new and

[1] 'As a God self-slain on his own strange altar,
Death lies dead.'—Swinburne, *A Forsaken Garden.*

p. 138. (lines 4-5) " though this is not a necessary part of the theory—", *read* " though this, I think, could be disproved— ".

deeper significance when we regard it no longer as a single and unexplained break in an unending life, but as part of the continually recurring rhythm of progress—as inevitable, as natural, and as benevolent as sleep. We have only left youth behind us, as at noon we have left the sunrise. They will both come back, and they do not grow old.

CHAPTER V

FREE WILL

112. THE question whether a man is free in his actions is ambiguous. We may distinguish four senses in which it may be taken. In the first place, we may say that a man is free to do anything which nothing but his own nature prevents him from doing. In this sense I am not free to draw a triangle with two right angles, since this would be impossible whatever my nature might be. Nor am I, in this sense, free to save a man's life if I am tied at a distance from him by a chain which I cannot break. For I should be equally unable to do it, whatever my nature might be. It is true that I could do it, if my body was sufficiently strong to break the chain. But a man's body is not generally held to be part of himself in such a sense as to make its characteristics part of his nature. Any one who made no distinction between a man and his body would, I suppose, hold that I was free, in this sense of freedom, to break the chain.

But if I do not save a man's life because I mistake the nature of his illness, or because it is too much trouble, then I am acting freely. For if my nature were such as to give me greater discernment, or such as to make me think more of human life and less of my own trouble, I should have saved him. And I should still, in this sense of freedom, be held to be acting freely, however certain it was that my action was absolutely determined by the character with which

I was born, combined with the circumstances of my life. I was not determined from without to be unable to save the life, and internal determination does not, in this sense of freedom, prevent me from acting freely.

113. Freedom, when the word is used in this sense, may be called freedom of self-determination. The use has some importance from a metaphysical point of view, but in ordinary life it is not often employed. Much more common is the second use of the word, according to which a man is free to do anything which nothing but his own will prevents him from doing. So far as a man is free in this sense he can direct his life as he chooses. We may call this, then, freedom of self-direction.

When the word is used in this sense, I should not be called free to save a man when I fail to do so because I mistake the character of his illness. This mistake comes from my nature, but not from my will. I may make it in spite of willing not to make it. But if I do not save his life because it would be too much trouble, I am acting freely in not saving it. I abstain from saving it because I choose to avoid trouble rather than save a life. If my choice—that is to say, my will—had been different, I should have saved him.

Here, as with the freedom of self-determination, I should not be held less free because my choice was absolutely determined by my character and my past history. I am free because I act as I choose, whether the choice is completely determined or not.

114. In the third place a man is said to act freely when he acts according to the ultimate ideal of his nature. The implication here seems to be that freedom is essentially the absence of such limitation as is felt to thwart and constrain the being who is limited, and that no person can be completely free from such constraint except by attaining the ultimate ideal of his nature. Thus it is often said that only the wise or the good are free, although it would be admitted that folly or wickedness might issue from the character of some men by the same inevitable determination which produced in others wisdom and virtue.

This use is extended by analogy to beings which are not believed to feel constraint. Thus we say of a tree that it grows freely when it grows to its normal size in the ground, and that it does not grow freely when it is stunted by being planted in a pot. And yet it is equally the nature of the tree to be stunted in the one case as not to be stunted in the other. The unstunted growth is called free because it is looked on as the ideal.

Virtue is certainly part of the ideal of man. And therefore virtuous action will be called free, in this sense, when wicked action is not. So, also, will a reasonable action as against a foolish action. For this there is also another ground. We often regard reason and conscience as more truly parts of our nature than desires or passions, which we speak of as though they were forces acting on us from outside. When I act according to a passion it is said to master me. When reason or conscience prevents me from doing so, I am said to master my passion. Thus virtuous and reasonable action will appear, by the suggestion of such phrases, as more truly self-determined than other action.

Freedom in this sense may be called freedom of self-realization. It has considerable importance in philosophy, but we shall not have much concern with it in the present chapter.

115. Freedom, finally, is used in a fourth sense,

which is the one which mainly concerns us here. In this sense a man is free in any action, if his choice of that action is not completely determined. The supporters of this view do not, I conceive, maintain that a man can ever act without a motive, nor do they consider that the existence of a motive is incompatible with freedom. But if the motive completely determined the act—either because there was no other motive, or because it was determined to be more effective than any other—then the act would not be freely done. It is essential for freedom that there should be motives prompting to different courses, between which the agent chooses. And it is essential that this choice should not be determined. We may call this freedom of indetermination. My object in this chapter is to consider whether it exists.

Freedom of indetermination is commonly spoken of as Free Will. This seems to be justified. If freedom were defined otherwise, the proper question might be 'Am I free to act?' not 'Am I free to will?' But, if freedom is to imply the absence of complete determination, it can only be the will that is free. The voluntary act is completely determined—in so far as it is not determined by outside circumstances it is determined by the volition on which it follows. No indeterminist would deny this. It is only the volition which is undetermined, and only the volition which is free. When an indeterminist says, for example, that a man has freely committed a murder, he means that he was free in willing to do it. Indeed, in so far as the will did not completely determine the act, as when a bullet meant for a tiger kills a man, the indeterminist would deny that the shooter had acted freely in killing the man.

116. The law of Causality asserts that every event

is determined by previous events in such a way that, if the previous events are as they are, it is impossible that the subsequent event should not be as it is. If this was the only general principle valid as to causality, however, we should not be able to accept as valid any of the laws of science which deal with causation. For these are all general laws, which assert that whatever has a particular quality produces an effect with a particular quality. Thus it is said that all alcohol, taken in large quantities, produces intoxication. But claret differs from whisky, and the effects produced by drinking them are not completely alike, nor are the effects exactly the same with all men. In order to have any warrant for such generalizations we need the additional principle that for any quality, *B*, in an effect, there is always a quality *A* in the cause, of such a nature that every other cause which has the quality *A* produces an effect having the quality *B*. In other words, the knowledge that exactly similar causes will produce exactly similar effects has no practical utility, since we could never know two causes to be exactly similar, even if it were possible that they should be so. What is required is the knowledge that partially similar causes will produce partially similar effects.

I do not propose to consider whether Causality and the Uniformity of Nature are valid of events other than volitions. To deny that they had any validity at all would involve almost complete scepticism, since no expectation of any future event would have the least justification, and all arguments for the existence of anything not perceived at the moment would be absolutely baseless. The indeterminist does not, as a rule, deny that all events except volitions must be completely determined by previous events. Indeed, all his arguments as to the goodness or badness of particular volitions imply that such volitions will result in consequences which will inevitably follow from them, unless interfered with by fresh volitions. He only maintains that volitions are not subject to the law of Causality in so far as to be themselves completely determined. It is this view which I propose to discuss in this chapter.

Some persons, no doubt, are indeterminists as to the will, because they reject the law of Causality altogether, and are indeterminists as to everything. But this position has not sufficient influence on religious thought in general to be of importance for our present purpose.

Determinists, on the other hand, maintain that our volitions are as completely determined as all other events. From this it is generally, and I think correctly, held to follow that it would be ideally possible to deduce the whole of the future course of events from the present state of reality—though, of course, a mind enormously more powerful than ours would be required to do it.

117. We have now to consider the arguments advanced by indeterminists in favour of their contention that volitions are not completely determined. These arguments may be brought under five heads. Firstly, it may be asserted that I have an immediate certainty of the proposition that my will is free. Secondly, that each volition is accompanied by a feeling of freedom in volition, and that this cannot be accounted for except on the supposition that the will is free. Thirdly, that with those volitions which are recognized by us as morally right or wrong is connected a judgement of moral obligation, which cannot be accounted for except on the supposition that the will is free. Fourthly, that the freedom of the will must be true, because its falsity would make all choice absurd. Fifthly, that it must be true, because of the disastrous consequences which would follow if it were not true.

With regard, first, to the persons who assert that they have an immediate conviction that the will is free, and that that conviction cannot be shaken by any arguments. I have given reasons in the second chapter for thinking that such a certainty, while of course decisive for the people who have it, has no force for those who do not have it. And it is beyond doubt that many people—including many believers in free will—have no certainty of this sort. It seems, indeed, not improbable that some, at least, of those who assert that they have such an immediate certainty, have made some mistake as to what it is of which they are immediately certain. They may have an immediate certainty that they can do (in certain cases) what they will to do—which is by no means the same as an immediate certainty that their will is not completely determined. Or they may have an immediate certainty that moral laws are binding on them, without an immediate certainty that this requires an undetermined will for its explanation. But of course if a man has, as some men may have, a certainty of freedom of indetermination, which is neither based on arguments nor capable of being shaken by them, all discussion is at an end as far as he is concerned. No one has any means to convince him, and he has no means to convince anybody.

118. We come next to the argument from that feeling of freedom which we experience in action. To prove that we have this sense of freedom an appeal must be made to introspection, and thus this argument is apt to be confounded with the assertion—just now considered—of an immediate certainty of the proposition that the will is not completely determined. They are, however, quite distinct. The position which we are now discussing does not say that we have an immediate belief, but that we have a feeling. It proceeds to argue that the existence of this feeling cannot be explained, except on the hypothesis that freedom of indetermination really exists. And so it affords some possibility of discussion between opponents, since arguments can be met by arguments.

The fact to which it appeals will scarcely be denied. When I make a false accusation or refrain from making it, when I draw my chair nearer to the fire or leave it where it was, I have a feeling of freedom in my decision which I do not have when I am thrown from a horse, or when I abstain from leaping over St. Paul's. Now, it is said, this feeling of freedom is incompatible with complete determination, and the only legitimate inference is that the decision which is accompanied by the feeling of freedom is one in which I am not completely determined.

119. I believe that we have this feeling of freedom because we are, in fact, free in these cases. But I believe that the freedom of self-direction is quite sufficient to explain the feeling, and that there is no necessity to accept freedom in the sense of indetermination.

On any theory, determinist or indeterminist, it is clear that I shall not make the accusation or draw up my chair unless I choose to do so. I may, in one sense of the word, do such an act unwillingly, because all the possible alternatives may be for some reason or the other repugnant to me. But whatever I do in these cases will be what I will to do in preference to the other alternatives which I recognize as being open to me. And my sense of freedom is just in proportion to the extent to which my action does depend on my will. If I draw a figure on paper I feel freedom in drawing a triangle and not a circle, but I do not feel free in abstaining from giving my triangle two right angles. Now I could draw either a triangle or a circle if I willed to do so, but no volition would enable me to draw a triangle with two right angles.

My sense of freedom, then, is proportionate to the extent to which my action is determined by my will. And I maintain that it is quite accounted for by the fact that the action is determined by the will, and that there is no need to hold that the determining volition is itself undetermined. The feeling of freedom which we experience is a feeling that constraint is absent. And constraint is absent in all cases where a man only acts because he wills to do so. How can constraint enter except in the form of a discord between the will and the facts? And when the facts depend upon the will there can be no such discord. If I were thrown from my horse because I had willed to be thrown from it, where would the discord be?

120. But, it is sometimes said, if we examine our volitions we perceive that they are not completely determined. If this is asserted to be an immediate conviction, we have gone back to a contention which has been already considered. If it is asserted on the basis of an examination of our volitions, I do not see how such a conclusion could ever be justified. We find, indeed, that all our most careful examination fails to show us the whole sum of conditions which are necessary in order that a particular volition should be completely determined. But this by no means proves that the whole sum of conditions is not there. For there is another alternative—that we have not powers of observation sufficient to discover them. And, except in the case of the human will, this alternative is always adopted. It is perfectly impossible for any one to explain why a particular drop of rain falls where it does rather than half an inch away. Yet no one supposes that this event is not completely determined. We all conclude that the series of events is so complicated, so numerous, and so unfavourably placed for observation, that our intellects are not able to follow it. It is clear, therefore, that we cannot logically come to a different conclusion with regard to our volitions unless we have already reason to think that the case for their complete determination is less strong than the case for the complete determination of the falling raindrop. And therefore such a conclusion must rest on a proof of free will, and cannot itself be used as such a proof.

121. It is sometimes urged, as an argument against the complete determination of volitions that a man can act as he believes to be right, although he would get, and knows that he would get, far more happiness by acting otherwise. This, I think, cannot be denied. And this is sufficient to disprove what is called Psychological Hedonism—that is, the doctrine that a man must will to do that which he believes will produce the greatest pleasure for himself. But this is quite distinct from determinism. We may maintain that a man can act from other motives than his own happiness, and yet quite logically assert that it is completely determined both what motives will be present to him, and which he will eventually choose.

122. We now pass to the third head. With those volitions which are recognized by us as being morally good or bad there is connected a judgement of moral obligation. I pronounce that one thing ought to be willed, and that another thing ought not to be willed.

And I approve of whomever wills the first or does not will the second, while I condemn whomever wills the second or does not will the first.[1] With this judgement of moral obligation the absence of complete determination in the will is asserted to be connected.

123. But what is the precise connexion? Is it the existence or the validity of these judgements on which the argument is based? And with what is it said to be incompatible? Is it the truth of complete determination or the belief in complete determination? It is always, I believe, the validity of judgements of obligation which is asserted to be incompatible with the truth of complete determination.

With regard to the other three possible combinations, it would, in the first place, be inconsistent with notorious facts to say that the belief in complete determination was incompatible with the existence of judgements of obligation. It is well known that many people are, and have been, determinists, and that the great majority of them, if not all, have made judgements of obligation respecting their own conduct, and that of others. This is decisive. For if it is replied that they ought not, from their own standpoint, to have made such judgements, the contention is changed, since it is no longer the existence of the judgements which is denied, but their consistency.

In the second place, it cannot be seriously maintained that the belief in complete determination is incompatible with the validity of judgements of obliga-

[1] The judgement of moral obligation is often spoken of as if it referred directly to actions. But it seems to me to refer only to volitions. For I do not blame myself for failing to carry out the most imperative duty, if my will to do so has been thwarted by external forces. And if external forces have hindered the realization of my will to do wrong I do not regard myself as innocent.

tion. In that case, if *A*, being a determinist, says that Nero ought not to have burnt Rome, the judgement is false, while if *B*, who is an indeterminist, makes the same statement at the same minute, it is true. This is clearly absurd. Or if I say this morning, being a determinist, that I ought not to have lost my temper last Saturday, it is false. But if I am converted to indeterminism this afternoon, and then repeat the same statement about the past, it will have changed from false to true.

In the third place, the statement that the existence of judgements of obligation is incompatible with the truth of complete determination is never, so far as I know, maintained, except on the ground that the truth of complete determination would make them invalid, and that, somehow or other, their existence proves that they are not invalid. Nor do I see how it could be maintained on any other ground. But if it is maintained on this ground it rests, of course, on the proposition that the validity of judgements of obligation is incompatible with the truth of complete determination.

And it is in this form—that the validity of the judgements is incompatible with the truth of the determination—that the argument, as I said above, is generally put forward, or intended to be put forward. It is, however, often stated inaccurately, so as to produce confusion between the validity and the existence of the judgements, and between the truth of the determination and the belief in it.

The argument from the judgement of obligation is perhaps the most usual argument for free will. It seems to me that it is also the strongest, though I cannot regard it as satisfactory. 'If the will is completely determined, judgements of obligation cannot be valid.' The first question which this suggests is the question whether judgements of obligation *are* valid.

I do not think that we need trouble to inquire how, if at all, the validity of judgements of obligation could be proved to any one who denied it—should such a person be found. Determinism has always, as a matter of fact, been defended, and, as I believe, can be successfully defended, on the basis that judgements of obligation are valid.

Let us, then, admit their validity. This does not, of course, mean that no such judgement is ever mistaken, but that there are possible judgements of obligation which would be valid when made, even if we have not as yet succeeded in our efforts to find them. Is this compatible with the truth of complete determination?

124. If the truth of complete determination were incompatible with the truth of any proposition logically presupposed in judgements of obligation, it is clear that it would be incompatible with the validity of those judgements, since they cannot be valid unless their presuppositions are true. Every judgement of obligation seems to me to have two such presuppositions. (*a*) Something is such that its existence would be good or bad.[1] (*b*) The person as to whom the judgement of obligation is passed can exercise, by his will, some effect in determining the existence or non-existence of that thing. No one would say that a man ought to will the existence of anything unless the thing willed was judged to be such that its existence

[1] When I use good and bad without any qualification, I do not mean only moral good and bad, but good and bad in the widest sense—that in which it may be said that happiness and beauty are good. I use virtuous and wicked as synonyms of moral good and bad, when the objects spoken of are volitions.

would be good. And, again, no man can will anything (though he may desire it) if he knows that he cannot possibly have any influence on the matter. I should not will that an eruption of Vesuvius should cease, though under certain circumstances I might desire it most passionately. And no sane man would say that I ought to will it, or blame me for not doing so. But if I were a magician, with powers so great that they might possibly stop an eruption, I might then will to stop it, and might possibly be morally bound to will it.

125. Would either of these presuppositions be necessarily false if complete determination were true? I cannot see that either of them would. Would the existence of anything cease to be good or bad because it was completely determined whether I should will its existence or not? Would my own possession of knowledge, or the satisfaction of my own hunger, or the relief of the distress of others, cease to be good because it was absolutely certain that I should will to bring them about, or because it was absolutely certain that I should not will to bring them about? Surely this cannot be maintained.

As to the second presupposition, it is clear that the complete determination of my will can make no difference to the question of the effect of my will on the result contemplated. Whether my will is completely determined or not, it is clear that I shall not learn classical Greek or satisfy my hunger unless I will to do so, while it is not improbable that I shall do both if I will to do them. Again, if I will to relieve the distress of others, it is at least possible that some distress will be relieved which would not have been relieved otherwise, and this is not in the least affected by the question whether my will is inevitably determined to take the course which it does take.

126. We pass from the presuppositions of the judgement to the judgement itself. Is a volition to produce a good result, or the man who makes it, to be less approved, is the volition to produce a bad result, or the man who makes it, to be less condemned, because the volition is completely determined? It does not seem to me that this should make any difference to the approval or condemnation. We approve or condemn whatever tends to produce good or evil results, without further consideration.

If I do not save a man's life because he died before I was born, I do not condemn myself for not saving him, since it is not my individual nature but the general nature of reality which prevents me from altering the past. If I do not save him, because I am tied with a chain I cannot break, do I condemn myself? If I had a stronger body, I could break the chain, and this would be a good thing to do. I shall therefore condemn the nature of my body for being unable to do it. If I regard the body as a part of myself, I shall condemn myself for this bodily imperfection. If I only regard it as an external reality with which I am in close connexion, I shall condemn the body and not myself.[1]

If I fail to save a man's life because I mistake the nature of his illness, and so treat him in the wrong manner, this is a purely intellectual mistake on my part, unless my ignorance is due to past or present misconduct. Postponing this latter possibility, I shall

[1] The intensity of the condemnation will, of course, vary according to the standard attained by similar bodies. We should think very badly of a man's body which was so weak that it could not break sewing-cotton. But if the chain that defied my efforts were the cable of a battle-ship, my condemnation would be no more than the recognition that I should have approved of a strength which is absent from my body, and from the bodies of all other men.

certainly condemn myself for the failure. For the failure is due to my want of knowledge, or of acuteness. These are qualities in my mind which tend to produce evil, and as my mind is certainly myself, whatever my body is, I shall condemn myself. I shall pronounce myself a worse person than I might have been. But I shall not condemn myself morally.

But now suppose that I do not will to save him, because I should be enriched by his death. Or suppose that I do will to save him, but that my efforts are frustrated by ignorance due to past indolence, or to confusion caused by intoxication. In these cases I shall again condemn myself. And in these cases the condemnation will be—as it was not before—moral condemnation. For the result does in these cases—as it did not before—depend upon my will.[1] If I had willed differently in the past, I should not now be ignorant or a drunkard. If I had willed differently at the moment, I should not have preferred my own wealth to the life of another.

I do not think that it would be denied by indeterminists that, even if the will were completely determined, moral condemnation of this sort would be possible. The will would still be, as the body and intellect had been in the previous cases, something which tended to produce a bad result. And there could be no reason why it should not be condemned, as they, although regarded as completely determined, were condemned in the previous cases.

127. The indeterminist, I conceive, would say that while the complete determination of the will would not destroy the validity of *all* approval or condemnation of volitions, yet it would destroy the validity of

[1] I do not say that all moral qualities are qualities of volition, but that all volitions have moral qualities.

the particular variety of approval or condemnation which is found in judgements of obligation.

Judgements of obligation are, of course, different from other judgements of approval or condemnation, or else they could not be distinguished as a class. But they are distinguished as a class by the fact that they are judgements which approve or condemn volitions. And we have seen that the complete determination of volitions could not destroy the validity of all approval or condemnation of them. It must be some other characteristic of judgements of obligation, and not their reference to volitions, which is incompatible with the complete determination of the volitions to which they refer.

Two such characteristics have been suggested. The first is the supreme value of right volition, which, as it is said, is affirmed by our judgements of obligation. The second is the sense of responsibility which follows on those judgements.

128. It is said that we approve right volition more than any other excellence, and that we condemn wrong volition more than any other defect. Some reason, it is said, is required for this fact, and the reason is found in the incomplete determination of the will. There was nothing which made it certain beforehand that we should will rightly or wrongly. And this makes right volition more precious and wrong volition more detestable.

I can see no reason whatever why the moral quality of an act should be regarded as intensified because it happened without complete determination. It seems to me that the moral quality of the act would be just the same, while that of the agent would vanish. The latter point will be dealt with later.[1] But however

[1] Cp. Sections 146–8.

this may be, it would be impossible to prove Free Will in this way, for two reasons. Firstly, if the alleged fact were true, it would admit of another explanation. Secondly, there is reason to believe that the alleged fact is not true.

Our judgement of the value of excellences which are not excellences of volition is different in different cases. We regard the intellectual excellence of Shakespeare with more approval than the excellence shown by the most brilliant punster. Each of them has excelled all other men in a particular direction, but we admire Shakespeare most, because we regard excellence in his direction as more important, in the general scale of values, than excellence in punning. Yet it would be universally admitted that Shakespeare's genius, on the one hand, and the absence of equal genius in myself, on the other hand, were facts completely determined. They do not depend on volition, and it is only in volition that the indeterminist denies complete determination.

If excellences which are admitted to be completely determined can be judged to have different values, so that one is placed above another, then the fact that one excellence is placed above all others is quite compatible with its determination. It would be quite adequately explained by our judgement that the presence of this excellence, however certainly determined, was better, and its absence, however certainly determined, was worse, than the presence or absence of any other excellence.

129. And, again, is it the fact that right volition is always placed above all other excellences? I think that few people would be prepared to assert this. A man who gives water to a thirsty dog has willed rightly. If that man were Shakespeare, or Newton, or Kant, should we be prepared to say that that volition had more value than anything in his nature except some other volition? Surely most people would regard the intellect which was capable of producing Hamlet, or the Principia, or the three Critiques, as of greater value.

Can we even say that the most important right volitions are approved more than any other excellence, and the most important wrong volitions are condemned more than any other defect? I doubt if we can say even this. It might be possible to maintain another proposition which is sometimes confused with the former—namely that the greatest moral excellence is approved more than any other excellence, and that the greatest moral defects are condemned more than any other defects. But the two propositions are very different.

The argument, it will be remembered, rests on the assertion that we can place nothing higher than right volitions, from which it is argued that they must be undetermined. Now, if we must place the greatest moral excellence highest, it is clear that the argument breaks down unless the greatest moral excellence consists in right volition.

The simplest way of proving this would be to show that all moral excellence was right volition. But what, in this case, are we to say of a loving disposition, a fervent patriotism, or a passion for humanity? They are not volitions, or tendencies to volitions, or habits of volition. Nor can they be obtained by willing. (They must, of course, be distinguished from resolutions to act in particular ways. A man's will can cause him to act as he would act if he loved his wife, or his country, or mankind. But it cannot make him love them.)

Love and patriotism, then, are qualities which, by

the indeterminists' own position, are as completely determined as artistic or literary excellence. Will indeterminists be prepared to say that, while justice and beneficence are moral excellences, love and patriotism are mere gifts of fortune, and have no moral import at all? I think that few of them would do so, in spite of the inconsistency in which their refusal plunges them. Kant, indeed, accepted the paradox rather than the inconsistency, but he had few precursors, and he has few successors. His attempt to prove that the teaching of Jesus is on his side can only be described as astounding.[1]

The indeterminist might save his position if he were prepared to maintain that, although certain completely determined qualities are to be called moral excellences, yet they are not to be ranked as the highest moral excellences, a position which is to be reserved exclusively for excellences of the will. But if he maintained this he would have against him the authority of most of the churches—certainly of the Christian church—and of most of the philosophers.

130. We have now to consider the second ground on which judgements of obligation are considered incompatible with the complete determination of volition. A man who is condemned by a judgement of obligation—who is condemned, that is, as having done wrong in what he has willed or omitted to will—is held responsible for his conduct. And people are not held responsible for anything else except an error of volition. In ordinary language we say that a man may be responsible for his ignorance, unskilfulness, or some other defect which is not a defect of volition. But what we really hold him responsible for is his will not to remove the defect, or his abstention from willing

[1] *Critique of Practical Reason*, Part I, Book I, chap. iii.

to remove it. If his circumstances were such, for example, that he could not have ceased to be ignorant, however much he had tried, we should not call him responsible for his ignorance. Even if the cause is not external, but internal, we do not call him responsible unless it is a volition or abstention from one. If I write a play, I am responsible for writing it, for I should not have done so if I willed not to do it. But, if I write it, I am not responsible for its inferiority to Hamlet, for the cause of that inferiority, though it is to be found in my nature, is not in any way dependent on my will.

It is asserted that this responsibility would be incompatible with complete determination, and that any one who is not prepared to reject responsibility must be prepared to deny complete determination of volitions.

131. Three sorts of responsibility have been asserted —to our fellow men, to God, and to self. With respect to the first I suppose that every determinist who need be reckoned with would admit that we are responsible to our fellow creatures for defects of will, and that this responsibility is only for defects of will and for their results.

But is this inconsistent with determinism? I cannot see that it is. For although the determinist does not hold that volitions are distinguished from all other events by not being completely determined, he admits, like every one else, that they are marked off from other events by being determinable by expectation of pleasure and pain. Expectations of pleasure and pain are not the only motives to will, but every one knows that they are motives. On the other hand, nothing but volitions can be directly determined by those expectations, though other things may be determined by them through volitions. The fear of pain may make a boy will to learn his lesson, or it may make him will it more earnestly. And if the only obstacle in the way was the absence or weakness of will, he will now learn it. But if it is entirely beyond his powers, the fear of pain may make him unhappy, but will not make him successful.

Society, therefore, is quite justified in giving rewards for right volitions and in inflicting punishments for wrong volitions, whether those rewards and punishments are deliberately bestowed by the state, or whether they are the less deliberate, but scarcely less powerful rewards and punishments of social praise and blame. For the expectation of such rewards and punishments may encourage right volitions and discourage wrong volitions. But to carry out a system of this sort with regard to good and evil qualities not dependent on volitions would be foolish, and (in so far as it was a system of punishments) brutal, since in these cases the expectation would produce no effect on the results.

132. Now I submit that my responsibility to my fellow men for my volitions consists in the fact that it is reasonable for them to reward and punish me for my volitions, and in that fact only. And, in support of this, we may notice that it is universally agreed that a man is not responsible in cases where his action cannot be affected by considerations of pleasure and pain. A lunatic who suffers from acute homicidal mania is not hanged for murder, because the expectation of such a punishment would not deter a man in such a condition. (It cannot, I imagine, be said that he is not punished because he has not willed the action. He has willed it as much as a sane murderer has.) But when the same murderer is in the asylum it is not thought wrong that he should be punished for infraction of rules by exclusion from an entertainment, because experience shows that the expectation of this may affect his conduct for the future. The homicidal maniac, then, is not held responsible for murder, but is held responsible for untidiness, because punishment will not prevent him from murdering, but may keep him tidy. On the other hand, the cases of certain of the more tyrannical despots, such as Nero, support the contention from the other side. Psychologically their states may have been quite as abnormal as those of the ordinary homicidal maniac. From a medical point of view they might perhaps be called mad. But no court would hold them to have been legally mad. It would have declared them responsible for their actions. And this, I think, would have been right. It is in the highest degree improbable that Nero would have committed any of his crimes if he had known that he would certainly have been executed for them within a month or two. And since the volitions of such men can be affected by the expectation of punishment, it is right to punish them—unless, of course, the punishment required to affect them is so severe as to be a greater evil than the crime.

133. It is clear from all this that the determinist is not in the least inconsistent in advocating that crimes should be punished. A preventive punishment is obviously defensible in exactly the same way for determinists and for indeterminists. Whether the will is free or not, it is clear that while a man is in prison he cannot be robbing on the highway or breaking into houses. Deterrent punishment is justified for the determinist by the fact that experience shows that the expectation of punishment will deter men from committing crimes which they would otherwise have committed. And other sorts of punishment are justified for him by the fact that experience also shows that a man's moral nature may in some cases be improved by influences brought to bear on him during the period of his punishment, or perhaps even by the punishment itself.[1]

There remains vindictive punishment. With regard to this it need only be said here that the justification of it is at least as easy for the determinist as for the indeterminist—or, rather, not more impossible. So far as punishment is vindictive, it makes a wicked man miserable, without making him less wicked, and without making any one else either less wicked or less miserable. It can only be justified on one of two grounds. Either something else can be ultimately good, besides the condition of conscious beings, or the condition of a person who is wicked and miserable is better, intrinsically and without regard to the chance of future amendment, than the condition of a person who is wicked without being miserable. If either of these statements is true — to me they both seem patently false—then vindictive punishment may be justifiable both for determinists and indeterminists. If neither of them is true, it is no more justifiable for indeterminists than it is for determinists.

As to vindictive punishment then, the two schools are, so far as we have yet seen, on a level.[2] But they are not on a level as to other sorts of punishment. The indeterminist may, indeed, believe in preventive punishment, since he attributes no indeterminate volition to bolts and locks. But, as we shall see later

[1] Cp. my *Studies in Hegelian Cosmology*, chap. v.
[2] Cp. Section 151.

on, he is quite inconsistent in supporting either deterrent or reformatory punishment.

134. Responsibility towards man, then, is not affected by determinism. But how about responsibility towards God? God's judgement—on the hypothesis that there is a God to judge—about the moral state of any man could not be affected by determinism. If the man is bad, he is bad, even if he is so necessarily, and an omniscient being would recognize this badness. But responsibility, as we have seen, involves more than this. A man is not called responsible to his fellow men because they do right to judge him evil, but because they do right to punish him. Now, it is argued by the indeterminists, it could not be right for God to punish men if their actions were inevitably determined by the natures which he had given them, and the circumstances in which he had placed them.

It seems to me that the answer is this. If there is an omnipotent God, we are not responsible to him for our sins either on the determinist view or the indeterminist. If there is a God who is not omnipotent, then we can as well be responsible to him for our sins on the determinist view, as we can on the indeterminist—or, indeed, better, as we shall see later on.

Punishment is painful, and pain is evil. Punishment, again, does not abolish the sin for which it is inflicted—that is in the past, and irrevocable. And sin is evil. Consequently no person can be justified in inflicting punishment if he might have avoided the necessity by preventing the offence, unless the final result of the sin and the punishment should be something better than would have happened without either of them.[1] And in this case he will not be justified

[1] Cp. my *Studies in Hegelian Cosmology*, chap. vi.

unless the good result which arises from the sin and the punishment could not be attained without them. For both the sin and the punishment are intrinsically evil.

Now on the determinist hypothesis an omnipotent God could have prevented all sin by creating us with better natures and in more favourable surroundings. And any good result which might follow from the sin and the punishment could be obtained by such a God, in virtue of his omnipotence, without the sin or the punishment. Thus God would not be justified in punishing sin, though man would be, because God could attain the desired results without the punishment, while man could not. Hence we should not be responsible for our sins to God.

135. But neither should we be responsible to an omnipotent God on the indeterminist theory. For such a God could have created us without free will, or without any temptation to misuse it, and then there would have been no sin. The common answer to this is that a universe in which we inevitably did good would be lower than one in which our action, whether for good or for evil, was not completely determined. Thus God is said to be justified in giving us free will, and in punishing us when we misuse it.

I cannot see what extraordinary value lies in the incompleteness of the determination of the will, which should counterbalance all the sin, and the consequent unhappiness, caused by the misuse of that will. If God had to choose between making our wills undetermined and making them good, I should have thought he would have done well to make them good. But we need not decide this point. For the defence is one which is obviously inconsistent with the idea of an omnipotent God—if the word omnipotent is taken seriously. The defence says that God could not secure the benefits — whatever they are — of undetermined volition without also permitting the evil of sin. But there is nothing that an omnipotent being cannot do. Even if the two were logically contradictory, a really omnipotent being cannot be bound by the law of contradiction. If it seems to us absurd to suggest that the law of contradiction is dependent on the will of any person, we must be prepared to say that no person is really omnipotent.

Thus, even on the indeterminist hypothesis, we are not responsible for our sins to an omnipotent God. For he could have prevented the sins without introducing any counterbalancing evil into the universe. And, consequently, he would not be justified in checking sin by pain, since pain is intrinsically evil. If God is omnipotent, then, responsibility is impossible on either theory of freedom.

136. But if there is a God who is not omnipotent, it would be quite possible for the determinist to hold that we are responsible to him for our sins. Such a God might be unable to create a universe without sin, or at any rate unable to do so without producing some greater evil. And he might find it possible, as men do, to check that sin by means of a system of punishments. In that case he would be justified in doing so—provided, of course, that the necessary punishments were not so severe as to be a greater evil than the sin.

And here the determinist is in a better position than the indeterminist. For the indeterminist, as we shall see later on,[1] has no right to assert that there is even a probability that the expectation of punishment

[1] Section 149.

will alter our volitions. And, without such a probability, no punishment can be justified except preventive or vindictive punishment.

It has sometimes been held that the freedom of the human will was the only way in which the goodness of God could be made compatible with the evil in the universe. The evil we perceive in the universe consists—at any rate chiefly, perhaps entirely—of sin and misery. If sin was due to man's free will, and not to God's decree, God, it was said, could not be condemned on account of the existence of sin. And the misery could be explained as the justifiable punishment of sin. On the other hand, it was said, if there was no free will, not only would it be impossible to justify the existence of misery, but the sin also must be referred to God as its ultimate cause. And it would become impossible to regard a being as good, to whose nature we must attribute the existence of all the evil of the world.

But, as was shown above, if God is omnipotent, it is impossible to account for the evil of the universe in this way. Indeed, if God is omnipotent, it is impossible that he can be good at all.[1] This would not be affected by the freedom of the human will, since the gratuitous permission of evil would be as fatal to the divine goodness as the gratuitous creation of evil. On the other hand, if God is not omnipotent, his goodness would not be impossible upon either theory as to the human will. For a being of limited power but perfect goodness might well create evil, and not merely allow it, supposing that the creation of the evil was the only way of avoiding a greater evil or attaining a greater good.

[1] Cp. chap. vi.

137. There remains the question of responsibility to self. I think that this must be admitted to exist—that a man does feel a responsibility to himself for defects of volition, or for defects caused by defects of volition, which he does not feel in cases of a defect with which volition has nothing to do. The analogy between this and responsibility to others seems to be that in the latter I recognize that the others do well to punish me, and in the former I recognize that I do well to feel shame and remorse. Now why should I recognize that it is well to feel shame and remorse for defects which are—directly or indirectly—defects of volition, and not for other defects? The indeterminist would suggest that it is because the defects of volition are not completely determined. But why should I judge it less good to feel shame or remorse for a defect because it is an essential part of my character? Surely, the more closely a defect is bound up with me, the more it is essential to my nature, the more reason I have to feel ashamed of it.

It seems to me that the real reason why it is good that I should feel shame and remorse in one case and not in the other is the same as the reason why it is good that other people should punish me in one case and not in the other—namely, that in the one case it may improve matters, and in the other case it cannot. The only part of our nature which is influenced by the expectation of pleasure and pain is the will. If, therefore, a defect is not a defect of volition, or dependent on one, it will not be in any way affected by the fact that I am miserable about it. And the misery, being useless and painful, will be evil, and it will be well to avoid it.

It is well that I should recognize my defects of all sorts, since ignorance of one's limitations often produces evil. But when I have once recognized that I cannot write a play as good as Hamlet, it is profitless self-torture if I am miserable about it, since my misery will certainly not remove this particular limitation.

With defects of volition, the matter is different. My will can be affected by expectations of pleasure and pain, and so, if the contemplation of a defect of volition, or its consequence, gives me pain, I may be led to cure the defect to escape from the pain. Or if the defect is in the past, and irrevocable, the dread of experiencing similar pain may keep me from similar faults. In such cases shame and remorse may bring advantages outweighing the evil of their painfulness, and, since they will be profitable, it will be good to feel them.

138. We now pass from the considerations drawn from the validity of judgements of obligation to the fourth division of the indeterminist arguments. This was that the will must be free because, if it were not free, all choice would be absurd. It may be conceded that scarcely any determinist would admit that all choice was absurd, and therefore, if it can be shown that this would be a result of determinism, they are logically bound to give up determinism.

It is said that it is inconsistent for a determinist to take duty as a motive for action. For he believes, it is argued, that it is already completely determined whether he will act according to his conception of duty, or whether he will act otherwise. And this, it is said, will render it unreasonable to choose to do his duty.

The absurdity of this particular choice is the one which is most often emphasized. But similar considerations would prove that any other choice is as absurd as the choice to do one's duty. For in each case the determinist would believe his action to be already completely determined, and if this made choice absurd in one case it would do so in all others.

139. I cannot, however, see the least ground for the conclusion that the belief in determinism makes choice unreasonable. Of course, if the belief of the determinist was that the end at which he was aiming was completely determined to occur or not to occur, irrespective of what he chose, then choice would be unreasonable.[1] I should be very unreasonable to choose that the sun should rise to-morrow, or that it should not rise. But the ordinary determinist, like everybody else, believes when he chooses any course that his choice may have some effect on the event. And he is quite consistent in this belief. He is a determinist because he believes that, while the event may well be determined by his choice, his choice is in its turn completely determined.

Why should the belief that, if I choose to shut the door, my choice to shut it was completely determined beforehand, make it unreasonable of me to choose to shut it? (This is all the information my determinism

[1] Such a belief has been held. Napoleon, for example, seems to have believed that the time of each man's death was fixed, independently of all other events. If I go here, I may be drowned, if I go there, I may be shot, but, wherever I go, I shall die somehow at that hour. Such a belief *does* render absurd all choice directed to the preservation of my life. Why should I protect my life? I shall either lose it to-day, even if I protect it, or keep it till another time, even if I do not protect it.

But this is not identical with determinism. It does not even involve it, for a man could hold this who held that my choice to protect life or not to protect it was not completely determined. It is compatible, no doubt, with determinism, but in this case the absurdity of choice would not be due to the determinism, but to this quite separate belief.

can give me on the question. For, so long as I am not omniscient, I can never be absolutely certain beforehand what I shall choose. My certainty may be very great but it can never be quite complete.) I cannot see that it should have any such paralysing effect. The contention that it ought to do so is, I think, due to a confusion of this belief with the other belief, mentioned above, which treats the choice as impotent to affect the result, and which asserts that the result is determined irrespective of it.

But suppose that I was omniscient, so that I could not choose anything without knowing beforehand that it was certain that I should choose it, would that render choice unreasonable? I find it rather difficult to conceive what would happen in circumstances so unlike those of which I have any experience. But I can see no absurdity in a choice which is preceded by a perfect knowledge that it would be made. It is to be observed that most theists would hold that God could predict with absolute certainty how he would will in any circumstances, and that they would not hold that this made it absurd in him to will.

140. There remains the defence of free will which is based on the disastrous consequences which, as it is asserted, would follow from the falsity of that doctrine. I have endeavoured to show, in Chapter II, that such arguments are never valid. But the practical consequences of the truth of any doctrine are always interesting, even if they tell us nothing as to its truth or falsity. Let us consider if any disastrous results would follow from the truth of determinism.

It would doubtless be a great disaster if it were absurd to recognize virtue as binding on us, or to adopt a course of action because we believed it to be our duty to do so. But we have seen that there is nothing in determinism which makes judgements of obligation absurd, or which renders it absurd to be moved by a regard for duty.

It would also be a great disaster if people did in fact —even without any logical excuse—no longer recognize virtue as binding on them, or no longer adopted a course of action because they believed it to be their duty. It would be also a great disaster if they did these things less frequently or less intensely. But there is no reason, that I know of, to suppose that a belief in determinism would tend to bring about these calamities. Many men, and many communities, have, at different times and for long periods together, accepted determinism, and I do not think that their morality has been observed to be inferior to that of communities whose general circumstances were similar, but who rejected determinism. Indeed, the usual course of indeterminist polemics has admitted that determinists are no less virtuous than other persons, and has devoted itself to attack what it asserts (for the reasons which we have already considered) to be their inconsistency in being virtuous.

141. It is true that a belief in determinism will tend to modify the emotion with which we regard those whom we hold to be acting wrongly. There is nothing inconsistent in an indeterminist pitying a sinner for his sinfulness. But, *ceteris paribus*, a determinist is more likely to do so. For he does not, like the indeterminist, hold that among the differences which separate sin from other defects is to be found the fact that sin is not completely determined, and that this difference is of fundamental moral importance. It is more natural, therefore, for him, than it is for the indeterminist, to look at sin, like other defects, as a calamity to the man who suffers from it. And the greater his hatred of sin, the greater will he consider the calamity, and the greater will be his pity.

The increase of pity for sinners, however, is not a calamity. It might be so if it were incompatible with hatred of the sin, or with the resolve to extirpate it by any remedy which would not be worse than the disease. But it is clear that there is no logical incompatibility between pity for sinners and the resolve to extirpate sin. And they are not psychologically incompatible, for they are often found together in great intensity. The little, for example, that we know about the life of Jesus suggests that he combined an invariable intolerance of sin with an almost invariable compassion for the sinner.

142. It is said that it would be intolerable for a man to believe that perhaps he was inevitably determined to be wicked in the future. But has the man in question any desire to be virtuous, or has he not? If he has no desire to be virtuous, he is not likely to find his life made intolerable by the possibility (it can never be a certainty for a being whose knowledge is finite) that he is inevitably determined not to be virtuous in the future.

If on the other hand he has a desire for virtue, he knows by experience that such a desire is an important factor in determining a man to be virtuous and not to be wicked, so that the chance that he is determined to be wicked is diminished by the existence of the desire. And the stronger such a desire is, the more likely is it to prevent his future existence from being wicked. Thus the more intolerable the prospect of future wickedness is to any man, the less fear is there that such a fate should befall him. Such a state of things is no great calamity.

Of course, a man's present desire to be virtuous is

far from being an absolute guarantee that he will not in the future be wicked. Many men have had such a desire who have afterwards become wicked. My present desire is one factor in determining my future moral state, and a very important factor. But it is not the only factor, and the tendency may be overcome by others.

But here the determinist is no worse off than the indeterminist. For the indeterminist, who desires to-day to be virtuous, cannot deny that other men who have desired to be virtuous have subsequently become wicked. The same fate may be his. He is in the same position of uncertainty as the determinist, except that the determinist may logically speak of a probability one way or the other, while the indeterminist has no right to do so. The indeterminist, indeed, can assure himself that, if he does fall into wickedness, no one will be able to give a complete explanation of why he has fallen. I must confess that I fail to see what comfort can reasonably be derived from that assurance.

If a man desires food, or love, or anything else, the important question for him is whether he will get it or fail to get it,—not whether his success or failure can be explained as the inevitable result of what has preceded. The question as to the manner in which the result has been determined may have a theoretical interest, but has no practical importance. Surely, in the same way, all that interests the man who desires to be virtuous, in so far as he desires it, is to know whether he will be virtuous or not. Whether virtue or wickedness comes to him from his own uncaused caprice in the future, or from the eternal nature of the universe, it will still be virtue or wickedness.

It is clear that neither determinism nor indeterminism, taken by itself, can settle the question whether virtue or wickedness will finally prevail, either with a particular person, or with the universe. But it is also clear that, if the question is to be settled at all by metaphysics, it can be settled only on the basis of determinism. For virtue and wickedness are dependent on the will, and if indeterminism is true it is impossible to predict the future state of the will of any being, or of all beings.

143. It has been said that, if we do not possess the freedom of indetermination, we shall be no better than machines. Kant speaks thus of the freedom of the Monads, of which Leibniz had asserted that they were free because they were determined internally by their own spiritual nature. 'It would', he says, 'be really nothing better than the freedom of a roasting-jack, which also, when it is once wound up, performs its motions of itself.'[1]

It would, doubtless, be a calamity if men stood no higher in the scale of values than roasting-jacks. But Kant seems to me to be wrong here. If a roasting-jack goes right, a joint is well cooked, if it goes wrong, it is badly cooked. If a will goes right, the man is virtuous; if it goes wrong, he is wicked. If the difference between virtue and wickedness is no more important than that between a well-cooked leg of mutton and one which is badly cooked, then, certainly, internal determination (which I have called above the freedom of self-determination) is of no more worth in a man than in a roasting-jack. But if, as Kant would certainly have admitted, the first difference is very much more important than the second, then freedom of self-determination in a man, which determines

[1] *Critique of Practical Reason*, Part I, Book I (p. 101, Hartenstein's ed.).

between virtue and wickedness, is much more important than the freedom of self-determination in a roasting-jack, which only determines whether the joint shall be well or badly cooked.

It must also be remembered that a man may be held to be free because he possesses, in many cases, what I have called freedom of self-direction. A roasting-jack cannot have this, since it has no will.

144. It would be difficult, indeed, to imagine anything more horrible than some of the determinist views of the universe which have been held in the Christian Church. But what made them horrible was not the belief in determinism, but the belief in hell. The belief that we are predestined to salvation is, as the 17th Article of the Anglican Church remarks, a belief which produces happiness, and not misery.

But is not a belief in hell even more horrible when combined with determinism than it would be without determinism? This has been asserted, but I think it rests on a misconception, or rather on two. The first is the belief that hell would be less unjust in a universe where our wills were not completely determined than in one where our wills are completely determined. But we saw above that our responsibility to God was not affected by the truth or falsity of determinism. This view, therefore, must be rejected.

The second misconception ascribes to determinism a horror which is really due to another belief—the belief that salvation cannot be obtained by any action dependent on the will. So far as people believe that salvation *can* be obtained by such actions, their fears—about themselves at any rate—would have some alleviation even if they were determinists. For in proportion as they were really anxious to obtain salvation they would be likely to obtain it, since a will to act in a particular way makes it likely that we shall act accordingly. On the other hand, if something is required for salvation which is in no way dependent on the will to obtain it, the tortures of apprehension might rise to any intensity for indeterminists, as well as for determinists. For then the desire for salvation, while it made the fear of losing it more intense, would not in any way make the chance of losing it less.

145. I have now considered the principal arguments brought forward by indeterminists in favour of their position. It remains to consider some arguments which may be brought forward against that position. The main argument against it is that which proceeds by establishing the universal validity of the law of Causality, and so showing that volitions, like all other events, must be completely determined. This argument, as I said at the beginning of the chapter, I do not propose to consider here. I shall only point out two inconsistencies in the position of the average indeterminist. The average indeterminist, like other men, admits the validity of morality; and he attaches some value to expectations that men will, under certain circumstances, act in certain ways. I maintain that indeterminism is inconsistent with both these positions.

146. In the first place indeterminism is inconsistent with the validity of morality. Determinism, as we have seen, was reproached with its inconsistency with the validity of judgements of obligation, and reproached wrongly. The accusation can be retorted with greater truth.[1] Judgements of obligation are judgements

[1] It is interesting to note in passing that this view is maintained by thinkers so different from one another as Hume and Green. Compare *Treatise of Human Nature*, Book II, Part III, Section 2; and *Prolegomena to Ethics*, Section 110.

which approve or condemn the person who wills a certain thing. I say that I myself, or some one else, is better or worse on account of a particular volition than would have been the case if the volition had not occurred. The approval or condemnation of the agent is essential to morality. If we are not entitled to say that a man is virtuous or wicked, what is left?

But how are we justified in passing from the volition to the person who makes it? There is, perhaps, no difficulty on any theory in saying that a man is good or bad at the moment when he is willing well or badly. But this is not all that we do say. Half an hour after ordering a murder, Nero may be eating his dinner, and thinking about nothing else. In the intervals of his labours, St. Francis, too, must eat, and may be too fatigued even to plan fresh labours. Yet we should call the one wicked, on account of his past crimes, and the other good, on account of his past services. The whole fabric of morality would be upset, if our approval or condemnation of a man for his volition had no right to last longer than the volition itself. Nor would any indeterminist, I imagine, be prepared to deny its right to last longer.

147. The determinist can explain this consistently with his position. According to him the volitions of each man spring from his character, and are the inevitable result of that character when it finds itself in a certain situation. The approval or condemnation of the agent is based on the belief that the character, indicated by the past acts, survives in the present, and is ready, on appropriate occasions, to manifest itself in similar acts. Nero is condemned in the present, because he still has the character which will probably cause him, when he is tired of eating, to amuse himself with another murder. St. Francis is approved in the present, because he still has the character which will probably cause him, when he has satisfied his hunger, to perform fresh works of benevolence.

But how can the indeterminist defend his judgement? According to him the volition in each case is a perfectly undetermined choice between two motives. When the volition is over, it has ceased to exist, and it has not, on the indeterminist theory, left a permanent cause behind it. For, according to that theory, it has no permanent cause at all. Directly Nero has ceased to think of a murder, nothing at all connected with it remains in his moral nature, except the mere abstract power of undetermined choice, which is just as likely to be exercised on the next occasion in an utterly different way. How then can the indeterminist venture to call Nero a wicked man between his crimes? And yet he certainly would call him so.

Are we to say that it is, after all, the same person who committed the murder and who is now being condemned, and that this forms a sufficient justification of the condemnation? I cannot see that this should justify it. For the judgement passed on Nero at dinner is not only that he was wicked when willing the murders before dinner, but that he is wicked now. But what is wicked in him now? Not his volition, for he is now only willing to gratify his palate, which is not wicked. Not his character, for his previous volition consisted in an undetermined choice of the wrong alternative, and this has no root in his character —or anywhere else.

148. Moreover, if the indeterminist adopts this defence, he involves himself in fresh inconsistencies. If a man is to be approved or condemned now, simply because he is the same man who willed well or badly in the past, then all past volitions are equally grounds for such an approval or condemnation. But there are cases in which every one, including indeterminists, would admit that past volitions are not equally grounds of approval or condemnation in the present.

We often will in our dreams to commit evil actions. And men often will, in a state of intoxication, to commit evil actions which they would not will to commit when sober. Now we never consider a man to be wicked, after he has awaked, on account of his evil volitions in dreams. And we do not consider him wicked, when sober, on account of the wickedness which he willed when drunk. In ordinary cases, indeed, we should blame him for getting drunk. But when this is not his fault—as in the case of a savage who tastes alcohol for the first time—then no blame whatever is attributed to him after he has got sober for the volitions he formed when drunk.

Such judgements are quite inconsistent with the theory in which the indeterminist has now taken refuge—the theory that a man may be approved or condemned in the present for any volition which he has made in the past. For the man who dreamed or was drunk is certainly the same man who is now awake and sober.

But the determinist avoids all inconsistency. Experience shows us that the conditions of dreaming or of intoxication so affect the moral character that no inference can be drawn from volitions made in one of these states as to the probable volitions of the same man when he is not in that state. I have no reason to think that the brutal murder, which I planned in a dream on Monday night, gives even the least indication that I should be likely to yield, when awake on Tuesday morning, to any temptation to commit murder. And therefore, when awake on Tuesday morning, I do not condemn myself for it.

Again, in so far as we believe a man to have really altered his character, we no longer blame him for what happened before it was altered. If, since he willed a certain crime, his conduct has shown that he can resist temptations similar to those to which he yielded before, we no longer condemn him. Even without this experience, if we have reason to believe that he has repented his crime so sincerely and effectually that he would not in future yield to a similar temptation, we condemn him no longer. It may be necessary to punish such men, either as an example to others, or because the law cannot safely take account of such delicate and doubtful matters. But from the point of view of morality, he is not condemned.

For determinists this is completely consistent. They pronounce a man to be wicked in the present, who has committed a crime in the past, because they regard it as evidence of a still-existing character of the kind which tends to produce crimes. But if they have reason to believe—such as amendment or repentance can give them—that his character has changed since the crime, and is no longer such as tends to produce similar crimes, they have no longer any reason to condemn him.

The indeterminist recognizes that amendment and repentance may remove wickedness as much as the determinist recognizes it. To deny this would be to break with every religion in the world's history, and with the moral judgement of all mankind. But his recognition of this is quite inconsistent with his indeterminism. We have seen that he can only condemn a man for a past crime at all, on the basis that it is sufficient ground for condemnation that he is the same

p. 181. (line 21-2) *Transpose* " to believe" from line 21 (before " such an amendment "), *to* line 23, *before* " that his character . . . . "

man who committed the crime. And if this is a sufficient ground, then it is clearly unjustifiable to condemn him the less on account of his amendment or repentance.

149. We pass to the second inconsistency involved in the position of the indeterminist. The indeterminist, like every one else, assumes that it is possible to predict, with some probability, though not with absolute certainty, how men will act under particular circumstances. To reject this would render impossible all trade, all government, and all intercourse with our fellow men.

We continually act on the faith of such predictions. We assume that a postmaster will sell a penny stamp for a penny, that he will not sell two for a penny, that a policeman will not try to kill us for walking along the Strand, that a soldier in battle will try to kill the enemy, and the like. There is, of course, no certainty. The postmaster may be drunk, the policeman a homicidal maniac, the soldier a disciple of Tolstoi. But we are confident of the probabilities. I am more likely to get one penny stamp for a penny than to get two. My life is more likely to be attempted in a fight at close quarters than in a walk through London.

The indeterminist admits that on his theory there can be no certainty of prediction. For all practical purposes the determinist must admit the same, since only an omniscient person could be quite certain what causes were at work, and with what strength. The indeterminist, however, thinks that his theory admits of statements of probability as to volitions.

If, however, indeterminism is true, there is no justification whatever for making any statement as to the probability of future volitions. The indeterminist theory assumes that in every case the choice between motives is undetermined. There cannot then be the slightest probability that this choice will be of one motive rather than another. Our only ground for supposing that a particular man will choose in a particular way, under particular circumstances, is that experience has shown us that he has previously acted in a similar way under similar circumstances, or else that most men, or most men who resemble him in certain ways, have previously acted in a similar way under similar circumstances. Now why should we suppose that similar circumstances will be followed by similar results? There is no reason to do so unless the circumstances determine the results, or the circumstances and the results are both determined by the same cause. Otherwise the expectation that the similar results would follow would be as foolish as the expectation that I should win at cards on one Lord Mayor's day because I had won at cards on the previous one.

According to the indeterminist theory our choice between motives is not determined by anything at all. And thus it follows that all ground for predicting the action of any man, so far as it depends on his volition, vanishes altogether.

One result of this is that the indeterminist is quite inconsistent in expecting one line of conduct from one man and another from another. It is just as probable that an English general to-day should eat his prisoners, as it was that a Maori chief should do so a hundred years ago. It is just as probable that the drunken man in the street should be Johnson as that it should be Boswell.

But this is a trifle. If the indeterminist is right we have no reason to expect any line of conduct from any one, rather than any other line of conduct which is physically possible. It is just as likely that the majority of Londoners will burn themselves alive to-morrow, as it is that they will partake of food to-morrow. I am just as likely to be hanged for brushing my hair as for committing a murder. When men commit suicide, or eat, or hang other men, their action depends on their volition, and their volition cannot be anticipated.

150. In the general chaos to which this would reduce our life, it is scarcely worth mentioning the result as to punishment. Preventive punishments might still be justified, because they trust to keeping the prisoner's body in a place where he will be harmless, and because their effect does not depend on his volition. Yet even here the punishment could not be carried out if the gaolers decided one morning to release all the prisoners. And on the indeterminist theory they are just as likely to will this as they are to will anything else.

All other non-vindictive punishments would be completely absurd. For they all depend on judgements as to the probability of future volitions. It is believed that a man is less likely to will to commit a crime which he desires to commit, if he knows that the commission of the crime will produce consequences which will be painful to him. And it is believed that a man who has been subjected to certain influences is less likely to desire to commit crime. If indeterminism is true, both these beliefs are absolutely baseless.

151. There remains vindictive punishment. It has often been believed that indeterminism would at least justify this—a belief which has sometimes been taken as the chief support of indeterminism. We admitted provisionally, earlier in this chapter, that, if vindictive punishment could be justified at all, it might be as well justified for the indeterminist as for the determinist. But there is a difficulty. Vindictive punishment is inflicted on a man because of his wickedness. It is seldom, however, that it can be inflicted at the very moment when he is sinning. And we have seen that to regard a man as wicked on account of a past volition is entirely inconsistent with indeterminism. Yet vindictive punishment does stand in a specially close relation to indeterminism. For at least we can say that, in those cases where the punishment begins before the sin ceases, vindictive punishment is not more absurd for the indeterminist than it is for other people.

CHAPTER VI

GOD AS OMNIPOTENT

152. By God I mean a being who is personal, supreme, and good. In calling him personal, I mean to assert that he is self-conscious, that he has that awareness of his own existence which I have of my own existence. In calling him supreme, I do not mean to assert that he is omnipotent, but that he is, at the least, much more powerful than any other being, and so powerful that his volition can profoundly affect the whole sum of existence. In calling him good, I do not mean to assert that he is perfect, but that he is, at the least, of such a nature that he would be rightly judged to be more good than evil.

All these three characteristics are, I think, implied in the word God, as used in Western theology. A reality which was not a person would not here be given the name of God. Cases can be quoted, no doubt, where the name has been used of an impersonal reality. But I think that such statements do not mean more than that the reality in question is a worthy substitute for a God, or that the belief in it is a worthy substitute for a belief in a God. They do not mean that the name is appropriate in a strict sense to an impersonal reality. When the schoolboy was told that the school was his father, his mother, and the rest of his relations, the meaning was that it ought to take their place with him. It is in this way, I believe, that we must interpret the statement that Law, or Nature, or Goodness, or Duty, is God.

It is sufficiently clear that a person is not called

God, unless he is supposed to be the supreme being in the universe, or, at least, one of a limited number of such beings. And it cannot, I think, be doubted that a supreme being, who was not believed to be good, would not be called God. It is true that some thinkers have admitted that the action of their God is not what would be called good according to human standards. But then they pronounce those standards to be unfit for application to God. In spite of those standards, they tell us, we must call him good, we must praise and worship him, and we have no need to despise ourselves for doing so. If a man believed in a supreme person whom he believed to be bad, he would not think him worthy of the name of God—a name which, when used by a believer in God, always implies reverence.

153. The usage in philosophy, however, is sometimes different from the usage in theology. In philosophy we have high authority—including Spinoza and Hegel—for a different practice. God is frequently defined by philosophers as the true reality, of whatever nature that reality may be, provided only that it possesses some sort of unity, and is not a mere chaos. If the word is used in this way, every person, except absolute sceptics or the most extreme pluralists, must be said to believe that a God exists. The question of the existence of God, on this definition, becomes very trivial. The important question is not whether there is a God, but what sort of nature he, or it, possesses.

If the usage of theology and philosophy differ, which ought to give way? It seems to me that it should be philosophy. It is possible to change the meaning of terms which are used by a comparatively small number of students, but impossible to change the meaning of so common a word as God in popular usage. Now popular usage is distinctly in favour of the narrower, or theological, use of the word, and philosophy ought to accommodate itself to this, to avoid a dangerous ambiguity.

Again, while the conception of the true reality is of fundamental importance for philosophy, the conception of a supreme and good person is also of great philosophical significance. It is desirable that each of them should have a separate name in philosophical terminology. For the second no name but God has ever been proposed, while the first is often called the Absolute. If God is used as a synonym for the Absolute, we should have two philosophical names for one important idea, and no name for the other.

Finally, philosophical usage is by no means uniform. Against Spinoza and Hegel we may put Kant and Lotze, both of whom use the word substantially in the theological sense. The balance of convenience, then, seems greatly in favour of confining the name of God to a being who is personal, supreme, and good.

154. Such a definition, of course, leaves many questions still open. Two of these may be regarded as of fundamental importance from a religious point of view. The first of these is whether God is Omnipotent in the strict sense of the word—whether he could do anything whatever, or whether there are things which he could not do. The second is whether all existent reality other than God has been created by him, or whether there are other beings—personal or impersonal—whose existence is as ultimate and uncaused as God's own.

If God is not creative, he cannot be omnipotent. If there are beings whose existence is as much an ultimate fact as his own existence, then he could not have prevented their existence, and therefore his power would be limited. But even a creative God need not be omnipotent. It is possible that he should have enough power to create this universe, or one of a rather different nature, or perhaps to have abstained from creating a universe at all, and yet that in creating he acted under limitations which would prevent him from doing certain things. We have therefore three possibilities, a creative and omnipotent God, a God who is creative but not omnipotent, and a God who is neither creative nor omnipotent. In this chapter I shall consider the first of these.

This theory scarcely requires further explanation, since it is familiar to every one. It holds that there is a reality other than God, but that this reality is entirely dependent on God. God, on the contrary, is not in any way dependent on this other reality. He is held to have created it, and to have been purely self-determined in that act of creation. The nature of what he created, and the character of whatever changes have befallen it, are held to be entirely due to his will, which is not believed to be acting under any limitations which can hinder its fulfilment.

155. What reasons are generally given for holding such a theory? We are often told by its supporters that they believe it because they have an instinctive and irresistible conviction of its truth. It is not necessary to recapitulate here what has been said in Chapter II on this ground of belief.

It is also frequently said that there must be a God, and that God must have a particular nature, because such disastrous consequences would follow from the non-existence of a God, or from the existence of a God with a different nature. The use of such considerations as a ground of belief has also been discussed in Chapter II. I shall, however, consider later on the practical effects of belief or disbelief in a God, not as bearing on the truth of the belief, but as a matter of practical interest.

We have likewise discussed in Chapter II the possibility of basing belief in the existence of God on miracles. It is to be noted, however, that this is not a very common ground for the belief. It is frequently admitted by those persons who accept certain dogmas on the evidence of miracles that the evidence of miracles depends on the belief that there is a God, and a God whose nature is incompatible with deceit or error. From this, of course, it follows that the miracles cannot be used to prove the existence of God.

Passing to more direct arguments, we find that Kant enumerates three, which he names Ontological, Cosmological, and Physico-Theological. I do not propose to discuss the Ontological argument. It had very little influence at any time except among professed metaphysicians, and, since Kant's destructive criticism, it has been abandoned by all schools of philosophy. (Hegel, indeed, asserts that Kant has not disproved it. But what Hegel calls the Ontological argument is not what was previously called so, and is not what Kant intended to disprove. Nor would what Hegel calls the Ontological argument suffice to prove a personal God.)

Kant's Cosmological argument resembles very closely the argument from the necessity of a first cause, while his Physico-Theological argument is what is more commonly called the argument from design. Both these arguments are in frequent use at the present day, and both will require our consideration. We shall also have to consider the argument that the truth of Idealism would involve the existence of an omniscient being, and that such a being could only be God.

156. The argument for a first cause may, I think, be

fairly stated as follows. Events continually happen in the world, and every event requires a cause. And the non-divine substances which exist in the world cannot have existed eternally. The commencement of the existence of each of these substances is also an event, and will require a cause. Now an event may be caused by another event, but then this earlier event will, like every other, require a cause. If we recognize no causes but events, every cause will itself require a cause, and the series will never be completed. We must, therefore, believe that the ultimate cause of all events is not an event but a being, who never began to exist, and who therefore needs no cause. And this being is said to be God.

This argument, even if valid, would not be sufficient to prove the existence of God. Even if it proved the existence of a being who was a cause without being itself causally determined, it could not prove that such a being was either personal or good. The *nature* of the effects that it produced might prove its personality and goodness, but the mere fact that it was a cause would be consistent with no personality or with an evil personality. Thus the argument could not reach the desired conclusion without calling in the aid of the argument from design.

157. But why, to go further, is a cause which is not an event wanted at all? (To speak accurately, we should say, a cause which does not include an event. For the full cause of any event always includes many conditions and circumstances which are not events.) Why should we not derive one event from another, and this again from another, backwards through unending time, without any first cause at all? As for the finite substances, they might either be conceived as existing through unending past time, or as brought into existence at some time. In the latter case the event of their commencing to exist would, like all others, be dependent on an unending series of previous events.

The supporters of the necessity of a first cause would argue against this as follows. The event *A*, with which we start, has a definite nature—certain predicates are true of it, others are false. The law of Causality tells us that the nature of *A* is entirely dependent on its cause. If (as the supporters of the unending regress assert) *A* is to be explained by an unending regress of events, then its immediate cause will contain an event, which we may call *B*. The nature of *A* is then dependent, among other things, on the nature of *B*. It cannot be determined unless *B* is determined. But *B* is an event, and, on the same principle, will have a cause containing an event *C*. Then *B* is not determined unless *C* is determined. And, consequently, *A* is not determined unless *C* is determined. And, similarly, *A* is not determined unless *D*, *E*, and so on are determined. The conclusion drawn is that *A* cannot be determined unless the earliest event in the chain is determined. But there is no earliest event in the endless series. Therefore *A* is not determined at all. And this is impossible. We must therefore either reject the law of Causality, which makes the determination of an event dependent on the determination of its cause, or we must assert that the series of causes is not endless. And this can only be done by asserting the existence of a first cause which is not an event.

158. I shall not inquire whether this conclusion is justifiable, nor is the inquiry necessary for our present purpose. Even if we grant, to the believers in a first cause, that an unending regress of causes is impossible, their position will be untenable. For the hypothesis of a first cause involves us in hopeless difficulties.

The argument conceives God's existence as having no beginning in time. But this leaves two possibilities open. Either God's existence is in time, and has no beginning, because he has existed through unending time in the past. Or else God's existence is timeless, in which case of course there could be no question of a beginning.

On the first alternative—that God exists in time—we have a substance which has persisted through an infinite past time. Now if one substance is admitted to exist in time without being caused, why should not other substances do so too? And, if any substance other than God can be uncreated, then the necessity of assuming the existence of a God to create them has disappeared. I cannot see why it should be said, of three substances existing in time, that God did not need a creator, but that a man and a pebble did. If God is held to be timeless, indeed, it might possibly be maintained that all substances existing in time required a creator, while God, who was out of time, did not require one. But we are considering at present the hypothesis that God's existence is in time.

The universe, however, does not consist merely of quiescent substances. It contains events. And the argument before us says that, apart from the creation of substances, God is required as the first cause of the events which occur to these substances. This contention depends upon the principle that every event must finally be derived from a cause which is not an event, in order to avoid the infinite regress which would ensue if every cause was an event, and therefore required a cause.

But how does God cause an event to happen at

a particular time which did not happen before? Is it by an act of volition which occurred at a particular time, and did not occur before? Then that act of volition is an event, and itself requires a cause. And if that cause is found in a previous event in God's mind, and so on, we should get back to the unending causal regress which the argument started by declaring impossible. We must therefore suppose that God causes changes without changing. Either he directly causes an event without forming a volition which is an event, or, if he does form such a volition, then the cause of the volition is not an event.[1]

But is this possible? How can that which is changeless be the sole cause of any event? A changeless state can, no doubt, be *part* of the cause of an event. But it would contradict the law of Causality to ascribe an event to a cause which contained no change. For in that case the cause would first exist without producing the effect, and would then produce it. And this change in the action of the cause would be itself an event which would have occurred without a cause.

159. If we pass to the second alternative about God's nature—namely, that it is timeless, it is clear that it is also incapable of change. And thus we get back the difficulties which we have just considered. An event happens, and makes the state of the universe different from what it had been before. The cause is said to be God's timeless nature. That nature is the same, however, before and after the event. (In itself, of course, there is no question of before or after. I mean that a human being who was judging of God's

[1] We are not yet discussing, it will be remembered, the hypothesis that God's nature is timeless, but the hypothesis that, while itself remaining unchanged in time, it can be the cause of an event—that is, a change in time.

nature before the event, and one who was judging of it after the event, would be right if they made the same judgement.) Then there is nothing in that nature which accounts for the change; and it cannot be the cause. If, while the so-called cause remains the same, the effect varies, it is clear that the variation of the effect—that is, the event—is uncaused.

As to the substances, other than God, if they are held to have come into existence at a particular moment of time, the event cannot be explained by a timeless nature in God. If, on the other hand, they are held to have existed through all past time, they have lost that characteristic — their commencement — on the strength of which it was asserted that a creator was necessary.

It has been suggested that the series of events in time will appear, to a timeless being, as a timeless reality, and may thus be due to an eternal and unchanging volition of that being. But, if the true nature of what appears as temporal is timeless, it is not really a series of events, and therefore the law of Causality does not apply to it. It needs a cause no more than God himself. And thus the argument breaks down.

It may perhaps be replied that these objections are valid as far as they go, but that God's nature is beyond our comprehension, and that in some way which we do not understand he may be the first cause of changes, in spite of his own changelessness. I have discussed in Chapter II the validity of such appeals to believe in something, which our reason tells us is impossible, on the ground that our reason is certainly limited, and may be wrong. With regard to this particular argument, however, it may be specially noticed that it requires us to be convinced, not only that we do not know the nature of God, but that we do not know the nature of a cause. The position we are discussing maintains that God is changeless and a cause. Our objections were directed to show that a (complete) cause could not be changeless. If this is to be doubted on the ground that the changelessness may be possible in some way which we do not understand, then what may be possible in this mysterious way is not merely a changeless God but a changeless cause. This means that a cause may be what our reason says it cannot be.

Now, if we do not understand the nature of a cause sufficiently to trust what our reason says about it, the whole argument for a first cause breaks down. If we are to be so sceptical about causes, we shall have no right to believe that every event must have a cause, or that an endless regress of causes is impossible, since these conclusions rest on what our reason tells us about causes. And the argument for a first cause depends, as we have already seen, on the exclusion of the alternatives of an uncaused change, and of an endless regress of causes.

160. Thus the hypothesis of a first cause is useless for the purpose of extricating us from the difficulties, whatever they may be, involved in an endless causal regress. If we are to avoid complete scepticism, it would be necessary for philosophy to show, either that such an endless regress is not impossible, or else that some other alternative has been overlooked. This question, however, does not concern us here, since our discussion of Causality has merely related to the asserted necessity of a first cause.

161. We must now consider the argument from design. It cannot, I think, be better stated than in the words of Kant, who takes a very sympathetic view of this argument, although he does not accept its validity. Kant, however, speaks only of the wisdom of the arrangement, and of the consequent wisdom inferred in God. The more ordinary form of the argument includes goodness among the qualities observed in the world, and inferred in God. I have therefore added goodness to Kant's statement.

'The principal points', he says 'of the physico-theological proof are the following.

'First. There are everywhere in the world clear indications of an intentional arrangement carried out with great wisdom' (and goodness) 'and forming a whole indescribably varied in its contents and infinite in extent.

'Secondly. The fitness of this arrangement is entirely foreign to the things existing in the world, and belongs to them contingently only; that is, the nature of different things could never spontaneously, by the combination of so many means, co-operate towards definite aims, if these means had not been selected and arranged on purpose by a rational disposing principle, according to certain fundamental ideas.

'Thirdly. There exists, therefore, a sublime and wise' (and good) 'cause (or many), which must be the cause of the world, not only as a blind and all-powerful nature, by means of unconscious *fecundity*, but as an intelligence, by *freedom*.

'Fourthly. The unity of that cause may be inferred with certainty from the unity of the reciprocal relations of the parts of the world, as portions of a skilful edifice, so far as our experience reaches, and beyond it, with plausibility, according to the rules of analogy.'[1]

[1] *Critique of Pure Reason*, first edition, p. 625. I quote from Max Müller's translation.

162. It is to be noticed that this argument does not assert, that all the part of the universe which we can observe is of such a nature that it could reasonably be supposed to be an end in itself for a good being. The argument is that what we observe is of such a nature that much of it suggests itself as being suitable *means* to an end such as a wise and good being would propose to himself; and, further, that it is of such a nature that we cannot believe it to have come into its present state except as arranged by such a being for the promotion of such an end.

It is clear from Kant's second paragraph that this is what he means. And this is the position generally adopted when the argument from design is used. It is never contended that all the facts which are brought forward in support of it are in every respect such as God might will for their own sake, but that in many cases they appear adapted as means to a divine purpose. The eye, for example, is not treated as something of intrinsic value, but as a means to sight. And sight again is held to be a divine means to a further purpose.

It would be impossible to base any valid argument on the assertion that all we observe is worthy to be itself a divine end. For such a conclusion would be absolutely unsupported by the facts. Very much of what we observe in the universe is of such a nature that we cannot conceive that it should have intrinsic worth in the sight of a wise and good being. How could we suppose that such a being should find the existence of one hair more or less on a man's head to have intrinsic worth? Can we suppose that the universe would be less good for such a being, because a particular man had one hair less? And then there is much in the universe which is positively bad, and this certainly cannot have any intrinsic worth for him. A being for whom sin or misery had intrinsic worth, could not be wise or good.

The force of these considerations cannot be avoided by the suggestion that perhaps all existing things have an intrinsic worth for a perfectly wise and good being, though our minds are too feeble to perceive it in all cases, and that, consequently, all things can be justified otherwise than as means. In the first place, the view that sin and misery can have intrinsic worth for a wise and good being seems absolutely untenable. There could be no justification for calling a being good, who approved of sin and misery for their own sakes. (To this point we shall return later.) And, in the second place, if such a view were possible, it would be quite irrelevant for our present purpose. For the relation of the facts of experience to ideals having intrinsic worth is not the conclusion of the argument from design, but the premise. And it is clear that we can only take as a premise the relations which we know to exist, and not those which may possibly exist beyond our knowledge.

Thus it is impossible to take everything as in itself a divine end. On the other hand, things which are intrinsically indifferent, or even intrinsically evil, may have worth as means to some end other than themselves.

163. It seems to me that, whatever worth the argument from design may have to prove the existence of a God who is not omnipotent, it is quite useless as a proof of the existence of an omnipotent God. If it proved the existence of a God at all, it would also offer a positive disproof of his omnipotence.

Kant points out that the argument could not prove the existence of a creative God. As the design has to be contingent to the material in which it is carried out, it gives us no reason to suppose that the being who carried out the design created the material. 'The utmost', he says, 'that could be established by such a proof would be an *architect of the world*, always very much hampered by the quality of the material with which he has to work, not a *creator* to whose idea everything is subject.'[1]

And, he goes on, we should have no reason to consider the power and wisdom of such an architect as infinite. We cannot logically infer to more power or wisdom in the cause than is necessary to produce the effect. There may be more, of course, but we have no reason to believe that there is more. Now the amount of the universe that we can observe, or infer, to exist, and the perfection of the arrangement that we see in it, may be very great, but they are certainly not infinite. It is not in our power to make empirical observations which shall be infinite. Accordingly, we may possibly infer the existence of an architect of the universe who is very much more powerful and more wise that we are, but not the existence in him of infinite power and wisdom.

The same, I may add, is the case with goodness. Quantitatively, however, the criticism has much more force with respect to goodness. If there is an architect of the world, our observation of the world will tell us that his power and wisdom must be enormously greater than ours. But it seems to me that a being of very moderate goodness might easily have designed a world with as large a proportion of good in it as we are able to observe in the facts around us. This point, however, will be treated more appropriately in the next chapter.

[1] Op. cit., first edition, p. 627.

164. We may go further than this. If a wise and good being has used means to an end, this is a positive proof that he is not omnipotent. For means are those things which have no worth in themselves, but which it is right to use because, without using them, some end which has worth in itself cannot be attained. Now there is nothing which an omnipotent God cannot do—otherwise he would not be omnipotent. He could get the ends without the means, if he chose to do so. And therefore it would be inconsistent with his wisdom to use them, since they are of no value except to get an end which he could get as well without them. In so far, therefore, as the nature of any fact in the universe suggests that it owes its existence to its utility as means for a divine purpose, it suggests, with just the same force, that the divine designer of the universe is not omnipotent.

But this is not all. The God whose existence it is attempted to prove is not only omnipotent, but good. Now there are many things in the universe which are not only intrinsically indifferent, but intrinsically bad. Such, for example, is pain. The argument from design justifies the existence of these things as means to some greater good. And when we are dealing with human beings, or with any being of limited power, the use of such means may be completely justified. A surgeon, for example, is often justified in inflicting very great pain. But this is because his end—an end whose good overbalances the evil of the pain—cannot be attained without the use of these means. To use an intrinsically evil thing as a means when the end could be obtained as well without it, would deprive the agent of all claim to goodness as well to wisdom. And this would be the position of an omnipotent God who used such means.

We may conclude, then, that, whatever force the argument from design may have in proving the existence of a God of limited power, it is worse than useless as a proof of the existence of an omnipotent God.

165. We need not consider here the argument that the truth of Idealism would involve the existence of an omniscient being, and that such a being could only be God. There seems no reason to conclude that omniscience implies omnipotence, and in that case the argument could not prove the existence of an omnipotent God. It is true that there is nothing in the argument to prevent the God, whose existence should be demonstrated in this way, from being omnipotent. But, since omnipotence is not a quality which can be assumed in any person without being demonstrated, it will be better to treat this in connexion with the arguments for a God who is not omnipotent. In the next chapter I shall endeavour to show that it cannot be used to prove the existence of a God of any nature.

166. We have now considered the chief arguments put forward to prove the existence of an omnipotent God. It remains to consider what objections there are to our belief in his existence of a more positive nature than the insufficiency of those arguments. God has been defined as personal, and as good. I maintain that omnipotence is incompatible with personality, and that, since the world around us is what it is, omnipotence is incompatible with goodness.

An omnipotent person is one who can do anything. The believers in an omnipotent God do not always hold, however, that nothing happens in the universe which is not in the long run completely determined by God's will. For the believers in free will hold that human volitions are not completely determined at all, and, in that case, they are not completely determined by God. But, if they also believe in an omnipotent God, they believe that these human volitions could have been prevented by God, if he had willed to prevent them. And they also believe that it is due to God's will that human beings were created and endowed with the power to will in this manner. If this were not so, God would not be omnipotent. For, if their existence was independent of him, then he could not have destroyed them.

Now suppose that God had willed to create a universe, and had not willed that the law of Identity should be valid. It seems that we have no alternative but to be inconsistent or to be completely unmeaning. To suppose that the universe would not have been created, although God had willed that it should, would be inconsistent with his omnipotence. But the assertion that the universe could be created without being a universe, and without being created, is surely unmeaning. And yet how can the universe be the universe, or creation be creation, unless the law of Identity is true?

Again, is there any meaning in the supposition that God could create a man who was not a man, or that he could create a being who was neither man nor not-man? But, if he could not, then he is bound by the law of Contradiction and the law of Excluded Middle, and, once more, he is not omnipotent.

The assertion that God is omnipotent implies that God could still be God, and omnipotent, whatever else was the case. Any other statement might, if God willed it to be so, be either true or false, and yet these two statements would remain true. But these two statements are not independent of the truth of all other statements—we have just seen that they are not independent of the truth of the laws of Identity, and so there are statements which God cannot make false. Consequently he is not omnipotent.

To take a less abstract instance, we may ask the old question: Could God create a being of such a nature that he could not subsequently destroy it? Whatever answer we make to this question is fatal to God's omnipotence. If we say that he could not create such a being, then there is something that he cannot do. If we say that he can create such a being, then there is still something that he cannot do—to follow such an act of creation by an act of destruction.

167. Another point must be considered in reference to omnipotent personality. Human personality is never found to exist without a recognition of the existence of something not itself. (We may follow Hegel's example in calling this the Other of the person. Other is a better term than Non-ego, since that may suggest that what is recognized by one person as not himself must not be any other person, but something impersonal. And this suggestion would be wrong, for what I recognize as not myself may quite well be another person.) We only realize our personality in so far as our consciousness has a content—a manifold to which the centre is formed by that I, awareness of which constitutes personality. And this content of consciousness involves for us the recognition of an Other. This may be direct, as when I know something other than myself, or have some volition regarding it, or some emotion towards it. But even when the Other is not involved directly, it is involved indirectly. It may be that that which directly occupies my consciousness is some part of my own nature, as when I think of past events in my life, or will to correct a fault in my disposition. But when we inquire into the nature of those events, or of that fault, we find that they include, or in the long run involve, the recognition of the existence of an Other.

Nor is this recognition, for finite personality, a limitation or imperfection, which it is impossible to remove altogether, but which hampers the fullness of self-consciousness. On the contrary, the more vivid, definite, and extensive is our recognition of the Other, the more vivid and definite becomes our self-consciousness. As consciousness of an Other becomes vague and indefinite, consciousness of self becomes vague and indefinite too. As we fall asleep the two become gradually faint together, and as we awake the two gradually revive together.

168. An omnipotent person, if one can exist, must be capable of being in a different position from this. He must be capable of existing out of relation to anything except himself. This does not, I think, follow from the conception of a personal creator, even if the universe is supposed to have been created at a particular moment of time. For the creator, although he would have existed before the creation as the only existent reality, might perhaps have found his Other by contemplating the universe which he proposed to create in the future. It is perhaps not necessary that the Other to be recognized should be co-existent with the recognition.

But it is necessary that he should be capable of existing out of all relation to an Other, if he is to be omnipotent. For, if he were not, then he could only be a person on condition that a universe had arisen or would some day arise. That is to say, it would be impossible for him to prevent the existence, some time or other, of a universe. And a person who cannot prevent something from taking place is clearly not omnipotent. There is perhaps no contradiction in the idea of a creator who must create, but it is impossible that there should be an omnipotent creator who must create.

169. It may be said that reality is wider than existence. The law of Contradiction and the multiplication table do not exist, but they are valid. And so, it may be said, they are real. Now perhaps an omnipotent God could find an Other, which was real though not existent, in eternal truths which he contemplated. And perhaps all that is essential for self-consciousness is the recognition of a real Other, whether it is existent or not.

Before this could be accepted, it would be necessary to discuss a very fundamental and a very controversial question in Metaphysics—how far the valid can be real independently of the existent. But without entering into this question, we can see, I think, that the suggestion will not help us here. For what could the eternal truths be, which the omnipotent God is to contemplate? They cannot be the laws of the universe, for that would imply that there was to be a universe, and so limit God's omnipotence. Nothing seems to remain but the possibilities to create a universe or not to create it, or to create a universe of one kind or a universe of another. That all this should be possible, it may be said, does not depend on God's willing it to be possible—on the contrary, the possibilities constitute his omnipotence. And so his omnipotence is not limited if we say that he inevitably recognizes these possibilities as real.

But when we look closer we see that for an omnipotent God, just because he is omnipotent, there are no possibilities to recognize. For me, who am not omnipotent, there are definite possibilities, and these possibilities are real, and are not myself. I can draw a triangle or not draw one. If I draw it, I can give it a right angle or not. But the existence of these definite possibilities for me to recognize depends on the fact that there is something, other than my own will, which prevents my doing other things. I cannot both draw a triangle and abstain from drawing it. Nor can I draw a triangle which is courageous, or which has two right angles.

Now with an omnipotent God it would be different. Nothing is impossible to him, and therefore there are no definite possibilities which he recognizes because his will must submit to their limitations. If we ask what exists outside an omnipotent God, the answer—not only about existence but about all reality—must be: What he wills. If we ask what exists outside an omnipotent God, independently of his will, the answer must be: Nothing whatever.[1] There are not even possibilities. There is nothing at all.

Since an omnipotent God, then, could exist even if he willed that nothing else should exist and that no laws should be true, and since his omnipotence leaves no possibilities outside him, but only nonentity, it follows that he could exist as the only reality, and consequently that he could exist without recognizing any other reality. His knowledge might be only of his own qualities and states, his volitions might concern nothing but those qualities and states, his emotions be directed towards himself only. And from these

[1] This is the case, even if we suppose, with the indeterminists, that human volitions, not being completely determined by anything, are not completely determined by God's will. For our wills are held to act in this way only because God has endowed them with the power to do so, and because he does not withdraw it. The volitions, although not completely determined by God's will, are still completely dependent on it, since they only take place because he wills them to do so.

qualities and states must be deducted all those that are determined by his will—for if these were essential to him, his will would be under limitations, since he could not dispense with them.

170. It would be too much to say that this gives us a second proof of the impossibility of an omnipotent person. Self-consciousness is not the same as consciousness of an Other, and we are not entitled to assert that they must inevitably be found together. But we have no knowledge of the first without the second, and it seems rather unwise to build on the abstract possibility that a being could exist, beyond the limits of our experience, who could have the first, without having the second.

And this will appear still more imprudent when we consider that, as was said above, the recognition of an Other is, for human beings, not a hindrance from which they cannot escape, but the condition of their development. If an omnipotent person can exist it follows that the recognition of the Other, while it becomes more and more definite and extensive as personality develops within our experience, becomes quite unessential to the most developed personality of all.

171. We now come to the relation of omnipotence to goodness. There is evil in the universe. It is not necessary to inquire how great or how small the amount of evil may be. All that is important for the present discussion is that there is some evil, and this is beyond doubt. A single pang of toothache, a single ungenerous thought, in the midst of a universe otherwise perfectly good, would prove the existence of evil.

The existence of evil is beyond doubt in the sense that no one denies the existence of pain and sin in experience, and that no one denies that pain and sin are, from the point of view of ordinary life, to be considered evil. But it has been asserted that the universe, when looked at rightly, may be completely good. Sometimes the standard is challenged, and it is suggested that pain and sin are really good, though we think them evil. Sometimes our comprehension of the facts is challenged; it is admitted that pain and sin, if they existed, would be bad, but it is maintained that they do not really exist.

The first of these alternatives means complete ethical scepticism. There is no judgement about the good of whose truth we are more certain than the judgement that what is painful or sinful cannot be perfectly good. If we distrust this judgement, we have no reason to put any trust in any judgement of good or evil. In that case we should have no right to call anything or anybody good, and therefore it would be impossible to justify any belief in God, whose definition includes goodness. This objection, therefore, cannot consistently be used, by the believers in an omnipotent God, against the existence of evil.

The second alternative is one which can only be supported by metaphysical arguments of a somewhat abstruse and elaborate nature. To expound and examine these arguments in detail would take us too far from our subject. I will only say briefly that the theory of the unreality of evil now seems to me untenable. Supposing that it could be proved that all that we think evil was in reality good, the fact would still remain that we think it evil. This may be called a delusion or a mistake. But a delusion or mistake is as *real* as anything else. A savage's erroneous belief that the earth is stationary is just as real a fact as an astronomer's correct belief that it moves. The delusion that evil exists, then, is real. But then, to me at least, it seems certain that a delusion or an error which hid from us the goodness of the universe would itself be evil. And so there would be real evil after all. If, again, the existence of the delusion is pronounced to be a delusion, then this second delusion, which would be admitted to be real, must be pronounced evil, since it is now this delusion which deceives us about the true nature of reality, and hides its goodness from us. And so on indefinitely. However many times we pronounce evil unreal, we always leave a reality behind, which in its turn is to be pronounced evil.

172. An omnipotent God is conceived as creating the universe. In that case it seems a natural inference that he is the cause of all the evil in the universe. But some people, who maintain the existence of a creative omnipotent God, maintain also that the choice of the human will between motives has no cause, and, therefore, is not ultimately caused by the creator. They admit, however, that God could have dispensed with the freedom of the human will, if he had chosen to do so.[1]

We may therefore say that an omnipotent God could have prevented all the evil in the universe if he had willed to do so. It is impossible to deny this, if omnipotence is to have any meaning, for to deny it would be to assert that there was something that God could not do if he willed to do it.

173. What bearing has this on the question of God's goodness? It is clear that man may act rightly in permitting evil, and even in directly causing it. It is

[1] It seems curious that believers in human free will should often accept the argument for God's existence from the necessity of a first cause. If human volition is not completely determined, the law of causality is not universally valid. And, in that case, what force remains in the argument for a first cause?

evil that a child should lose his leg, for the loss deprives him of much happiness, and causes him much pain. But the surgeon who performs the operation, and the parent who allows it to be performed, may be perfectly justified. For amputation may be the only alternative to evils much greater than those it produces.

And, again, the production of sin may under certain circumstances be justified. Supposing that it were true—fortunately there is no reason to believe that it is true—that employment as an executioner tended to degrade morally a large proportion of those who were employed, it would by no means follow that men ought not to be induced to act as executioners. The evil results which might follow from having no hangman might far outweigh the evil done to morality by having one.

But the justification in these cases depends entirely on the limited powers of the agents. The father and the surgeon, for example, are justified because it is only through the evils of amputation that worse evils can be avoided. If they could have avoided those worse evils by some other course that would not have been evil at all, they would not have been justified in deciding on the amputation.

174. Now the power of an omnipotent God is not limited. He can effect whatever he wills. If he wills to have *A* without *B*, he can have *A* without *B*, however closely *A* and *B* may be connected in the present scheme of the universe. For that scheme also is dependent on his will. It thus appears that his action cannot be justified as the amputation was. It rather resembles that of a father who should first gratuitously break his son's leg, or permit it to be broken, and should then decide for amputation, although a complete cure was possible.

If a man did this we should call him wicked. We do not wait to call a man wicked till he does more evil than good. If a man should, at the risk of his life, save all the crew of a sinking ship but one, and should then, from mere caprice, leave that man to sink, whom he could easily have saved, we should say that he had acted wickedly. Nor is it necessary that a man should do evil for the sake of evil. To desire to attend a concert is not a desire for evil as such, but if I killed a man in order to acquire his ticket, I should have acted wickedly.

Now in what way would the conduct of an omnipotent God, who permitted the existence of evil, differ from the conduct of such men, except for the worse? There are palliations of men's guilt, but what palliations could there be for such a God? A man may have lived a long life of virtue before he fell into sin, or, again, we may have reason to hope that he will repent and amend. But could we have any reason for hoping that the omnipotent God would repent and amend? It seems difficult to imagine such a reason. Again, a man may be excused to some extent for his sin, if ignorance or folly prevents him from realizing the full meaning of his action. But if an omnipotent God is not omniscient (and it seems most natural to suppose that he is), at any rate he could be so if he chose. Or again, a man may have a genuine repugnance for his sin, and only commit it under extreme temptation. A man who betrays his country under torture is less wicked than if he had betrayed it for money. But an omnipotent God can be forced to nothing, and can therefore not be forced to choose between wickedness and suffering.

175. Such conduct, then, as we must attribute to an omnipotent God, would be called wicked in men, although the amount of evil for which any man is responsible is insignificant as compared with the sum of all evil, and although men have in most cases excuses which would not apply to an omnipotent God. Yet this being is still called God, by people who admit that goodness is part of the definition of God. Why is God called good, when his action is asserted to be such as would prove a man to be a monster of wickedness? Two lines of defence have been tried. The first is, in substance, that the omnipotent and good God is not really good, the second that he is not really omnipotent.

The form in which the first is put by its supporters is that goodness in God is of a different nature from what it is in man. Thus Mansel says that 'the infliction of physical suffering, the permission of moral evil' and various other things 'are facts which no doubt are reconcilable, we know not how, with the infinite Goodness of God, but which certainly are not to be explained on the supposition that its sole and sufficient type is to be found in the finite goodness of man'.[1] And he goes on to say that the difference is not one of degree only, but of kind. Pascal is still more plain-spoken: 'What can be more opposed to our wretched rules of justice than the eternal damnation of a child without any will of its own for a sin in which it seems to have had so little share that it was committed six thousand years before the said child came into existence.'[2] Nevertheless Pascal continued to call good, and to worship, a God whom he believed to have done this.

176. But why should the word good be used in two senses absolutely opposed to one another? The senses are not merely different, as they would be if, for example, it was proposed to use the word good to indicate what

[1] *Limits of Religious Thought*, fourth edition, Preface, p. xiii.
[2] Works, ed. Brunschvicg, ii, p. 348.

is generally meant by the word scarlet. For what is called good in God would be called wicked in men, and good and wicked are predicates directly contrary to one another.

Is the alteration to be considered as one of mere caprice? Are the people who say that God is good, while Nero was wicked, in the same position as a man who should call Everest a valley, while he called Snowdon a mountain? It seems to me that there is more than this involved, and that the real ground of the alteration is that good is a word of praise, and that wicked is a word of blame, and that it is felt to be desirable to praise God rather than to blame him.

But why is it desirable to praise him? Certainly not for the reasons which make us praise Socrates and blame Nero. For the conduct which in God we call good is conduct for some faint and imperfect approximation to which we blame Nero. What other reason is left? I can only see one—that an omnipotent God is, and will remain, infinitely more powerful than Nero ever was.

On this subject Mill has spoken,[1] and it is unnecessary to quote words which form one of the great turning-points in the religious development of the world. Yet when Mill says that rather than worship such a God he would go to hell, it is possible to raise a doubt. To call such a being good, and to worship him, is to lie and to be degraded. But it is not certain that nothing could be a greater evil than to lie and to be degraded. It is not impossible that God's goodness, as explained by Pascal and Mansel, should include the infliction of such tortures, physical and mental, on one who refused to worship him that they would be a greater evil than lying and degradation. Unless it is

[1] *Examination of Hamilton*, chap. vii.

said that moral degradation is absolutely incommensurable with suffering—and I doubt if this can be maintained—the case does not seem impossible. Nor need the motive of the worshipper be selfish. The goodness of God, like the wickedness of some men, might include the torture of the culprit's friends as well as of himself.

177. We may doubt, then, whether we should be bound, or justified, in refusing to misapply the predicate good to such an omnipotent being, if the use of the word would diminish our chances of unending torture. But it seems just as likely to increase them. There are, no doubt, men who are prepared to inflict suffering on all who do not flatter them, even when they know that the flattery is empty and undeserved. But, granted that God has some qualities which would be called wicked in men, it does not follow that he has all qualities which would be called wicked in men, and there is no reason to suppose that he has this particular quality. Many men, bad as well as good, are not appeased by such flattery, but rather irritated by it, especially if they know it to be insincere, or to have been insincere when it began. God may resemble these men rather than the others. Indeed, the probability seems to be that he would do so, since pleasure in such flattery is generally a mark of a weak intellect, and even if God's goodness is like our wickedness, it can scarcely be suggested that his wisdom is like our folly. Or, again, God's goodness may induce him to damn us whatever we do, in which case we shall gain nothing by lying.

When everything is so doubtful there does not seem to be the least prudence in flattery. Nor can we rest our actions on any statement made by God as to the conduct which he will pursue. For, if goodness in God is different from goodness in us, we should have no reason to believe a statement to be true rather than false, even if it were certain that it came from God. Divine goodness may not exclude the desire to destroy our happiness by false statements.

178. There remains the attempt to save the goodness of an omnipotent God by giving up the reality of his omnipotence, while retaining the name. Various elements in the universe have been taken either as good or as inevitable, and the evil in the universe explained as the necessary consequence of the reality of these elements. Thus, for example, the sin of the universe has been accounted for by the free will of the sinners, and the suffering explained as the necessary consequence, in some way, of the sin. Thus all the evil in the universe, it is asserted, is a necessary consequence of free will, and it is said that free will is so good that God was justified in choosing a universe with all the present evil in it, rather than surrender free will.

Or, again, it is said that it is impossible that there should not be some evil in a universe which was governed according to general laws, and that to be governed according to general laws is so great a perfection in the universe that God did well to choose it with all the evil that it involves.

It seems to me rather difficult to see such supreme value in free will that it would be worth more than the absence of all the present evil of the universe. It might be doubted, even, whether the advantage of unbroken general laws is so great that the evil of the universe would not be cheaply removed at the cost of frequent miracles [1]. But we need not discuss this.

[1] The supporters of this view of the supreme value of unbroken general laws, have often, it may be noted, been men who believed that God did well in permitting the human will to be undetermined, and in working occasional miracles.

For it is quite evident that a God who cannot create a universe in which all men have free will, and which is at the same time free from all evil, is not an omnipotent God, since there is one thing which he cannot do. In the same way, a God who cannot ordain a series of general laws, the uniform working of which would exclude all evil from the universe, is not an omnipotent God.

Or, once more, it is said that a universe without evil would involve in some way the violation of such laws as the law of Contradiction or of Excluded Middle, and that these laws are so fundamental that the existence of evil in the universe is inevitable.

Even if there were any ground for believing that the absence of evil from the universe would violate such laws as these, it is clear that a God who is bound by any laws is not omnipotent, since he cannot alter them. If it is said—as it may very reasonably be said—that these laws are so fundamental that it is unmeaning to speak of a being who is not bound by them, the proper conclusion is not that an omnipotent God is bound by them, but that, if there is a God, he is not omnipotent.

It is necessary to emphasize this point because, remarkable as it may appear, it is not an unusual position to maintain that God is absolutely omnipotent, and, at the same time, to believe that there are certain things he cannot do, and even to be quite certain what those things are.[1] As against such a view as this it seems necessary to emphasize the tolerably obvious fact that, if there is anything which God could not do if he wished, he is not omnipotent.

[1] Cp., for example, Flint's *Theism.* The omnipotence of God is asserted : I. 2, III. 1, IX. 2. In VI. 1 and VIII. 1 we find statements of some of the things which God cannot do.

179. It may be said that we are attaching too much importance to a slight inaccuracy of language. If people say that there are certain things which God could not do, then they do not believe him to be omnipotent, and they are simply using the wrong word when they say that they do believe him to be omnipotent.

But then why do they use the word? It seems to me that the confusion of language covers a confusion of thought. Many people are unwilling to accept the idea that God is not omnipotent. It is held to detract from his perfection, and to render it difficult to regard him as the creator of the universe.

And there is another point of grave importance. If God is not omnipotent, the fact that God exists and is good gives us no guarantee that the universe is more good than bad, or even that it is not very bad. If God exists and is good, the universe will of course be as good as he can make it. But, if there are some things that he cannot do, how can we tell that among these impossibilities may not be the impossibility of preventing the world from being more bad than good, or of preventing it from being very bad? If it could be shown that God's power, though limited, was strong enough to prevent this, it could only be by a determination of the precise limits of his power, and, if this could be done at all, it could only be done by an elaborate metaphysical investigation. Such investigations are open to few, and their results are frequently highly controversial. It is not strange that popular theology is unwilling to accept the position that the goodness of the universe can only be proved in such a way.

And thus popular theology has two conflicting impulses. It desires, among other things, to show that the universe is more good than bad—at any rate in the long run. The only means at its disposal for showing this—if it is to remain popular—is its belief in the existence of a God to whose will all evil is repugnant, and who is powerful enough to effect the predominance of good. But if God is to be taken as omnipotent, it is certain that all evil is not repugnant to his will, and if he is to be taken as not omnipotent, it is not certain that he is powerful enough to effect the predominance of good.

The inaccurate use of the word omnipotence hides this dilemma. When popular theology is pressed to reconcile the present existence of evil with the goodness of God, then it pleads that omnipotent does not mean omnipotent, but only very powerful. But when the sceptic has been crushed, and what is wanted is a belief in the future extinction of evil, then omnipotence slides back into its strict meaning, and it is triumphantly asserted that the cause which has an omnipotent God on its side must certainly win. The confusion is unintentional, no doubt, but it is dangerous.

It seems to me that when believers in God save his goodness by saying that he is not really omnipotent, they are taking the best course open to them, since both the personality and the goodness of God present much fewer difficulties if he is not conceived as omnipotent. But then they must accept the consequences of their choice, and realize that the efforts of a non-omnipotent God in favour of good may, for anything they have yet shown, be doomed to almost total defeat. It is not a very cheerful creed, unless it can be supplemented by some other dogmas which can assure us of God's eventual victory. But it is less depressing and less revolting than the belief that the destinies of the universe are at the mercy of a being who, with the resources of omnipotence at his disposal, decided to make a universe no better than this.

180. In this chapter I have only discussed the view which makes God a being separate from the universe, though all-powerful over it. I have not thought it necessary to consider the view—which has been maintained—according to which the whole of the universe is one omnipotent person, so that God is the sole reality, and we are not his creatures, but parts of himself. This view has not had much influence on religious thought. (Pantheism, indeed, has been and is very powerful, but the prevailing type is that which denies personality to the unity of all things.) And it is so little known, and of so obscure a nature, that I could scarcely have done it justice without expounding the whole philosophical system of each of its principal adherents. It is clear that the arguments given above to prove the inconsistency of omnipotence with personality and goodness would apply to God equally, if this theory of his nature were true. In addition to these there would be the further difficulty that it would require us to regard ourselves as parts of God. The belief that one person could be part of another would, I think, be found very difficult to defend.

CHAPTER VII

A NON-OMNIPOTENT GOD

181. WE must now proceed to consider the theory that God exists without being omnipotent, so that there are results which his volitions could not produce. On this hypothesis it is possible to hold either that God created all existent reality except himself, or that the other existent reality exists co-eternally with God, and independent of his will. In the latter case God would act on his environment in the same way that men act on theirs. His claim to be considered as God would rest on the very great excess of his goodness and power over that of all other beings.[1]

What grounds have we for believing in the existence of a non-omnipotent God? His existence is sometimes maintained, as in the case of an omnipotent God, on the ground of an instinctive and irresistible conviction, on the ground of the disastrous consequences which would result from his non-existence, or on the evidence of miracles. These grounds of belief were discussed in Chapter II, and need not be considered here.

It will also be unnecessary to consider here the Ontological argument, both for the reasons mentioned in the last chapter, and also because it has always, so

[1] The belief in a creative God who is not omnipotent has been recently urged with great force by Dr. Rashdall in his essay on *Personality Human and Divine* in the collection entitled *Personal Idealism*. The conception of a non-creative God has been brilliantly expounded and defended in *The Limits of Evolution* by Dr. Howison.

far as I know, been employed to prove the existence of a God who is omnipotent.

The objections brought in the last chapter against the validity of the argument for the necessity of a first cause, will apply here also, since none of them depended on the omnipotence of the first cause. In the case of a non-creative God, indeed, there will also be additional objections to the argument. A first cause was said to be required, both for non-divine substances and for events. But the hypothesis of a non-creative God implies that non-divine substances can exist eternally and in their own right, so that no creator is required for them. And, as for events, the argument for a first cause asserts that it is a sufficient explanation of them to refer them to an eternal and uncreated being for their first cause. But if this is so, then the existence of a God is not required to explain them, for, by the hypothesis, the non-divine beings are also eternal and uncreated, and therefore could be the causes required.

The position of the argument from design is different. The objections made to that argument in the last chapter rested on the fact that its truth would be compatible with the existence of a God who was not omnipotent, and, indeed, incompatible with the existence of a God who was omnipotent. Such an objection cannot, of course, apply to the attempt to prove, by this argument, the existence of a non-omnipotent God. But this argument will not give us any help in determining whether God is or is not creative. A creative God without unlimited power might find it necessary to use means to carry out his ends, since the limitations on his power might preclude the possibility of attaining his ends directly. In this case he would produce a universe such as is asserted to exist by the argument from design. On the other hand it is quite possible that the universe might have been organized as means for an end by a being who did not create the reality which he dealt with, but arranged and modified it as a watchmaker arranges and modifies the metal which he cannot create.

In the same way the argument that a God is necessary because all reality must be known to some being tells us nothing as to whether that God is a creator. Such an omniscient being might also be the creator of all the existent reality, other than himself, which he knows. But we can know things which we have not created, and, if there is an omniscient being at all, there seems no reason why he should not know various existent realities which do not owe their existence to his will.

182. Since these arguments give us no help in deciding between the two alternative forms of a belief in a non-omnipotent God, let us consider whether there are any other reasons which should lead us to prefer either alternative to the other. I shall endeavour to show that the hypothesis of a creative God, even when he is conceived as non-omnipotent, labours under serious difficulties which do not affect the hypothesis of a non-creative God.

Before considering these difficulties, however, we must make a further distinction. A creative, but non-omnipotent, God may be conceived either as free not to create, or as not free not to create. It may be held, that is, that the limitations of his power left him free to remain permanently the sole reality of the universe, should he choose to do so. In this case the limitation of his power would consist in the fact that, if he did choose to create, he could not create anything that he chose, but had only the choice between certain alternatives. Or it may be held that he had no power to abstain from creating reality other than himself, although he had power to decide, within certain limits, what sort of reality he would create. The second objection to God's personality mentioned in the last chapter would also apply to a God who was free to abstain from creating.[1] But it need not apply to a God who was compelled to create, since the created universe might afford him his necessary Other.

183. The difficulties which, as I have said, seem to me to arise from the hypothesis that the non-omnipotent God is creative, arise from the goodness which we decided to be part of the definition of God. We saw in the last chapter that it was impossible that an omnipotent being should be good, in view of the fact that there is evil in the universe. The believers in the limitation of God's power assert that they have saved the possibility of his goodness, because it is possible that a non-omnipotent God might wish to make the universe much better than it is, and yet be unable to do so. That this is possible with a non-creative God, is, I think, beyond doubt. But I am not so clear that it is possible with a creative God. It is quite possible, no doubt, that there are some things that the creator of the universe—if there is a creator—cannot do. But I cannot satisfy myself that it is possible that there could be anything which he willed to do, and which yet he could not do. And he would not be good—and consequently would not be God—unless he did will to remove the evil which he could not remove.

[1] Sections 167–70. These objections, however, would not apply to a non-omnipotent God, if it were held—as some philosophers hold—that it is possible for a truth to be real without reference to any existence.

184. In one sense, indeed, it is clear that nothing exists except as God wills it, if God is creative. For nothing exists unless he decides to create it—unless, that is, he prefers its existence to its non-existence. But we often will to produce a result, and yet say that we do so unwillingly, meaning that the result is the one most desirable under the circumstances, but is at the same time one which, in many respects, is undesirable.

The old distinction between antecedent and consequent volition is useful here. We will antecedently that which we desire in all respects. We will consequently that which, under the circumstances, we prefer to any other alternative which the circumstances leave possible. The two would be coincident for an omnipotent being, but for others they may diverge, and very frequently do so. A good man does not antecedently will to produce anything which is not good. But he often wills consequently to produce much that is bad. He wills, for example, to inflict pain in order to avoid worse evils.

With the exception of the undetermined volitions of non-divine beings—if such undetermined volitions exist—everything in the universe must be held to be caused by God, if God is conceived as creative.[1] And what is caused by God must be in accordance with his consequent will. But need it be in accordance with his antecedent will?

The will of any being is said to be thwarted in so far as he cannot act in conformity with his antecedent will. If I wish to enter a certain field, and abstain from doing so because there is a savage bull in it, my

[1] It would be due to the will of God, also, that any beings did form undetermined volitions, though the character of the volitions they formed would be due to nothing.

action is in accordance with my consequent will. The bull cannot prevent me from entering the field, and I only abstain from entering because I prefer being disappointed to running a serious risk of death. But my will has, nevertheless, been thwarted. I did not will to enter the field at great risk, but I did will to enter the field. It is this latter volition, the antecedent volition, which has been thwarted.

185. If the evil of the universe thwarts God's antecedent will, the fact that it has all arisen by his consequent will is no more reflection on his goodness, than the pain caused by amputation is on the benevolence of the surgeon. But it is essential that it should thwart his antecedent will, since God has been defined as good. God must feel the same impotent hatred of the evil which he cannot remove as is felt by a good man. Indeed, he must feel more. For whether God is conceived as perfectly good or not, he is always conceived as appreciably better than the best man. From this it would follow that evil must be more repugnant to him than it is to the best man.

This does not involve that God is more dissatisfied with the state of the universe than a good man would be. If God is much better than man, he must not only revolt more intensely against the evil, but he must rejoice more intensely in the good. Again, it is possible that a divine knowledge, which embraced the whole universe, might be able to see that the proportion of good to evil in the universe was much greater than it appears to us who see such a small corner of the whole. And thus it is possible, though only possible, that God's satisfaction might enormously outweigh his dissatisfaction. But, however much the good in the universe may exceed the evil, there is evil, and this must be more repugnant to God than it can be to any one else.

The only way to escape from this conclusion would be to deny that any evil did exist in the universe, or to maintain that God's goodness was so different from ours that his antecedent will could be in harmony with a state of things with which the antecedent will of a good man could not be in harmony. These suggestions were considered in the last chapter.

If, indeed, we were to say that the universe was created by a being who was not good, it would not follow from the existence of evil in the universe that the will of such a being must be thwarted. Such a being, however, would not be a God, of whose definition, as we have seen, goodness is a part. Nor would the discussion of such a view be of any practical interest, since, as far as I know, the theory of a personal creator who is not good is not one which commands any support. It has been maintained that the creator's goodness was of a different nature to man's, but goodness has always been attributed to him.

186. Why is it that any person wills consequently that which is contrary to his antecedent will? It is because things are so connected that, if he did not will this consequently, he would produce a result still more repugnant to his antecedent will. I remain outside the field, in the previous instance, although it is repugnant to my antecedent will to do so, because otherwise I should put my life in great peril, and because that is more repugnant to my antecedent will than staying outside the field would be. In the same way, we are told, God creates evil things, which is an act repugnant to his antecedent volition, because if he did not do so, he would have to create still worse things, or abstain from creating things with an amount of good which more than outweighs the evil. And either of these courses would be still more repugnant to his antecedent volition than the course which he actually takes.

In every case where the consequent volition has an element repugnant to antecedent volition the explanation is the limited power of the agent. If I could pacify the bull by a look, I should enter the field safely, and thus gratify both my antecedent volitions. If God could have abstained from creating the evil he did create, and at the same time abstained from creating any greater evil, and created all the good he did create, he would have created a universe which was all good and no evil, and was therefore in complete harmony with his antecedent volition.

There is often considerable unwillingness among theists, as was said at the end of the last chapter, to admit that God is not omnipotent. But when that has once been admitted, it seems to be generally taken as a matter of course, that God might will consequently to create, and so create, that which was repugnant to his antecedent will. We have continual examples in daily life of men willing consequently what is repugnant to their antecedent will. It seems to be thought that so soon as we are in a position to say that God is like man in not being omnipotent, we are entitled to believe that he may act repugnantly to his antecedent volition.

187. But there is another very important difference between man and a creative God, even if that God is not omnipotent. No characteristic, and therefore no impotence, of a man can be explained entirely from his own nature. He is part of a universe, all the parts of which are connected. Nothing can happen in the rest of the universe which does not affect him, nothing can happen in him which does not affect the rest of the universe. And, therefore, when a man wills to do something and cannot do it, his impotence is never due entirely to his own nature.

This is clearest when the thing which I wish to do, and cannot do, is to produce some effect on some being other than myself. Then it is clear that success or failure depends not only on my own nature, but also on the nature of the being I am trying to affect. In ordinary language it would sometimes be said that a failure was due entirely to my own nature, if the circumstances were such that an average person, in my place, would have succeeded. But it is obvious that this leaves out an essential element. However feeble my effort, its failure cannot be explained merely from its feebleness. For we cannot know that it was *too* feeble to succeed, until we know the nature of the being it was attempting to influence.

But the proposition is also true when the effect which I vainly endeavour to produce is a change in my own nature. My nature, in all its characteristics, is dependent, not on itself only, but on the rest of the universe. How far it will be changed, in any case, by the influence of my will to change it, will depend on the result produced by my will in combination with all the other factors which are influencing it. If my will fails to change it, the failure cannot be explained by my nature alone, but will depend also on the strength of the other factors which opposed the change which was willed, and on the feebleness of the other factors which supported the change.

188. With a creative God the matter is different. At the moment at which he creates nothing exists except himself. He is the only existent reality. Whatever happens must be explained from his nature, and from his nature alone, for there is nothing else anywhere.

It is from his own nature, then, that we must explain the limitation of his power, which, according to the theory we are considering, accounts for the existence of evil in the universe in spite of his antecedent volition for something different and better.

But God endeavours to produce whatever he wills antecedently. The defeat of an antecedent volition means a defeated effort. And what I am unable to see is the possibility of explaining the defeat of the effort solely from the nature of the being who made it. He only acts by his will. And if his will is directed to a certain end, can there be anything in his nature which can hinder its execution?

The result of answering this question in the negative would not be to make the creator omnipotent. We could still say that there were things which he could not do, but we should hold that it was also impossible for him to will to do them, since the impossibility must be found entirely in his own nature, and could only act through his will. We should not be compelled to believe—as the upholders of his omnipotence must believe—that he could have created a universe in which the laws of Identity and Contradiction did not apply. But, since we should believe that whatever he willed would find nothing to hinder it, we should conclude that the impossibility of creating such a universe proves the impossibility of his willing to create it. For the impossibility of creating it rests entirely on his nature, and his nature in acting is expressed simply by his will.

But if this is the case, the creator of the universe cannot be a God. For then the cause of the evil in the universe is not that the creator could not do what he antecedently willed to do. Whatever he antecedently willed to do has been done. But a person whose antecedent will includes the production of evil cannot be good, although, as we have seen, a being may be good whose consequent will includes the production of evil. And a being who is not good is not God. Even if we say that the limitations on the creator's nature rendered it impossible for him to will anything better, that would not make him good, but only assert that his badness was inevitable. Under no circumstances can a person be called good, whose will is not thwarted by the production of evil.

I do not know that I can make this important and difficult point any plainer, except by clearing away a few objections. It is not fair to argue that, because men can will all sorts of impossible things, it must be possible for God to will things which it is impossible for him to carry out. A non-creative God could doubtless do so, because the impossibility of his carrying them out would not depend exclusively on himself. His efforts to do so might be thwarted by the nature of some other being co-existent with him. It is only when everything is completely dependent on God's nature—as it must be in the case of a creative God—that we can argue from the non-existence of a result to the non-existence of any will on God's part to produce it.

189. We must also be on our guard against methods of expression which treat God's nature as if it consisted of different beings, capable of working in opposite directions and neutralizing one another in the same way that the will of one diplomatist may be opposed by the will of another, or the will of a carver by the nature of the marble. Thus it is said, for example, that God is prevented from completely realizing his antecedent volitions by the law of his own nature. The will of God and the law which prevents its realization are conceived of as so separate that their opposition appears to present no difficulty.

But this is unjustifiable. A law is not another existent thing, apart from the thing of which it is a law, and capable of acting on it, as a wall may check the course of a bullet. The law is simply the statement of how the thing will act under certain circumstances. In other words, the law is not something which controls the thing's nature from without. We are often tempted to give it this significance—probably from confusion with the laws of jurisprudence, which do control our acts from without. But this is to confuse two quite different conceptions, which have nothing but the name in common. The laws of which we speak here are not commands, but statements of facts. The law of a thing's nature does not control it, but expresses it. When we say that the law of the nature of wax is to melt at a certain temperature, this is not an outside authority to which the nature of the wax submits. It *is* the nature of the wax.

And so the difficulty remains unsolved—how can God's nature at once impel him towards an end and yet be the sole obstacle to his realizing that end?

190. Or, again, God's will and God's power are taken almost as separate beings.[1] The tendency to realize the antecedent volitions is ascribed to the nature of the will, the failure to realize them completely is ascribed to the nature of the power—that is to say to its limitation. And, as we have seen, there is no difficulty in maintaining that the antecedent volitions which are due to the nature of one being may be hindered from complete realization by the nature of another being.

But this view involves a disruption of God's nature which is indefensible. If there is a God, he is a person,

[1] Cp. Dr. Rashdall's *Personality Human and Divine*, quoted above.

and not an abstract quality.[1] Still less is God to be resolved into a couple of abstract qualities which can be treated as opposing one another. God's power—the power of a creative God for whom there are no external obstacles—can only mean the extent to which his own nature does or does not permit him to perform things. And we are no further towards a solution of the difficulty how his nature can stop him from doing anything except by stopping his willing it.

Whatever a creator does, he is completely self-determined in doing it, for there is nothing but his own nature to determine him. Therefore he is wholly self-determined in producing, among other things, much that is evil. Now when a being who is completely self-determined produces evil, knowing that it is evil, can we say that such a being is good? I do not see how we can do so. A person who consciously produces evil can be good, if he is not completely self-determined, for then the evil may be due to the external forces which determine him, as when the surgeon is forced to give pain to prevent greater pain. But a person whose nature is such that he spontaneously produces what he knows to be evil—what is this but the definition of a wicked person?

191. If we combine this result with that attained in the last chapter it would lead us to reject the idea of a creative person who is either omnipotent or thwarted in his volitions. This does not absolutely exclude the possibility of a creative person. It would be possible that a non-omnipotent person should exist for whom the present universe would be in every

[1] No one has realized this truth more clearly than Dr. Rashdall, or expressed it more forcibly. But I confess that it seems to me that, in his treatment of the relation of God's will to his power, he has temporarily lost sight of his own principle.

respect desirable for its own sake, and for whom nothing which is excluded from that universe would be desirable for its own sake. In that case his antecedent volition would be for this universe, and for nothing else, and it would therefore not be in the least thwarted by his consequent volition to produce this universe and nothing else. But such a person could not be a God, because he would not be good. It is, as we have seen, impossible that any person should be good to whom some features of the present universe were not intrinsically repugnant[1].

192. I have spoken so far of a creative and non-omnipotent God who is distinct from that which he creates. But it is also possible to believe in a creative and non-omnipotent God who is the sum of all existence, and whose acts of creation consist in producing modifications within his own nature, and not beings outside it. Lotze, for example, appears to take this view. This conception, I think, does not require separate discussion. It is obvious that the difficulties, already considered, of regarding a person as self-thwarted, will be just as great if his creation operates within himself as it would be if his creation produced separate realities. And then, as was said in the last chapter, the conception of God as the sum of all existent reality involves the additional difficulty—which seems to me wholly insuperable—of regarding one person as part of another person.

[1] Another argument against the possibility of a creative God would be supplied if we found reason to believe that all existent reality was eternal and ultimate. In that case there could not be a creative God, or a creator of any sort, because there would be nothing for him to create. It seems to me that by following out the lines of Hegel's philosophy we are led to this conclusion, as I have endeavoured to show in my *Studies in Hegelian Cosmology*, chap. ii.

193. We now pass to the theory that God is neither omnipotent nor creative. According to this theory all the non-divine existent beings of the universe are co-eternal with God, and have not been called into being by his will. Their existence is an ultimate fact, and a fact which God has simply to accept, as we all have to accept it about one another. God can affect the condition of these other beings, in the same way that they can affect the condition of one another, and, presumably, of God. So far there is no difference between God and other persons. The difference is quantitative. God is conceived to be so much more perfect in goodness than his fellow persons, that the due attitude of all of them, even the highest, towards him is that of reverence and adoration. And he is conceived to excel them so much in wisdom and power that his efforts are capable of producing important effects, not only in one small corner of the universe, but in every part of it. His position towards us is that of a schoolmaster towards his scholars. He does not create us. He cannot destroy us. His power over us is limited. And we can resist his power, and in some cases our resistance is effectual—at any rate for a time, perhaps permanently. But, on the other hand, his power is greater than the power of any one of us, and is so great that it can do much, though not all, of what he wishes to do throughout the universe. Independently of his exertions the universe would not be completely bad, since beings who are capable of improvement cannot be completely bad. In spite of all his exertions, he has not yet succeeded in making the universe completely good. It is uncertain what his eventual success will be. But it is at any rate certain that the universe is better because he is working in it.

194. Of the three theories of God's nature which

we have to consider, this seems to me by far the most tenable. God has been defined as good and as a person. We have seen that, if God is held to be omnipotent, it is, at the least, very difficult to conceive him as a person, and absolutely impossible to conceive him as good. The creative God who is not omnipotent presents less difficulties. But it is almost as difficult to conceive him as a person, unless he is conceived as not free to abstain from creating. And, in any case, we have seen that he can only be conceived as good if he is conceived as self-thwarted, and that the possibility of this is, at any rate, very doubtful.

Neither of these difficulties applies to the conception of God which we shall now discuss. There is no more difficulty in believing such a God to be a person than in believing myself to be a person, since he, like myself, is one member in a universe, none of the other elements in which are dependent on him for their existence. These other members, therefore, may form the Other of his personality. Nor does the existence of evil in the universe reflect, of necessity, on his goodness, since it may possibly all be due to defects in the constitution of the other beings co-eternal with him. In that case, of course, we should know that God's power was not sufficient to remove these evils, but this need not imply defective goodness in him, any more than it would in a man. He is only responsible for making the evil as small as he can. And the existence of evil does not prove that he has not done this.

We may admit that there is nothing antecedently impossible in the existence of such a God as this. Persons do exist. And, of these persons, some excel others in virtue, some in wisdom, and some in power. It happens not infrequently that one person surpasses another in all three. There seems no reasons why one person should not surpass all others in all three to such an extent that his goodness would fit him for a universal worship, and his wisdom and power would enable him to dominate the universe as much as an efficient schoolmaster dominates his school.

195. But this is not enough. There is nothing antecedently impossible in the supposition that the next six dice I throw will come up 4, 1, 4, 3, 5, 5. Indeed it may be said that, in a sense, there is no antecedent improbability, for they must come up somehow, and this series is just as likely as any other, if the dice are honest. Yet, if the dice are honest, the odds required for a prudent bet on this series would be enormous. There is nothing antecedently impossible, again, in the supposition that at this moment a play equal to Hamlet is being written in Gower Street. The existence of Hamlet proves that such a feat is possible to mankind. If one such play has been written, another may be, and it is just as likely to be written now in Gower Street as at any other time and place. But we should want a good deal more than this negative evidence before we should believe that the great play was actually being written.

We must now inquire what evidence can be brought in favour of the existence of such a God. Immediate conviction, the disastrous consequences of his non-existence, revelation, and the ontological argument present no new features when God is conceived in this way. And such a God is not a first cause. But the argument from the necessity of all reality being known to some one has not been considered at all, and the argument from design has not been considered as applied to a non-omnipotent God. Let us first consider the argument from design.

196. It is doubtless the case that much of what we observe around us in the universe could be easily explained as the means for realizing some end which is good in itself, or for realizing some end which may in its turn serve as means to a further end which is good in itself. Now if reality is so arranged that it becomes means to ends, it is a simple and natural explanation to suppose that it has been so arranged by some conscious being who wills the end, and brings about the means for its sake. Much of what appears to be so arranged would require much more than human wisdom and power to arrange it. From this it is a natural inference—though not strictly logical, as we shall see later on—that it was arranged by a being of sufficient pre-eminence to deserve the name of God. Since omnipotence precludes the employment of means, such a God could not be omnipotent.

I have thought it convenient to discuss this argument while speaking of a non-creative God, because we found reason for thinking that, if there was a God at all, he was not a creator, and therefore the alternative of the non-creative God was the only one which remained. But the argument from design itself tells us nothing as to whether the directing God creates things so as to form certain arrangements, or whether he arranges what exists independently of him, as the watchmaker arranges the metal of the watch, and does not create it. I shall endeavour to deal with the argument in such a way that my remarks will be applicable to either alternative, although, for the reasons mentioned above, we have come to the conclusion that, if any God is proved by this argument, he will not be a creator.

The facts of the case would be met, as I have

admitted, by the hypothesis that the order and goodness to be observed around us are due to the influence of a person who antecedently willed the good, and who, though not omnipotent, was very powerful. Such a person would be entitled to be called God. But before we can legitimately infer from this that God does exist, we must inquire whether any other hypothesis would explain the facts as well. Would the order, and the tendency to produce good, which we can observe, in certain parts of our experience, and to a certain degree, be explicable on the supposition that the reality around us was not under the influence of a God?

197. Much of what we observe in experience appears, at any rate, not to be spirit but matter. And the traces of order and goodness are to be observed in this part of our experience as well as in others. Now suppose that this appearance is correct, and that those parts of the universe, which present themselves *prima facie* as matter, really were matter. In that case we should have existent reality which was unconscious, which was not actuated by final causes, since it could desire nothing and judge nothing good, and which was actuated only by causes of a mechanical nature. Moreover, it would either be infinitely divisible, or divided into a great number of very small parts, and its parts would have no intrinsic connexions which should arrange them in a definite order, but would enter into various combinations according to the external forces which actuate them.

If such matter shows an order tending to the good, which does not arise from the action of a conscious being with an intention to promote the good, such an order can only arise, as is commonly said, by chance. This does not mean that the events which brought about the order had no cause, for every event has a cause. (Even the systems which deny this of human volitions would not deny it of matter.) What then is meant by chance?

198. If a roulette table were constructed in which letters were substituted for numbers, and if the letters indicated by consecutive settlements of the ball spelled out the received text of Hamlet, we should say, provided we were certain that the table was an honest one, that this was a most extraordinary chance. Yet the result was absolutely determined. With sufficient knowledge, and sufficient power of reasoning, the result could have been inferred with absolute certainty before it happened.

There is no contingency in the connexion of the particular cause with the particular effect. We cannot get contingency unless we describe the cause and effect respectively by some general class to which each of them belongs. And then we get contingency if the nature of the general class to which the cause belongs has no tendency to ensure that the effect shall be of the general class to which, in point of fact, it does belong. Thus it is not contingent that a roulette table of the sort I have described should produce an effect which is a succession of letters. The nature of such roulette tables ensures that they should produce such an effect. It could not, for example, produce a succession of numbers, because the holes are not marked with numbers, but letters. But if we bring the effect under another general class to which it belongs, and call it not merely a succession of letters (which it is), but also a copy of the play of Hamlet (which it also is), then the connexion is contingent. For there is nothing in the nature of such roulette tables as a class which makes it necessary or probable that its effect should come under the general class of copies of Hamlet. Thus we do not say that it is a chance that the table produces a sequence of letters, but we do say that it is a chance that it produces Hamlet.

If then, matter uninfluenced by mind should assume a form which contained ordered means towards a good end, we should say that this was a chance, not meaning that the particular cause could have produced anything but what it did produce, but meaning that there is no necessity or probability that a cause which answers to the description of matter uninfluenced by mind should produce such an effect as answers to the description of ordered means towards a good end.

199. If we are perfectly sure that no cause can be found for the effect which would have a tendency to produce an effect of this nature, we must accept the view that it has happened by chance, as explained above. But when the chance would be antecedently a very small one, we are unwilling to accept this view. I suppose that no evidence which our imperfect human knowledge admits would convince us that a roulette table spelled out Hamlet by chance. We should always prefer the belief that it was influenced, in some way unknown to us, and perhaps by some law as yet unknown to science, by a mind which had for some reason resolved that it should spell out Hamlet. Even supposing—which is a closer analogy to the state of the world as we perceive it—that the table should at intervals, interspersed with long series of letters without significance or coherence, give us a sentence, now of Hamlet, now of Paradise Lost, mutilated and distorted, but still to be recognized, we should probably insist on attributing this to the action of a mind, however unable we were to explain how a mind could act on the table.

The reason of this unwillingness to accept chance is, it would seem, that if we accept as a cause a mind which wills to produce the result, there is a reason why a significant result should be produced rather than any other, while, if we hold that all that we know about the cause is that it is matter uninfluenced by mind, we have to assume that a result has taken place against which there was an enormous antecedent probability. The uninfluenced roulette table is just as likely to produce any one combination of letters as any other, and the number of combinations of letters which have no significance are enormously greater than those which have a significance. This is true even if we take a series of a hundred letters, much more if we take so long a series as that of the letters in Hamlet.

200. On this principle the argument from design urges that the traces of order directed towards good which we perceive in the universe render the hypothesis that matter is directed by mind more probable than the hypothesis that it is not directed by mind. In the first case the order is accounted for at once. In the second case we have to make the additional hypothesis that it has been brought about by causes which were just as likely to produce any one of many results which excluded such an order, and therefore were more likely to exclude the order than to produce it.

There is certainly force in this contention, but it is not as strong as it is sometimes supposed to be. It is sometimes put as if the antecedent improbability was that of precisely the actual arrangement of the universe occurring among all the possible arrangements which undirected matter could fall into. But this is wrong. For many other arrangements of the universe would have given us as good reason to trace order directed towards good as the present arrangement can. Consequently, to account for the present state of the world, we should have, after assuming a directing mind, to assume that it had chanced to produce this particular arrangement, when it might just as well, as far as we can see, have produced any one of many others, and was therefore less likely to have produced the existing one than some one of the others.

Of course, if the present order is produced by a directing mind there must be a sufficient cause why it produced this order rather than another. But then, if the present order were produced by undirected matter, there must be sufficient cause why it produced this order rather than any other arrangement. The argument was based on the fact that all we know about the nature of undirected matter was equally compatible with an enormous number of other arrangements. And it must accept as relevant the corresponding fact that all we know about the nature of a mind which wills the good would be equally compatible with a number of different orders.

Thus the greater improbability of the hypothesis which excludes a directing mind is not to be expressed, as is sometimes maintained, by the proportion of a large number to unity, but of one large number to another. But the number of arrangements which would show some traces of such an order is very small as compared with the total number of arrangements of which undirected matter is capable. And thus the argument, if not as strong as has been sometimes supposed, retains considerable strength.

201. But there is another point to be considered. The improbability of a result arising by chance depends on the number of times that it does happen as compared with the number of times when it might have happened and did not. If I cast a die ten times, and threw a six each time, I should have little doubt that it had been loaded. But if I cast it sixty million times, and got only one run of ten sixes, I should find no difficulty in supposing that it came by chance.

Now it is possible that all the traces of order in the universe are in the position of the run of ten sixes among sixty million throws. Our present discussion is based on the hypothesis that matter does exist, and that its existence is not necessarily connected with spirit. In that case it would be possible that by far the greater amount of the universe at this moment does not exhibit the least traces of order, since it is quite possible that by far the greater amount of the universe is beyond the range of our observation. And it would be possible that by far the greater amount of past time did not exhibit, and that by far the greater amount of future time will not exhibit, any traces of order in any part of the universe. The proportion of the amount of the universe which shows such traces to the amount which does not may be so small as to make the order which we see as explicable by chance as the run of ten sixes in sixty million throws.

In answer to this it has sometimes been said that the times and spaces which would correspond to the sixty million throws would be so great that even to write the figures expressing them would be fatiguing. But this would only be a valid objection if there were any reason to suppose the world of matter to be limited in time and space in such a way as to make it smaller than this. And, on the hypothesis that there is a world of matter at all, there seems no reason to suppose that there is any finite duration or magnitude which is too great to be possible for it.

The improbability that the traces of order should be due to chance is thus lessened, but it is not removed. For the existence of vast areas of reality in which no trace of order is to be observed, while certainly possible, is not more than possible.

The conclusion so far seems to be that, if any reality is rightly conceived as matter, then there is a considerable probability—though by no means a certainty—that any traces of order in it are due to the action of a directing person. Such a person would be greatly superior in wisdom and power to ourselves, and might be—though this would not necessarily follow—also superior in goodness. His superiority in all three over all other beings might be sufficient to entitle him to be called God.

202. But the existence of matter is not universally admitted. It has often been maintained that nothing exists except selves, and that the reality which lies behind the appearance of matter is in truth spiritual. In that case all traces of order are to be found in spirit only, because nothing else exists. How does this affect the probability of a directing God?

We must distinguish two varieties of the doctrine. According to the first, the selves, taken separately, are spiritual, but they do not form a spiritual unity. They form a unity, no doubt, for they form the universe, and the universe is certainly more or less of a unity. But the arrangement of that unity is determined by laws of a purely mechanical nature. The relations in which selves find themselves with other selves are determined by laws analogous to those on which, according to the theory which accepts the existence of matter, one particle of such matter is brought into relation with other particles.

203. If we hold this view to be the truth, it will not be so difficult, as it would have been on the hypothesis that matter existed, to account for traces of order without the agency of a directing God. For every unit in the whole universe will be a self. It is absurd to suppose that matter, if it is really matter, should will the good, or take steps to carry out that will. But it is by no means absurd to suppose that selves should do so. However much the forces which combined and separated selves were blind forces regardless of the good, still if all or many of the selves which they combined and separated strove towards the good in whatever circumstances they found themselves, some traces of order would naturally arise in the universe.

In such a case the universe might be compared to a space into which human beings had been flung by some natural force—an earthquake or a cyclone. That they were in that place at all, and all their original arrangement in it, and much of their future arrangement, would be due to this blind natural force. But if they kept any control of their actions, their state would soon show some efforts towards ends. They would try to escape, or to alleviate their position. Some would sacrifice the advantages of others to their own, some would sacrifice their own advantage for the sake of others. An observer would soon be assured that they were thinking and willing persons, and not statues or automata.

But while a directing mind could thus be dispensed with, on this hypothesis, with less improbability than if matter really existed, there would still be some difficulty in dispensing with it. We perceive traces of order which extend over such large areas of the universe, and which are so minute and exact in their arrangements, that it is impossible to regard them as due to the efforts of a single self no higher than we are. And it seems very difficult to suppose them due to the unconscious co-operation of many such selves, if the relations and juxtapositions of those selves are due to blind forces. On the other hand, if we suppose it to be due to the conscious co-operation of selves, we cannot suppose that those selves are no higher than our own, since the knowledge required in order to plan and carry out such a work would require far more than human capabilities. It is simpler and more probable to fall back on the supposition of a directing person—or possibly a plurality of such persons—of a much higher nature.

204. But there is a third hypothesis. We may deny that matter exists, and we may deny that selves are only connected by blind forces. We may hold that reality consists of a system of selves, and we may hold that the nature of that system can to some extent be determined. We may hold further that what we can determine about that system is such that it shows it to exhibit an order directed towards the production of something of spiritual significance and value—of something which is either completely good, or, at any rate, more good than bad. Such a view as this is the basis of the systems of Fichte, of Hegel, of Lotze.

Now, if we hold this view, it seems to me that the directing mind is not wanted at all to account for the traces of order in the universe. The nature of reality has been seen to be such that it inevitably manifests itself in order directed towards the good. It is a harmonious system—no longer a mere aggregate, whether of atoms or souls—and so it must manifest itself in order. And it is a system of such a nature that it is directed towards some end which is, on the whole, good. And therefore the order in which it manifests itself must be an order directed, to some degree at any rate, towards what is good.[1]

205. We may be asked how such a harmonious system of selves came into existence, and it may be said that its production would require a directing mind. But this is not valid. For, if this theory is true, the harmonious system of selves is the fundamental fact of the universe. And, on any theory, there must always be a fundamental fact which is accounted for by nothing, and which accounts for everything. If it were a fatal objection to this theory that it takes a harmonious system of selves as an ultimate fact, which cannot be explained any further, it would be just as fatal an objection to the opposite theory that it takes the existence and nature of God as an ultimate fact, which cannot be explained any further. If it is asked, 'Who made the system of selves, and secured that it should be harmonious rather than chaotic?' it may as well be asked, 'Who made God, and secured that he should be good rather than bad?' The fact is that both questions are unjustifiable, since the system of selves, on the one hand, and God on the other hand, are both put forward as ultimate facts.

If matter, or selves mechanically arranged, are accepted as real, the probability of a directing mind arises from the fact that nothing that we know about

[1] The point is not merely that we know that the nature of reality is such as to produce the traces of order. We knew that before, since we knew that it did produce them. The point is that the qualities which we have determined reality to possess are such that they are seen to involve the production of such an order, and there is no longer any chance or contingency in its production.

the nature of the matter, or the nature of the selves, would explain the traces of order, and that therefore we had a tendency to postulate an external cause whose nature would explain them. But here the nature of the system of selves does explain the traces of order, and there is no need to go further.

206. Such a harmonious system of selves, if it existed, would be the fundamental reality of the universe. But its existence is, of course, by no means self-evident, and we must prove its truth before we are entitled to believe in it. Such a proof cannot be attempted here, since it would involve a discussion of a complete system of metaphysics. The theory is, at any rate, one which is widely held. And the onus of disproving it lies on the supporters of the argument from design. Their position is that the hypothesis of a directing God is the only one which, without great improbability, can be used to explain the traces of order in the universe. They are bound, therefore, to disprove an hypothesis, which, if true, would explain the traces of order in the universe without any improbability at all.

The existence of such a harmonious system of selves would not *disprove* the existence of a directing God. It might well be that among those selves was one who, in goodness, wisdom, and power, so much excelled all the others that he might appropriately be called God. And so powerful a being would doubtless have a large share in carrying out the order of the universe. But, although the existence of a harmonious system of selves is not incompatible with the existence of a directing God, it is, as we have seen, incompatible with any possibility of proving his existence by the argument from design. The order in the universe would be there, on this hypothesis, whether there was a God or not, and cannot, therefore, be used to prove his existence.

207. Idealism and Theism are generally held to be theories which have a natural affinity. But they are perfectly separable. It is quite possible to believe that there is no reality except spirit, and yet to reject the conception of a God. On the other side, most people who accept the existence of God have no doubt that matter is as real as spirit. And we see now that under certain circumstances the interests of Theism may lie in disproving Idealism. If there is matter, there is much in the arrangement of matter which seems to require a God to direct it. But if all reality is a harmonious system of selves, it is perhaps itself sufficiently godlike to dispense with a God.

The weight which Mill attaches to the argument from design must in any case be an interesting and significant fact.[1] But considerations which affected him would have no force for a thinker who believed, as Mill did not believe, that reality, of its own nature, and without any direction, formed a harmonious spiritual system.

208. We must now proceed from the argument from design to the argument from the necessity of everything being known to some one. This argument has been stated by Dr. Rashdall in a criticism with which he honoured a previous book of mine. 'Mr. McTaggart (whatever we may say of the "Pluralists") feels that the world must be a Unity, that it consists not merely of souls but of related and inter-connected souls which form a system. But a system for whom? The idea of a system which is not "for" any mind at all is not open to an Idealist; and the idea of a world each part of which is known to some mind

[1] Essays on Religion, III, i.

but is not known as a whole to any mind is almost equally difficult. Where then, in his view, is the Mind that knows the whole? i.e. the whole system of souls with the content of each.'[1]

If there is no omniscient person there is doubtless a possibility that some things may exist which are not known to anybody—or, at least, not fully known to anybody. And in that case there can be nobody who knows everything—no one, that is, who knows the system of selves in its entirety. And, again, an omniscient person might very probably be—though it is not certain that he would be—a person of such power and goodness as to be rightly called God.

209. But I cannot see that it is at all necessary for an idealist to admit that nothing can exist except that which is *for* a mind, in other words, except that which is known. There is, no doubt, a school of Idealism which maintains this. It has been maintained that to Be is to be Perceived, or that to Be is to be Thought. To such Idealism, certainly, Dr. Rashdall's argument applies. If all reality is a system, and if only that has being which is known, then some person must know the system, and so know all reality.

There is, however, another form of Idealism—the form which seems to me to be true—which is not liable to these criticisms. This form of Idealism does not say that nothing can be real except what is known. It says that nothing can exist but persons—conscious beings, who know, will, and feel. To the traditional expression of the first-mentioned school, *Esse est percipi*, the adherents of the second view might, for the sake of antithesis, oppose the maxim *Esse est percipere.* But it must always be remembered that

[1] *Personal Idealism*, Essay VIII, p. 393.

such a formula sacrifices accuracy to antithesis, since persons have other activities as fundamental as knowledge.

Now if we take this view, there seems no difficulty at all in saying that certain aspects of reality are unknown to every one. The theory maintains that nothing exists but persons connected in a unity. Accordingly, whatever exists must either be a conscious person, or a quality belonging to him, or an event happening to him, or else it must be one of those relations which connect these persons, and make up their unity. In the latter case, while it does not actually fall within any one person, it involves a quality which does. For if *A* and *B* are in relation, then *A* has the quality of being related to *B*, and *B* has the quality of being related to *A*. Thus there is no reality which cannot be expressed in a proposition about conscious persons.

But it does not follow from this that whatever exists must be known to some one. A proposition about one conscious person stands in no different relation to any other conscious person than a proposition which was not about a person at all would do. If a true proposition about a conscious person cannot remain unknown, and the reason of this is that it is about a conscious person, it can only be because such a proposition must be known to the person himself. But this is certainly not the case. It is often a true proposition about a person that he is vain, humble, or the like, without his knowing it. Again, it must be true of every conscious person either that he was created by a God or that he was not. But many persons do not know either of these propositions to be true—either because they are in doubt, or because they are too young or ignorant to have thought about them. In these cases something must be true about a person which he does not himself know, and in this event the form of Idealism which we are now discussing can offer no opposition to its being true without any one knowing it.

If I am right, then, we must reject Dr. Rashdall's argument that Idealism involves an omniscient person. My counter-argument has, of course, not been directed against Dr. Rashdall's view that one form of Idealism does involve an omniscient person, but has only pointed out that another form of Idealism exists which does not.

210. Another point remains for consideration. If it were proved that there was a person in the universe who greatly excelled all others both in wisdom and power, yet this would not by itself prove the existence of a God. For God has not only to be wise and powerful, but also good. How are we to prove that this director of the universe is good enough to be called God?

In the first place, he could not, as it seems to me, be perfectly good. He is one self in a universe which contains other selves. He is continually acting on them. They, in their turn, are continually acting on him, sometimes helping his plans, sometimes thwarting them, sometimes rejoicing him, sometimes grieving him. Selves in such a union as this form a society. We have to consider, then, the director of the universe as one of a society of selves.

Is it possible that one member of a society should be *completely* perfect while others are not? We see, of course, in everyday life, that people of very different degrees of perfection may be closely united. But I do not see how there can be any unity at all if each is not helped by the perfection, and hindered by the imperfection, of every other. Any hindrance must prevent the person hindered from being quite perfect, and this seems to render God's perfection impossible.

'No doubt', it might be replied, 'God is not completely perfect—at any rate, as yet. To be perfect he would have to be in perfect harmony with his environment, to be perfectly acquiescent and happy. And this he cannot be in a world which contains sin and pain. But this does not prevent him from being completely perfect *morally*. He can be completely good without being completely happy.'

It is surely, however, a false abstraction to maintain that any cause can work an effect on one aspect of a person's life and leave the others untouched. A person is not a mere aggregate of water-tight compartments. He is essentially a unity, although that unity is manifested in a plurality of activities. And, consequently, nothing can be a hindrance to the perfection of any side of his nature without affecting that unity, and, through it, all the other sides of his nature. One cause, no doubt, may have much more effect on one side of his nature than on other sides, and so the sides may develop unevenly. Thus three people, if arranged in the order of their intellectual perfection, might be placed—*A*, *B*, *C*; if in the order of their moral perfection, *B*, *A*, *C*; and if in the order of their happiness, *C*, *A*, *B*. But every cause must have *some* effect on each aspect of each nature, and so, if any cause exists which causes some imperfection in any aspect of God's nature, it will be impossible to regard him as completely perfect in any respect.

211. The possibility would remain that the director of the universe, although not perfectly good, was very much better than any other person. This would justify us in calling him God. Such a comparative perfection would suffice for worship. If worship is to be anything higher than selfish propitiation of the powerful, it requires that the being worshipped shall be conceived as morally better than the devotee. But, if this is secured, it does not seem essential that it should be accompanied by an assertion of the absolute perfection of the object of worship. Thus the director of the universe, if he exists, may be a God. But it is also possible that he may not be a God. For that would require that he should be distinctly better than the best man. And I do not see that it is impossible that he should be even worse than the worst man. Absolutely bad, indeed, he could not be. Evil, though not a *mere* negation, is nevertheless of a distinctly negative nature, and could only exist as limiting and confining the good. An absolutely bad person —one without any goodness in him—would be an impossibility.

But it is not impossible that the director of the universe should be worse than the worst man. Our only ground of inference as to his moral nature is the present condition of the universe, which would be due largely to his influence. It was admitted that much of what we observe around us in the universe could be easily explained as the means for realizing some end which is good in itself. And if it is to be explained this way, we might argue that the director of the universe must be good. But it seems to me that the facts which we observe could just as easily be explained as the means for realizing some end which is bad in itself. Many of the ends to which facts of the universe appear to be adapted as means are partially good and partially bad. Some of the ends to which the facts of the universe appear to be adapted as means seem to be purely bad. If we believe the director of the universe to be good we say, in the first case, that he brings such ends about for the sake of the good in them, and because the good outweighs the evil with which it is necessarily connected. In the second case, when the ends achieved seem to be purely bad, it is said that in some way which we do not know they may in their turn be indispensable means to some end whose good outweighs their evil.

And all this is quite possible. But then, it seems to me, the contrary hypothesis is also quite possible—that the director of the universe has proposed to himself an end which is distinctly bad. The existence of the good could then be explained in the same way as the existence of evil was by the more cheerful theory. It would be something which the director of the universe unwillingly brought about, because the constitution of the universe prevented him from producing the evil without producing this amount of good also. It would no more prove his goodness than the refreshments administered in the intervals of tortures proved the humanity of the torturers.

Nor would this possibility be removed, even if we could prove that good far outweighs evil in the universe. It would still be possible that the aim of the director of the universe was to produce a much worse result, and that the excess of good merely proved that the conditions under which he worked were unfavourable to his purpose.

212. I cannot see, therefore, that any reason has been given for supposing a director of the universe to be good rather than bad. But even if we assume that he is more good than bad, it would not follow from this that he would be a God. He might be no better than the average good man. The size and complexity of the universe—even of that little part of it which we imperfectly observe—is so enormous that a being who directed it must very greatly excel human beings in wisdom and power. But it is not equally necessary that he should excel them in goodness. For it is not certain that the universe excels the works of men in goodness at all, and still less certain that it excels them very greatly in goodness. Indeed most men would, I imagine, be distinctly relieved if they were certain that good bore as large a proportion to evil in the universe as a whole as it did in the work of such men as Buddha, Aquinas, or Mill. Of course, a universe which was proportionately much more evil than Mill's work *might* have been produced by a person much better than Mill, for the evil *might* have been due almost exclusively to the limitations of his power. But it is also possible that the conditions might have allowed of a better state of things, and that some of the existing evil is due to the defective virtue of the agent.

It is possible, for example, that, while good is attractive to the director of the universe, other things are also attractive. And, when the two attractions lead to different courses, he may sometimes be tempted, like less wise and less powerful persons, and choose the worse alternative. Or, again, to produce the best possible result may well cause him fatigue and pain, and it is possible that the amount of these which he is prepared to encounter is limited. The universe might have been better if his self-sacrifice had been greater.

213. And, once more, if the director of the universe is finite, why should we be certain that there is only one? Many of the facts of experience, while they are compatible with the theory of a single director working under limitations, suggest at least as strongly the idea of several such beings, working in opposition, or possibly — as patriotic Tories work with patriotic Liberals—partly in harmony and partly in opposition. The opposition might be direct, between powers whose ends are intrinsically contrary, or indirect, between powers which had different ends, not intrinsically opposed, but capable of clashing under certain circumstances.

Or, supposing that only one director is at work in the part of the universe which we know, still that part may be very small compared with the whole. How shall we tell that there are not other regions—perhaps separated from ours by vast ungoverned intervals—in which other beings, higher or lower than he whose work we perceive here, are working out other independent and isolated purposes?

There is nothing, perhaps, which should prevent us from giving the name of God to each of several beings simultaneously existing, or to one such being, existing simultaneously with others, who equal him in wisdom and power, but not in goodness. It may not be impossible to revert to polytheism, or to conceive God as striving against other persons who equal him in everything but goodness. But the name of God seems to imply that the person to whom it is applied is of appreciable importance when measured against the whole universe. A person who was only one among millions of similar beings would scarcely be allowed the name. And yet this may be the case with the person, if there is one, to whom we owe all the order and purpose which we can observe in the universe.

214. If we make God to be less than a creator, we make it possible that he should be a person, and that he should be good. And it is sufficiently certain that his wisdom and power would excel our own. But when we come to his relation to the universe, Hume's suggestions are more easily ignored than disproved. 'In a word, Cleanthes, a man who follows your hypothesis, is able, perhaps, to assert, or conjecture, that the universe, sometime, arose from something like design: but beyond that position he cannot ascertain one single circumstance, and is left afterwards to fix every point of his theology by the utmost licence of fancy and hypothesis. This world, for aught he knows, is very faulty and imperfect, compared to a superior standard; and was only the first rude essay of some infant deity, who afterwards abandoned it, ashamed of his lame performance: it is the work only of some dependent, inferior deity; and is the object of derision to his superiors: it is the production of old age and dotage in some superannuated deity; and ever since his death, has run on at adventures, from the first impulse and active force, which it received from him. You justly give signs of horror, Demea, at these strange suppositions: but these, and a thousand more of the same kind, are Cleanthes's suppositions, not mine. From the moment the attributes of the deity are supposed finite, all these have place.'[1]

215. Finally, it is necessary once more to emphasize the fact that, if God's moral character is saved by limiting his power, we have no right to be confident as to the eventual victory of those ends in which God is interested. We know that he will work for them, and we know that they will be the more triumphant or the less defeated because of his efforts. But we do

[1] *Dialogues concerning Natural Religion*, Part V, *ad fin.* I may remark that it seems to me that Hume's most important contribution to the philosophy of religion is to be found in these Dialogues, and not in the more famous discussion on Miracles in the *Enquiry*.

not know that they will be completely triumphant. Nor is this all. We do not even know that they will not be almost completely defeated. The fundamental conditions of the universe may prevent it from being anything but very bad, and all that God's utmost efforts may be able to do is to make the inevitable calamity a little less calamitous.

That is all that the doctrine of a non-omnipotent God can give us—a person who fights for the good and who may be victorious. But it is at any rate better than the doctrine of an omnipotent person to whom good and evil are equally pleasing. And it is fortunate that, as we have seen, the more attractive of the two ideas is also the more probable. Indeed, when the non-omnipotent God is also taken as non-creative, there seems to me, as I have said, only one reason why we should not believe in his existence—namely, that there is no reason why we should believe in it.

CHAPTER VIII

THEISM AND HAPPINESS

216. If the results which I have reached in the last two chapters are valid, it would seem that we have no reason to believe in the existence of a God. It remains to discuss the effect which such a conclusion would have on the happiness of those who hold it. The fact that the belief in a proposition would render us happy or miserable gives us no reason whatever for accepting or rejecting the proposition. But this does not prevent the inquiry being important. Indeed, except for those few students who pursue knowledge for its own sake, the main interest of the inquiry into the existence of God lies in its bearing on our happiness and on that of our fellow creatures.

Men's desires on this subject are very diverse. Some people passionately desire the existence of a God; some are indifferent; some are desirous that God should not exist. Now a thing may be desired either for its own sake, or as a means to something else which is desired for its own sake. And, when a thing is desired for its own sake, any difference of opinion on the subject may prove to be an ultimate difference not susceptible of alteration by argument. It is sometimes possible to alter a desire for an end by argument. For example, a man who desired the existence of an omnipotent God for its own sake, might be convinced by argument that such an omnipotent God would be wicked, and might then cease to desire his existence. But it is also possible that of two men who held exactly the same idea of what the nature of an omnipotent God would be, one would desire that he should exist, and one would desire that he should not exist. In this case, it would be impossible to alter the opinions of either of them by argument. In the same way, if one man desires to drink claret rather than burgundy, because he prefers the taste of claret, and another desires to drink burgundy rather than claret, because he prefers the taste of burgundy, it is useless to try to alter the opinion of either by argument. In the latter case the futility would be generally recognized. It is admitted that there is no disputing about tastes. But with those desires, which relate to our deepest needs and highest aspirations, the uselessness of argument is often ignored where it should be admitted.

When a thing is desired as a means, however, the desire is never so ultimate as to make argument irrelevant. If a man desires *A* only for the sake of *Z*, it would always be relevant to prove to him that *A* will not produce *Z*, or that *B* will produce it better, or as well. In the first case he will cease to desire *A* at all; in the second case he will only desire it if *B* is impossible; in the third case he will be indifferent whether *A* or *B* exists, so long as one of them does.

The interests which men conceive themselves to have in the existence of God may be divided into two classes. In the first place, there are the desirable results which we may expect will be produced in the universe by a person who is pre-eminent in goodness, wisdom, and power. We may call this our interest in God's works. In the second place, the very existence of such a being, apart from the beneficent results which his action may produce, may be considered desirable. This may be called, to distinguish it from the other, interest in God's person.

217. If God is desired through our interest in his works, he is desired as a means. The universe—the sum total of existence other than God—will be more desirable, it is said, if he exists than if he does not exist. And for this reason God's existence is desirable. About such a desire as this it is not useless to argue. We can inquire how far the existence of God would guarantee a desirable universe, and whether anything else could guarantee it if God did not exist.

It is clear, from what has been said in Chapter VI, that the existence of an omnipotent creator would afford no guarantee as to the goodness of the universe. Such an omnipotent creator, we saw, could not be supposed to be attracted by goodness as such, nor to be repelled by badness as such. For if he were, everything that existed would be good, and nothing would be bad. And this is notoriously not the case.

Some things in the universe are good, and some are bad. And, since everything would be exactly as an omnipotent creator would like best to have it, such a creator must sometimes like things which are good and sometimes things which are bad. Therefore we have no reason at all for anticipating what the nature will be of those parts of the universe which are so far removed from us, either in space or time, that we do not know them directly. They may be all good, so that evil is to be found nowhere except where we already know that it exists. Again, they may be all evil, so that there is nothing good except what we already know to be good. Or anything between these extremes is possible.

The knowledge that the universe was created by

an omnipotent creator can tell us nothing about the character of the universe that we did not know already. If we can see in the universe traces of a divine design, we might be able to infer what God wanted to produce everywhere. But omnipotence, as we have seen, can have no designs, for it needs no means. All we could infer would be that everything which we know to exist was such as to please the creator for its own sake. And as what we know to exist consists of good and evil, in proportions which vary from place to place, and from time to time, it is impossible to predict how much good and how much evil will be pleasing to the creator in places and times which we do not know.

Thus the existence of an omnipotent creator—to whom, as we have seen, the name of God would be inappropriate—would give us no reason to expect any goodness in the universe which we should not have expected otherwise. And therefore, from the point of view of our interest in his works, we lose nothing by the non-existence of such a creator.

218. The existence of an omnipotent creator has, no doubt, sometimes been made the basis of an optimistic view of the universe. Some people have been able to believe that the creator of such a universe as this could be both omnipotent and good. And they have also believed that, while a certain amount of evil in the universe would not be incompatible with his goodness, a greater amount would be. In particular, it is often held that, although temporary evil is compatible with God's goodness, permanent evil is not.[1]

[1] Cp. Lowell (*Biglow Papers*, Second Series, VII) on the conflict between freedom and slavery:

'Set the two forces foot to foot,
An' every man knows who'll be winner,
Whose faith in God hez ary root
Thet goes down deeper than his dinner.'

Such a belief would bring happiness to those who held it. It would enable them to believe that the evil in the universe would not exceed a certain amount. It might also enable them to believe that the evil diminished as time went on, and perhaps died away entirely. And a man who lost such beliefs as these would lose much happiness.

But the position rests on a basis which is untenable. It is not possible that the creator can be both omnipotent and good. And, if this difficulty was removed, and he could be both, then his goodness would be completely untarnished by the existence, in the present and the past, of some evil in the universe. And, if any evil can exist without tarnishing it, it is impossible to prove that it would be tarnished by any amount of evil, however permanent.

Optimism which rests on such a basis would not need for its destruction the rejection of the belief in an omnipotent creator. It would destroy itself as soon as the believer in an omnipotent creator realized what his own belief meant. A believer in an omnipotent creator, if he were not hopelessly illogical, could get no optimism out of his belief, and would lose no optimism by ceasing to believe in such a being.

219. Let us pass to the conception of a non-omnipotent being who was either the creator or the director of the universe. If non-omnipotent, he may be good, though we found reasons in the last chapter for supposing that, if he is good, he would not be creator, but only director. If he is good, then he may be called

But since slavery existed in 1862, when the poem was written, God had clearly been either unable or unwilling to abolish it up to that date. If the recognition of that fact is compatible with faith in God, I can see no reason why a man should be thought faithless who doubted as to God's power or intention in the future.

God. From the point of view of our interest in his works, do we gain much by believing in such a God, or lose much by disbelieving in him? It seems to me that we gain very little, whether we take him as director only, or whether we waive the difficulties which stand in the way of taking him both as good and as creator.

Let us consider first the non-creative God. If such a God exists, and if (as would be perhaps more probable) he never dies, and never deserts the cause of the good, then the universe is better than it might possibly have been. This, so far as it goes, is a gain. But it goes a very little way. The amount that God may be able to effect in making the universe better may be almost indefinitely small. It is true that we should not call him God unless his power were very great in comparison with ours, and unless it were so great as to have *some* appreciable effect on the universe as a whole. But the conditions under which his power is to be exerted—conditions which he cannot change—might be such that, however great be his power, however wisely it be exercised, it could only be said of him, as of the general of a hopelessly beaten army, that his efforts had made the result slightly less disastrous than it would have been without him.

And, again, even if we suppose that God's exertions in the cause of the good have produced a result which is very greatly better than anything which would have happened without his exertions, still what is greatly better may yet be very bad. Those fundamental conditions of all existence which he cannot change may have such evil effects that, even after God has succeeded in introducing very much good into the universe, it may still be very much more bad than good.

If we put these two considerations together—the uncertainty of how much God may be able to do, and the uncertainty of how much there is to be done—it would seem that the hypothesis of a non-creative God can give us no appreciable help towards a cheerful view of the universe. For such a view we require evidence of how good or bad the universe is. The hypothesis gives us no help here. And for our present purpose it is useless to be told that circumstances could be imagined under which the universe would be worse than it is.

220. The same principles apply in the case of a non-omnipotent God who is a creator. He will make the best universe he can, but we cannot tell how bad the best possible universe may be. The conditions under which he works may be such that the best possible may be very bad indeed.

'At any rate,' it may be said, 'if God creates the universe, we have a certainty that it is not, on the whole, more bad than good. For, if it were more bad than good, it would have been better to have created nothing at all, than to have created it. And so the fact that God has created it proves that the evil does not outweigh the good.'

But this implies that God was free to abstain from creating at all. Of course this is possible. Much would depend on the will of a creator, even if he were not omnipotent. And among the things which depended on it might be whether any created world should ever exist, or whether he should remain in eternal isolation. But it is also possible that among the things which the constitution of the universe imposed as necessities on God was that he should create something. In that case, the existence of the universe only proves that it was the best thing that

God was able to create. It gives us no ground for believing that the universe is good on the whole or even that it is not, on the whole, very bad.

221. Is there any way by which we can escape from the shadow of such dreary possibilities? It seems to me that there is only one way. If we can so determine the fundamental nature of reality as to see what limitations it imposes on the accomplishment of God's volitions, we might find that, while it made it impossible that the universe should be entirely devoid of evil, it did not make it impossible that the good should always exceed the evil. We might also find that the question of whether the good should exceed the evil depended on God's volition. Now God has been defined as good, and if we have any reason to believe that a God exists, we may be sure that he would will that the good should exceed the evil. In that case we might be sure that it did always exceed it.

Or we might find that the limitations on God's power, while they did not admit of a universe originally more good than evil, yet did admit of a progressive amelioration of the universe in time, if God willed it. And, as God certainly would will it, we should then be certain that this progressive amelioration would take place, and would be carried as far as was permitted by the constitution of reality—which might be to the point of the complete extirpation of evil.

Both these results, again, might be combined. We might find reason to believe that it was in God's power to ensure that good should always predominate over evil, and also that the predominance of good over evil should increase till only good remained. And we might be certain in that case that God would bring about these desirable results.

222. Thus, although the belief in a God, taken by itself, cannot lead us to optimistic conclusions about the universe, yet it might be possible to establish a metaphysical position, which included the belief in a non-omnipotent God and led to optimistic conclusions. But it might also be possible to establish a metaphysical position, which would lead to equally optimistic conclusions, and which did not include the belief in a God. Even with a God, we are not entitled to be optimistic unless the nature of reality, independent of God's volitions and logically prior to them, is such as to *permit* the predominance of good. Now it is quite possible to maintain that the nature of reality is such as to *ensure* the predominance of good, independently of the volitions of a God. In that case our optimism would not be affected if we denied God's existence.

I cannot here examine whether the nature of reality is such as to bring about the predominance of the good, whether by means of God's volitions or independently of them. The only way of answering this question would be by the establishment of a complete system of metaphysics. I merely wish to point out that the existence of a God striving for the good is neither sufficient nor necessary for an optimistic view of the universe. There might be a God, and yet the universe might be, on the whole, bad. There might be no God, and yet the universe might be, on the whole, good.

The statement that the existence of God is not necessary for an optimistic view of the universe requires some explanation. I only mean by it that it is possible to conceive a theory of the nature of reality which excludes the existence of a God, and yet leads to an optimistic view of the universe. Such a theory can be conceived, and, in fact, theories of this sort have been held by great philosophers.[1] But, of course, it might be contended that all such theories break down on further examination, while the theory which bases optimism partly on the belief in a God does not break down. I do not agree with this contention; but I certainly do not wish to assume its falsity. My position is merely that the belief in God will not justify optimism, unless it is supported by other metaphysical conclusions (which, as far as our present investigation goes, may or may not be true), and that there are metaphysical conclusions (which, as far as our present investigation goes, may or may not be true) which would justify optimism without a belief in God.

223. It follows from this that we must reject the very usual assumption that theism, as such, is an adequate basis for optimism, and the only adequate basis. A man who believes in God, it is said, is logically bound to take an optimistic view of the universe, while a man who does not believe in God has no right to take such a view. In fact, however, the theist requires much more than his theism before he is entitled to pronounce the universe good, and the atheist requires much more than his atheism before he can reject optimism as untenable.

What is the cause which leads so many people to the view that optimism and theism are so closely connected? I believe it is the same as that which makes the argument from design plausible—the difficulty of apprehending the position of Idealism.[2]

We may hold that all existent being—other than

[1] E. g. Fichte, in his earlier system; Mr. Bradley; and, as it seems to me, Hegel.

[2] Cp. Sections 196-207.

God, if there is one—is matter, or that some of it is matter and some of it spirit, or that all of it is spirit. If we hold that it is all matter, we should have no reason to take an optimistic view of the universe, unless we supposed a God who directed and controlled it. The nature of matter has no tendency to bring about the good more than the bad. It may do so if it is controlled by a person who desires to produce the good. But, if it is left to itself, it can only realize a good result by chance, and that it should do this seems very improbable, since, so far as we can judge, the arrangements of matter which would thwart the good are much more numerous than the arrangements which would promote it.

A similar result follows if we hold that, apart from God, both spirit and matter exist. In this case spirit exists in the midst of matter. It is continually affected by matter, and it cannot carry out its designs—in many cases, perhaps in all—except by employing the agency of matter. Even if spirit should aim at the good, then, its success in attaining it will be conditional on matter. And the extent to which such spirits as ours can affect matter is extremely limited. We have experience every day sufficient to convince us that our efforts cannot always make matter subservient to our purposes. Unless the matter is controlled by a spirit much more powerful than ours, the predominance of the good will be largely dependent on the undirected action of matter. And it will only be by chance—and that an improbable chance—that the undirected action of matter will realize the good, or permit it to be realized.

Thus, if we accept the existence of matter at all, optimism, it may reasonably be held, does find the existence of a God essential to it. Even if a God did exist, it would not be certain that he could realize the good, but without him it seems almost certain that the good would not be realized. And the same result would happen if we substituted for matter anything else which was not spiritual.

Even if we take all the existent beings of the universe as spiritual, the question arises whether the individual spirits are a mere aggregate, whose juxtapositions and relations are decided by laws resembling those of matter. If this is so, the chance of a predominance of good in the universe, without a directing God, is still not very large. It is larger than it would be if matter existed, for the reasons which we considered in the last chapter, when speaking of the argument from design. But, for the reasons which were also considered then, the probability is not great. In order that a system of individuals shall be good, it is necessary that the relations between them shall be satisfactory. If these relations are of such a nature that they are as likely to thwart the good as to promote it, they will only promote it by chance. They may, indeed, be modified by the efforts of the related individuals. But we do not know how far such efforts will meet with insuperable obstacles.

224. Thus the existence of a God seems to be necessary for optimism unless we are able to hold that all existence is spiritual, and that all spirits form a system such that it has a greater tendency to produce good than to produce evil. And this is the metaphysical view which is most removed from the attitude of every-day life.

A civilized man who does not reflect on metaphysical subjects almost always accepts both matter and spirit as existent realities. He conceives himself and his friends as spiritual, while their bodies and clothes and tables are material. Matter is lower and less important than spirit, in his view, but it is equally real. If he believes, as he generally does, that the universe is on the whole good, he believes it because he holds that the universe is created and controlled by a God. The intrinsic nature of the universe—or at any rate of one side of it—is no more calculated to produce the good, than the intrinsic nature of canvas and paint is calculated to produce a beautiful picture.

If a man does not hold this view, he is more likely to hold that the universe is completely material than to hold that it is completely spiritual. The arguments —such as they are—for the first view can be learned and appreciated without the systematic study of metaphysics, and without using any ideas but those which are known to every educated man. The arguments for the second view, though they are much stronger, almost inevitably require a systematic study of metaphysics, and introduce a way of looking at things which is very unlike our everyday way of regarding them, though it may be much more correct. And if the entire universe is material, there is no ground for optimism unless all this matter was controlled and directed by a God behind and above it.

Finally, of the different forms which can be assumed by the belief that all existence is spiritual, the form which makes it an aggregate of mechanically connected selves is better known, and appears at first sight simpler and more probable than the view which makes it a really spiritual unity. The former seems more probable because it has a greater resemblance to the views of relation which are adopted in the physical sciences, while the latter involves ideas which are scarcely known except in metaphysics. As we have seen, the former would almost inevitably require the existence of a God to secure a desirable result.

It is not wonderful then that it should be so generally believed that optimism requires theism as a basis. But it is quite possible to conceive the universe as a spiritual unity of such a nature that it necessarily manifests itself in more good than evil, or in continually increasing good and in continually diminishing evil. In such a casé an optimistic view of the universe would be justifiable, which did not depend on the existence of a God. Such a theory must necessarily take us far away from the standpoint of ordinary life. It must make us look on matter as only an appearance of spirit, and it must make us look on unity as equally real with differentiation. It will not be easily understood, or easily proved. But it may be true.

225. Before leaving our interest in God's works, it may be worth while to discuss the relation of the belief in God to the belief in immortality. These beliefs are often supposed to be logically joined. If the existence of God is accepted, it is often held that from this alone —independent of any alleged revelation on the subject —the immortality of man may be either proved, or, at least, shown to be highly probable. And, on the other hand, it is held that, if the existence of God is rejected, not only has one argument for immortality gone, but there is no chance of proving it at all, or rendering it in the least probable. Atheism must necessarily involve disbelief in immortality.

Let us consider the first of these assertions. Would the certainty of God's existence support the belief in human immortality? If it does so, it must be on account of God's goodness. His wisdom and power might possibly be arguments for proving that he could make man immortal if he wished to do so, but they could throw no light on the question whether he would will to do so or not. The only way of deciding this—and it is a way which is often taken—is to say that immortality is very good, that its absence would deprive the universe of almost all its value and significance, and then to argue that God, who is good, could not refuse us this gift.

226. But if immortality is to be proved in this way, it is necessary to be certain that it is good. And this would be difficult. Many people do not desire immortality. There are some who desire no sort of immortality—who would rather cease to exist at the death of their bodies than continue to exist in any way whatever. There are others who would not be unwilling to encounter an immortal life of rest and tranquillity, but who would prefer extinction to an immortality which involved a continuance beyond death of the pain and struggle of this life, even if that struggle should be comparatively short, and should lead to eventual repose. In the far East, again, we find two of the greatest religions of the world teaching that personal immortality is an evil, and that the highest consummation of a wise and virtuous life will lead us to lay down life altogether.

Even if we were able to put these difficulties on one side, and assume that human immortality was certainly good, should we be entitled to base a belief in immortality on a belief in God? I do not see that we are justified in this, whether God is held to be omnipotent or not.

If God is omnipotent, then it is clear, as we saw in Chapter VI, that there are some good things which he does not antecedently will to exist, and some bad things which he does antecedently will to exist. For some good things do not exist, and some bad things do. Now how can we tell that immortality is not one of the good things which he does not will to exist, and the annihilation of persons one of the bad things which he does will to exist? To reply that immortality is better than most things, and annihilation worse than most things may be true, but is irrelevant. For we saw above that, if any evil in the universe was consistent with the goodness of God, it was impossible for us to determine any limits to its amount.

But if God is not omnipotent, then his goodness is no security for immortality. There are some good things which we know that he cannot realize, since we know that they do not exist. How can we be sure that human immortality is not among such things? There are some bad things which we know that he cannot prevent from existing, since they do exist. And among such things may be our annihilation at the death of our bodies.

If immortality can be proved at all, it can only be proved by arguments of a different sort. If we are to do anything, we must be able so to determine the nature of reality as to show that every self is an eternal part of the eternal reality, and that its eternity necessarily manifests itself in an existence throughout all future time, or we must, in some similar way, prove the immortality of the self as a direct consequence of its own nature. Such a line of argument, if possible at all—I believe, as I have said earlier, that it is possible—is difficult and arduous. But nothing less will suffice.

Now it seems clear that such a deduction as this would not be helped by a demonstration of God's existence. If God is taken as director, and not as creator, then my existence is independent of his will. And if my immortality is a consequence of my nature, then my immortality is involved in my existence, and is likewise independent of God's will. And in no other way than by his will could the existence of a directing God be supposed to bear on the question. The mere fact that the universe contained a being who greatly excelled me and all others in perfection could not be a ground for believing that my existence would be unending.

227. If we go back to the hypothesis that God is a creator, and that, among other things, he creates ourselves, then, so far from the existence of God rendering my immortality more probable, it seems to me that it makes it less so. The idea of creation is generally held in a form which makes the created being begin to exist at a point in time, so that there was a time, however distant, when that being had not yet begun to exist. Whether this form is essential to the idea of creation or not, it is the form in which it is almost always found. Indeed the hypothesis of creation is often supported by the assertion that it is impossible for finite beings to have existed through all past time. Now if for every man there was a time when he did not yet exist, I cannot see how his immortality is to be proved. If his relation to the universe is compatible with his non-existence in past time, how shall we be able to prove that his relation with the universe is not compatible with his non-existence in future time? Metaphysics have not yet given us the right to discriminate in this manner between the past and the future.

Of course the difference between the past and the future is very considerable from the point of view of our own interests. We are much more interested in what is about to happen to us than we are in what has happened to us. And this might be important, if the proof of immortality rested on the goodness of the universe or of its creator. To annihilate existing persons might well be a much more serious blemish on the universe than to postpone the creation of persons not yet existent. And so, if immortality could be based on this ground at all, we might prove that a being would never cease to exist in the future, although he had formerly not existed. But we have seen that immortality cannot be based on this ground, and on any other it seems impossible to give any reason why that which was once created should not be again annihilated.[1]

228. Thus we see that there is no logical connexion between the belief in God and the belief in human immortality. And there has not always been a historical connexion. Fichte, in his earlier system at any rate, believed in immortality without believing in God. The same may be said, in my opinion, about Hegel, though this is disputed. Buddhism, again, which has no God, holds immortality to be the natural state of man, from which only the most perfect can escape. And, in modern times, Schopenhauer is in the same position. On the other side we find Lotze. Of all the theists of the nineteenth century he is philosophically the most important. And he regards immortality as quite undemonstrable and as very doubtful.[2]

What is the cause of the opinion that a belief in immortality requires a belief in theism? Partly, perhaps, it is the fact that the majority of theists do believe in immortality, and that the majority of Western believers in immortality are theists. But,

[1] Cp. chap. iv.

[2] Lotze's defence of theism will be found in his *Microcosmus* (Book IX, chaps. iv and v) and his doctrine of immortality in his *Metaphysics* (Section 245). Both these works are translated into English.

in addition to this, it must be remembered that materialism would make any belief in immortality perfectly unreasonable, and that scepticism makes all beliefs unreasonable.[1] Now there is a very common idea that an atheist must either be a materialist or a sceptic, and, therefore, that it is unreasonable for him to believe in immortality. But this, like many other common ideas, is erroneous.

229. We must now pass from our interest in God's works to our interest in his person. This interest may be due, in the first place, to the guidance which, it is maintained, we can procure by imitating a character so superior to our own. In this case argument is still possible. For the existence of God is here desired as a means to an end which we should all admit to be good—namely, our guidance to right action. The question is only how far the contemplation of the character of an existent God is a necessary means to that purpose. And this is a question which admits of argument.

If the belief in God is rejected, we lose along with it the belief in the present existence of any person who is, from a moral point of view, absolutely perfect. The belief in a being who was morally absolutely perfect, but whose wisdom and power were too limited to allow him to be called God, is perhaps not absolutely impossible. But it seems impossible to see how the existence of such a being, as distinguished from one whose perfection was very great, could be proved. And, historically, absolute moral perfection has never been attributed to any person except God, unless that person

[1] Materialism—the belief that *all* existent reality is material—must be distinguished from the belief mentioned above (Section 223) that all *non-divine* existent reality is material.

was conceived as the incarnation of God, or as his specially favoured minister. (In the following discussion I will, for the sake of brevity, use 'perfect' to mean morally perfect.)

230. But, as we have already seen,[1] this loss, if it is one, does not depend on the denial of God's existence. Even if a God does exist, he could not be absolutely perfect so long as the society of selves of which he forms a part is by no means perfect. It is impossible that any one member of the society should be unaffected by the defects of his fellows. And, if this is so, the disbelief in God's existence loses us in this respect nothing which ought not to have been lost already.

God might be looked at, no doubt, as destined to become eventually perfect. But he could only become so if all other persons were perfect too. And, if they were perfect, they would need no moral guidance. It would be superfluous for them to look to God for an example of moral perfection if they were equally examples of it.

Still God, though not at present perfect, would at any rate be much better than any other person. If we were certain that God existed, we should be certain of the existence of a being whose character, so far as it was known to us, and so far as its lessons were applicable in our circumstances, would be a far safer ideal for our actions than the character of any man could be. If we lose the belief in God's existence, we lose this ideal. Let us inquire how serious the loss would prove.

231. There are cases, to begin with, in which it is clear that it is possible to see what is right, without having an ideal in a God conceived as existent. Many

[1] Section 210.

pagans—and many other people—practise virtues of which no trace is found in the conduct which they attribute to their Gods, and would shrink with horror from vices to which they believe their Gods addicted. Atheists, again, who believe in no God at all, can distinguish between right and wrong, and their judgements would often be accepted as correct by theists. The possession of a divine ideal, then, is not always essential for the knowledge of the right.

In many cases, however, the knowledge of a person good enough to serve as an ideal is of the greatest value, not only as a stimulus, but as a guide. It may be so, I conceive, in two ways. In the first place, it may suggest to us that a quality is desirable which we should never have thought desirable if we had not seen a person who possessed it. It is quite possible, for example, that the goodness of self-control in grief might not occur to some people until they saw a man who practised self-control, and that it would be acknowledged by them when it did occur to them. In the second place, when something has been recognized as desirable, a person who exhibits that quality may indicate to us by his example shades of that quality, too delicate to be determined by any abstract rule. It does not need the contemplation of a courteous person to teach us that courtesy, in the abstract, is good. But for most people there is only one way of learning in detail what courtesy is—to live with those who are courteous already.

232. It must be admitted then that a personal ideal —by which I mean a person believed to exist, not merely imagined as possible—may be of great use as a guide to action. But then such an ideal need not be God. It can be another man. And it very frequently is another man. We are all of us guided, more or less, by our knowledge of the characters of other men, whom we recognize as our superiors in certain qualities, and whom we endeavour to imitate in respect of those qualities.

Thus to lose God would not involve losing a personal ideal. It might be objected that a man who had reached higher than any of those known to him in any particular direction could not have a personal ideal in that direction—unless he mistakenly followed a man lower than himself, which might lead him wrong. To this it may fairly be answered that the imitation of another person, though often useful, is not indispensable to right action, and that a man who had got so high as this would probably be able to see what was right without waiting for any one else to show him the way. Nor would it follow that such a man had not the advantage of feeling reverence and veneration. Different good qualities are distributed in different ways, and a man who would be mistaken if he thought that he knew of any one braver than himself might perhaps find a man worthy of his imitation in respect of industry or unselfishness.

At the risk of appearing fanciful, I will also suggest that it is not impossible that two men might each make an ideal of the other, with respect to the same quality, and yet each might have found a true ideal. *A* would think *B* excelled him in that quality. *B* would think he was excelled by *A*. Both could not be right. But, if they happened to love each other, each might see in the other the eternal perfection of which the temporal imperfection—which is all a man can see of himself—is only an imperfect manifestation. To pursue this possibility, however, would take us too far into the metaphysics of personality.

233. But non-divine beings, it may be said, must

always be defective as personal ideals, unless supplemented by an ideal of a divine person. I may take the wrong man as my ideal. Or, even if I take the right man, the best man whom I know, still he may be mistaken just on the point on which I am imitating him, and so I may be misled.

Doubtless this may be so. But we are no better off with a divine ideal. It is true that there cannot be a better ideal than God, if he exists, and that the chance that he is acting wrongly in any particular case, though it exists, is much smaller than it is in the case of any particular man. But, on the other hand, we are much more likely to make mistakes about what God's character is than we are in the case of a man. We can only gather God's character from his acts. And as to those acts there is much doubt. It has been, for example, a much disputed point whether he has or has not predestined certain of his creatures to eternal damnation. Even if we know what he has done, we may not be certain whether he has willed it for its own sake, or as a means; and, if as a means, we may not be certain for what end. Now this makes all the difference as to his character. If God has caused pain to a wicked man, for example, we can tell nothing from this as to his character, if we do not know whether he did so simply because the man was wicked, or to reform him, or to deter others, or to spare him greater pain, or for some other reason.

If we believe that there is a God, we shall certainly believe that he has acted well, since a goodness exceeding that of all other persons was part of the definition of God. But this belief, by itself, will give us no guidance. If we know that God has acted well, and also know why he has acted, we shall know what good action is under certain circumstances, and this may afford us guidance. But if we merely know that God acted well, without knowing what he did or why he did it, we shall get no more guidance from the nature of God than we could have got from our abstract notion of the good, without reference to God at all.

234. And there is another difficulty which meets us if we try to take God as the ideal which is to guide our actions. His circumstances, and his character in non-moral aspects (such as his wisdom and his power) are so different to ours that it is very difficult to apply his example so as to guide us in our difficulties. The example, no doubt, is not altogether irrelevant. The moral nature and the moral problems of one individual have always some analogy to those of any other. And if God is conceived as not omnipotent, and not absolutely perfect, though much more powerful and more good than any other person, then we can conceive that his duties, his perfections, his imperfections, his temptations, would have, so far as we could know them, many lessons for our guidance. But it is obvious that they would have far less application than those of a person whose conditions resembled our own more closely. If there is a God, he would be morally much superior to Socrates. But Socrates was sufficiently superior to most of us to afford us an ideal. And Socrates acted under conditions so much more like our own than those under which God would act, that it seems to me we should derive more guidance from his example than from God's—even if we knew as much about the character of God as we do about the character of Socrates.

235. This difficulty is, to a great extent, removed if God is considered to be incarnate in some man or men whose history is known. The conditions under which an incarnate God acted would be far more like the conditions under which an ordinary man acts than the conditions under which an unincarnate God acted could be. Thus we could obtain more guidance. In the Christian religion, for example, we see that moral guidance is more frequently sought from the earthly life of Jesus than from the action of God in creating and governing the world. And this is, doubtless, one of the reasons—I do not say the chief reason—for the the singular fascination of the idea of an incarnate God.

But what guidance shall we lose if we hold that a person who has been regarded as an incarnation of God was in truth an ordinary man? This opinion will not prove that such a man did not exist, or that he was not a good man. All that goodness, which history tells the believers in his divinity that he exhibited, may still be held—if there is sufficient evidence—to be his. The believers in his divinity, indeed, may *infer* from his divinity the existence of greater goodness in him, of which no manifestations are recorded in his history. And those who reject his divinity will have no grounds to infer such greater goodness. But goodness which is merely inferred cannot give us moral guidance, for we cannot infer it unless we already know it to be good. It is only goodness which is *observed*—either directly or through history—which we can recognize as good without having previously known of its goodness. And so it is only goodness which is observed which can give us moral guidance. Whatever goodness is observed in a person who is believed to be an incarnation of God will not cease to be there, or to be good, if he is believed to be a man of the ordinary kind. And thus he will not be a less satisfactory ideal for moral guidance.

'But,' it may be said, 'if you no longer believe this

man to be an incarnation of God, you cannot know that his actions are good, and so you cannot be safe in taking them as your ideal.' I conceive that this objection may be validly answered by a dilemma. When we observe an action, either we are competent to judge of its goodness or we are not. In so far as we are competent, then we can pronounce it good, even if its author is not an incarnation of God. But in so far as we are not competent, then it is impossible for us to tell whether the being of whom he is asserted to be an incarnation is properly called God. For no being is to be called God unless he is good, and what evidence can we have of the goodness of the being incarnated, except that the action of the being who incarnates is good?

And if the incarnation is not the incarnation of a good being it can give us no moral guidance. However wise and powerful the being who was incarnated might be, we should have no reason to follow his example if he was not good. To follow the example of any person merely because he was wise would be foolish, since he might be using his wisdom as a means to bring about undesirable ends. And to follow the example of any person merely because he was powerful would be contemptible. It would not even be prudent, unless we were reasonably certain that he would be pleased with flattery and servility.

236. Moreover, the example of an incarnate God, although much more useful for our guidance than that of an unincarnate God, is much less applicable than the example of an ordinary man. For the position of an ordinary man is much more like ours, who are ordinary men, than is the position of a being who is the incarnation of God. We have reason, for example, to believe that Jesus behaved with courage and dignity at his trial and execution. This fact has much more value for those who do not believe in his divinity than for those who do. For the former class it shows—as, of course, many other examples show—that man can rise above pain and the approach of death. And what men have done, we, who are men, may hope, if the need comes, to do also. At any rate, the fact that it has been done by a man raises humanity. But it by no means follows that, because these things can be done by a being who is both 'perfect God and perfect man' that they can be done by us, to whom this description does not apply.

Again, most people would now be inclined to admit that Jesus was right in declining to be bound by various rules of his national church—as to the strict observance of the Sabbath, for example. And, if he is considered as simply a man, we may derive guidance for ourselves from our perception that he was right as against his contemporaries in these matters. But, if we accept his divinity, I do not see that we have any guidance. For it might well be that a being who was both God and man might be entitled to dispense with rules, while beings who were only men were not. (I am speaking here, of course, only of what may be gained from example. The question of explicit teaching is therefore irrelevant.)

God could, no doubt, be held to be incarnate without adopting the extreme view that the being in whom it took place was perfect God and perfect man. And, in so far as that being resembled an ordinary man, in so far his example would be more applicable for our guidance. But then, in so far as he resembled an ordinary man, in so far his example would only help us in the way that the example of an ordinary man would help us, and so we should lose nothing by denying that he was an incarnation of God, and considering him merely as a man.

Some systems of philosophy, again, treat every man as an incarnation of God. In this case it is clear that whether the doctrine is true or not, we can hope for no special guidance from it. Every possible example offered to us will be that of an incarnation of God, and many of them will lead us in different directions. The question will still remain which of them we ought to follow, and which to avoid.

237. It would seem then that we should lose little, if anything, in the way of moral guidance by rejecting a belief in God. But moral encouragement is another matter. If any man finds that he is encouraged to do right by a belief in God's existence, taken in itself and not as a means of producing the good, or guiding men's actions, this is ultimate—in his case, and while it lasts. If a man feels morally helped by hearing music of a particular sort, and that sort only, it would be foolish to maintain that such a man lost nothing when he could hear no music, or only music of another sort. And, in the same way, a man who feels discouraged in right action when he rejects the belief in a God, does lose something by his rejection.

Not all men would feel this, but some would. At the same time it must be noticed that it does not follow that the loss would be permanent in the cases in which it is real. A man who has been accustomed to do right in the name of God may feel a loss when he ceases to believe in God. So a man who has been accustomed to be loyal to his country in the name of a king may feel his loyalty shaken if his country becomes a republic. But loyalty, as the history of republics shows us, can do very well without a king, when the king has once gone. And so it may be—

I do not say that it always will be—with morality and God.

238. And the rejection of the belief in God may bring discouragement of a different sort. Without depriving us of stimulus, it may deprive us of comfort. It may well be that some people find some consolation in the thought that the struggle for the good has a leader who can, at any rate, survey the whole field, of which each of us sees but a corner. We have seen that the mere existence of such a leader tells us nothing about the results of the struggle. It may be defeated with such a leader, or it may be victorious without one. But if a man finds some comfort in the existence of a leader for its own sake, and without reference to the result, then his comfort will be diminished by the rejection of the belief in a God. Here, as in the last case, it is possible that a desire which cannot be removed by argument may be removed by time. And here, as in the last case, it is also possible that it may not be removed.

239. In a universe without a God there will be no one to worship, and there will be one person less to love. And the loss—if any—which results from this change is again a thing which each man must estimate for himself. With regard to worship, however, it is to be remembered that no metaphysical conclusion can deprive us of the power to feel reverence, and to feel it justly, because it is certain upon any metaphysical theory that there are many men who are worthy of reverence. What we shall lose is the opportunity of reverencing a person who is held to excel all other persons in a very high degree. The loss in this will depend very much on what each man finds to reverence in his fellow men. And it must also be remembered that an object of reverence is only of value to us in so far as we appreciate it. God is a better object of reverence for me than Socrates, not in proportion as he is superior to Socrates, but in proportion as I can realize his superiority to Socrates. And, if I cannot realize his superiority to Socrates at all, then, even if God exists, my reverence for Socrates may be of more value than my reverence for God. In the same way, a boy's reverence for the captain of the eleven may be of much more value than his reverence for God, however sincere the latter may be. For it is possible that his idea of the captain of the eleven may be one much more adequate to excite reverence than his idea of God.

240. There remains love. By love of God I mean something entirely distinct from reverence and admiration and gratitude. I mean a feeling of one person for another, which is not unworthy to bear the same name as the feeling of friend for friend. That, of course, must go, if it is believed that the person that was loved never existed.

Love will not cease. There are other persons to love. And the non-existence of God would leave it as possible as it was before that love should be the central fact of all reality. It might still be true that nothing else had value. It might still be true that nothing else had existence, except lovers and their love.[1] But some love would have been poured out on a dream—or rather a reflexion—which could not return it. Whether the friends whom all men may find could compensate for the friend whom some men thought they had found is a question for each man to answer. It is a question which can never be answered permanently in the negative while there is still a future before us.

[1] I have endeavoured to develop this theory in my *Studies in Hegelian Cosmology*, chap. ix.

CONCLUSION

241. THE result of our investigations has been almost entirely negative. We have, indeed, come to the conclusion that dogma is important. But when we inquired how it could be established, we only found that some of the most common ways of establishing it were inadmissible. We found reason to think that immortality, if true, would involve pre-existence, and that some of the usual objections to the truth of immortality were untenable. But we found no reason for a positive belief that immortality was true. Again, we were able to see that there was no reason why human volitions should be exceptions to any law of the complete determination of events, but we did not establish any such law. And our conclusion that there was no reason to suppose that God existed gave us no information as to what did exist.

All this was inevitable. The only way of coming to any conclusions on matters of religious dogma is by means of metaphysical arguments. This was the result of our consideration of the question in Chapter II. And since I have not put forward here any positive metaphysical position, it was impossible to hope for positive conclusions. Negative conclusions on matters of dogma can be arrived at without the standpoint of a positive metaphysical theory. We may point out that the arguments for a certain dogma are untenable, and that therefore there is no reason to believe it, or we can go further and point out that the dogma is self-contradictory, or incompatible with indubitable facts, and must therefore be false. We can do this, even if we are not prepared to establish any other dogma on the same subject.

To refute a dogma may thus sometimes be easy, while to establish a dogma is always hard, especially as the subject-matter of various dogmas is so closely connected, that it is difficult to establish the truth as to one of them unless we can also determine the truth about all the rest. And in order to establish such dogmas as may form a basis for religion it seems necessary to establish a complete system of metaphysics. We need, for religion, to be able to regard the universe as good on the whole, and it does not appear how we could do this, except on the basis of a general theory as to the ultimate nature of reality.

242. We are sometimes justified in basing action or emotion on a proposition whose truth we have not ourselves investigated. A man who has never examined the evidence for the law of gravitation may reasonably act on the assumption that it is true, because the consensus of opinion among competent students of the subject is so overwhelming that he has good grounds to believe it on their authority. But we are not justified in assuming in this manner the truth of dogmas. For on these there is not the necessary consensus. No dogma—at any rate, no dogma of religion—is asserted which is not also denied by able students.

It follows that a man is not entitled to believe a dogma except in so far as he has investigated it for himself. And since the investigation of dogma is a metaphysical process, and religion must be based on dogma, it follows further that no man is justified in a religious attitude except as a result of metaphysical study. The result is sufficiently serious. For most people, as the world stands at present, have not the disposition, the education, and the leisure necessary for the study of metaphysics. And thus we are driven to the conclusion that, whether any religion is true or not, most people have no right to accept any religion as true.

This result is serious because, if this theory is true, it will probably win increased, though not general, acceptance, as inquiry in matters of religion becomes more general, and the weight of authority and tradition becomes less. The number of people who wish to hold a religion, but are unable to do so, will become larger. And this will increase the amount of human suffering.

But it seems inevitable. What people want is a religion which they can believe to be true.[1] Since they are confronted on all sides with religions different from their own, and with the denial of all religion, it is inevitable that they should ask themselves why they believe their religions to be true. And when the question is once asked, what can avert a widespread recognition that the truth of religion can only rest on foundations too controversial to be taken on trust, and too obscure for many people to investigate?

The result may be evil, but that is, unfortunately, no ground for denying its truth. It is no more evil than cancer, famine, or madness, and these are all real. But it is not as evil as may appear at first sight.

243. In the first place, supposing that the universe as a whole was good, so as to form a satisfactory basis for a religion, this would not be affected by the fact that most people on this planet at present were not entitled to believe it, and that a large number of them

[1] The sense in which it can be said that a religion is true is explained in Section 8.

did not believe it. Religion involves believing in something good, and the belief in religion is itself something good. If a religion is true, but not believed, the second good vanishes, but not the first. Thus if it should be true that all men are immortal, and are progressing to a state of great perfection—to take one dogma of religion which is sometimes maintained—the evil inflicted on any of them by their present lack of religion would be only temporary. Like all other evils it would be destined to be removed some day.

It is necessary to be clear on this point, because the two goods are occasionally confounded. We are asked, for example, to consider how evil the world would be without the belief in immortality, and, in expounding this, a confusion is occasionally made between the happiness which we have before death in believing in immortality, and the happiness which we may have after death if immortality is true. But the latter would not be lost by losing the belief in immortality, for men would not perish when their bodies perished because they had previously believed that they would do so.

244. In the second place, it must be remembered that the man who has no religion cannot have a bad one. If the mass of Englishmen ceased to believe in any religion, many of them would lose much happiness by ceasing to believe in heaven, but many of them would gain much happiness by ceasing to believe in hell. If a loss of happiness would result from the loss of belief in God, there would be a gain, both in happiness and otherwise, in freedom from the belief that the creator of such a world as this was omnipotent, and was yet to be worshipped. Loss of religion might be an evil to the average man, but would certainly not be an unmixed evil.

245. And, thirdly, the extent to which religion would be lost may be exaggerated. The study of metaphysics will perhaps never be very common, but it may be more common in the future than it is at present. The world's leisure is increasing, and much of it may be devoted to study. And if study at present is rarely study of metaphysics, that is largely because metaphysics seems unpractical. If, however, people find that they cannot have religion without it, then it will become of all studies the most practical. Its results, indeed, may not be more practically useful than those of some other subjects. For some results of study are, in our present civilization, essential to life, and life is a condition precedent of religion. But elsewhere we can enjoy the results without investigating them ourselves. I can eat bread, although I have never learnt to plough or bake. I can be cured of an illness, though I have never learnt medicine. But if —and this is the case at present—I have no right to rely on any metaphysical result which I have not myself investigated, then the study of metaphysics will be for many people the most momentous of all studies. And this may produce important results. For, after all, one great reason why so few people have reached metaphysical conclusions for themselves, is to be found in the fact that so few people have tried to reach them.

Once more, if our interest is for the happiness of mankind, we may console ourselves with the reflection that the large majority of men, while human nature remains what it is, are not likely to give up traditional opinions merely on the ground that they have no logical right to hold them. Like opium-eaters, they will preserve their happiness at the expense of their intelligence, though, more fortunate than opium-eaters, their dreams will not unfit them for practical life, and will—sometimes—not quit them before death. And when the average man has changed so much that he rejects all beliefs that he is not logically entitled to hold, he may well have changed so much as to have some logical right to a religion.

Finally, it is possible that a time may come when metaphysics may attain the same certainty in a higher sphere which is now often reached by science in a lower sphere. If there was the same consensus of expert opinion that immortality, for example, could be proved as there is now that the law of gravitation can be proved, men in general might accept the truth of immortality without investigating it, in the same way that they now accept the law of gravitation without investigating it. And in this way, perhaps, sufficient dogmas might be accepted to form the basis for a religion.

There is no impossibility in this. It would be rash to infer that metaphysics will never pass out of the controversial stage because they have not done so yet. But they have not done so yet, nor is there any sign that they are about to do so. Any school of philosophy which has for a few years a very marked predominance over its rivals is tempted to teach its conclusions dogmatically to those who have no time or capacity for its arguments, and to assure them that they can take the results on trust because now, at last, all philosophic opinion is on the same side. But a few years are sufficient to show that such agreement as had ever existed was only temporary. There is not now, and there is not likely to be soon, such an agreement on metaphysics as would justify any man in accepting any dogmas on authority.

Many dogmas, indeed, are supported by such a weight of authority that, even without investigating them, we may reasonably conclude that they are not transparently absurd, and that there is much to be said for them. And this is something. But we want more than this—especially when incompatible dogmas are supported in this way, as is often the case.

246. In spite, then, of the alleviations which I have just pointed out, we are here confronted with one of the great tragedies of life. Many men desire passionately to know the truth as to the great problems of religion. And no man may believe any solution of these problems to be true unless he has tested it himself. Even if he tests for himself, and comes to some conclusion, his conclusion must lack that confirmation by the unanimous agreement of inquirers which plays so great a part in knowledge elsewhere.

This is sad, and would be sad even if dogma were not essential to religion. For whether dogma is essential to religion or not, it is clear that many men do desire, and will desire, to know the truth about such dogmas as the existence of God and the immortality of man.

It would not, perhaps, be a dispiriting conclusion that truth on these great matters can only be attained by long and toilsome efforts, if we were certain that it would some day be attained. But this certainty must itself be dependent on dogma, and cannot, therefore, be available for the comfort of those who have not attained it. It is evident that various persons die in a state of uncertainty about these dogmas, and others are certain of incompatible conclusions, so that some at least must be wrong. We should have therefore to be certain, at least, of a life beyond death, if we were to be certain that we should all eventually know the truth on such subjects.

247. It is sad, but I do not know why it should be

thought strange. Is knowledge so easy to get that the highest and deepest of all knowledge is likely to be had for the asking? Or is everything good so common, that we should expect that religion—almost the best of all earthly things—should be never absent where it is desired?

The matter would be different if we held to the old opinion that it was a sin not to reach the true religion in this life. For then religion must be open to all who choose to take it, and cannot be dependent on metaphysical ability, which does not depend on the will. And again, the matter would be different if the true religion was essential to morality. For it is notorious that the comprehension of metaphysics is not essential to morality. But it would seldom be said now that the attainment of true religion was either a duty or a condition of dutifulness, but only that it was a great happiness. And, in this case, what right have we to expect that it will not be rare?

An exclamation reported[1] of Jesus has been, rather unfairly, twisted into a canon of knowledge declaring that the kingdom of heaven is hidden from the wise and prudent and revealed unto babes. Such a principle is sure to be popular, for it enables a man to believe that he is showing his meekness and humility by the confident assertion of propositions which he will not investigate and cannot prove.[2] Yet some other words

[1] Matt. xi. 25; Luke x. 21.

[2] This criticism applies, naturally, not to the teacher who made the exclamation, but to the teachers who turned it into a principle. It may be remarked that the principle is applied rather capriciously. Many men would be prepared to use it as a ground for distrusting Hegel, and for trusting the peasantry of Ireland or Wales (as the case may be). But they would not admit it as a ground for accepting the peasantry of Morocco as a safer guide in religion than Thomas Aquinas. And yet Thomas Aquinas was a wise man, and the religion of a peasant in Morocco would be eminently

reported[1] of the same teacher might be remembered. 'The kingdom of heaven is like unto a man that is a merchant seeking goodly pearls: and having found one pearl of great price, he went and sold all that he had, and bought it.' All that he had,—but if it is too little? The greater the price, the fewer can pay it.

Sixteen centuries after the death of Jesus, the Jewish race produced another great religious teacher, in whom philosophical insight and religious devotion were blended as in no other man before or since. 'If the way'—so he ends his account of the beatific vision which frees man from all sorrow and all sin, and makes death the least of all things—'if the way which I have pointed out as leading to this result seems exceedingly hard, it may nevertheless be discovered. . . . But all things excellent are as difficult as they are rare.'

Perhaps it will not always be so. Perhaps time as it goes on will bring its imperfection nearer to the perfection of eternity. But, here and now, dare we deny that Spinoza is right? 'Omnia praeclara tam difficilia quam rara sunt.'

childish. But, of course, it is only ignorant orthodoxy that is childlike simplicity. Ignorant heterodoxy is childish superstition.

[1] Matt. xiii. 45.

THE END

Classic Works in the History of Ideas

Also Available in this series:

ACTION, EMOTION AND WILL
Anthony Kenny
ISBN 1 85506 319 0 : 1963 Edition : 256pp : £15.99/$26.95

ARISTOTELIANISM
John Leofric Stocks
ISBN 1 85506 222 4 : 1925 Edition : 174pp : £12.99/$19.95

AUGUSTE COMTE AND POSITIVISM
John Stuart Mill
ISBN 1 85506 219 4 : 1865 Edition : 202pp : £14.99/$28.95

BERKELEY
G. Dawes Hicks
ISBN 1 85506 168 6 : 1932 Edition : 346pp : £16.99/$

BERKELEY – THE PHILOSOPHY OF IMMATERIALISM
Ian Tipton
ISBN 1 85506 352 2 : 1974 Edition : 406pp : £16.99/£26.95

COMMONPLACE BOOK 1919–1953
George Edward Moore
ISBN 1 85506 231 3 : 1962 Edition : 426pp : £16.99/$29.95

DESCARTES
Anthony Kenny
ISBN 1 85506 236 4 : 1968 Edition : 256pp : £9.99/$14.95

THE DIVINE RIGHT OF KINGS
John Neville Figgis
ISBN 1 85506 349 2 : 1914 Edition : 420pp : £16.99/$28.95

ECONOMICS OF INDUSTRY
Alfred and Mary Paley Marshall
New Introduction by D. P. O'Brien
ISBN 1 85506 320 4 : 1879 Edition : 248pp : £16.99/$27.95

AN ESSAY ON PHILOSOPHICAL METHOD
R. G. Collingwood
ISBN 1 85506 392 1 : 1933 Edition : 240pp : £14.99/$24.95

ESSAYS ON SOME UNSETTLED QUESTIONS OF POLITICAL ECONOMY
John Stuart Mill
ISBN 1 85506 160 0 : 1844 Edition : 172pp : £12.99/$19.95

ESSAYS ON SUICIDE AND THE IMMORTALITY OF THE SOUL
David Hume
ISBN 1 85506 167 8 : 1783 Edition : 132pp : £10.99/$16.95

ETHICS
Peter Kropotkin
New Introduction by Andrew Harrison
ISBN 1 85506 224 0 : 1924 Edition : 366pp : £16.99/$28.95

FOUR DISSERTATIONS
David Hume
New Introduction by John Immerwahr
ISBN 1 85506 393 X : 1757 Edition : 258pp : £14.99/$24.95

FRANCIS HUTCHESON
William Robert Scott
ISBN 1 85506 169 4 : 1900 Edition : 318pp : £14.99/$28.95

GOD AND THE SOUL
Peter Geach
ISBN 1 85506 318 2 : 1969 Edition : 140pp : £12.99/$19.95

HOBBES
George Croom Robertson
ISBN 1 85506 216 X : 1886 Edition : 250pp : £14.99/$

HUMAN NATURE, OR THE FUNDAMENTAL ELEMENTS OF POLICY
bound with
DE CORPORE POLITICO
Thomas Hobbes
New Introduction by G.A.J. Rogers
ISBN 1 85506 351 4 : 1840 Edition : 228pp : £14.99/$24.95

AN INTRODUCTION TO THE PHILOSOPHY OF HISTORY
W. H. Walsh
ISBN 1 85506 170 8 : 1961 Edition : 176pp : £12.99/$19.95

JOHN STUART MILL
Alexander Bain
ISBN 1 85506 213 5 : 1882 Edition : 216pp : £14.99/$24.95

KANT ON EDUCATION
Annette Churton (trans.)
ISBN 1 85506 165 1 : 1899 Edition : 146pp : £10.99/$

LOCKE
Samuel Alexander
ISBN 1 85506 181 3 : 1908 Edition : 102pp : £12.99/$19.95

LOCKE AND THE WAY OF IDEAS
John W. Yolton
ISBN 1 85506 226 7 : 1956 Edition : 248pp : £15.99/$28.95

MENTAL ACTS
Peter Geach
ISBN 1 85506 166 X : 1971 Edition : 148pp : £10.99/$19.95

OUTLINES OF A PHILOSOPHY OF ART
R. G. Collingwood
ISBN 1 85506 316 6 : 1925 Edition : 110pp : £10.99/18.95

OF THE CONDUCT OF THE UNDERSTANDING
John Locke
New Introduction by John Yolton
ISBN 1 85506 225 9 : 1706 Edition : 160pp : £12.99/$19.95

ON THE AESTHETIC EDUCATION OF MAN, IN A SERIES OF LETTERS
Friedrich Schiller (Translated by Reginald Snell)
ISBN 1 85506 322 0 : 1954 Edition : 150pp : £14.99/$26.95

OUTLINES OF THE HISTORY OF ETHICS
Henry Sidgwick
ISBN 1 85506 220 8 : 1886 Edition : 310pp : £14.99/$19.95

THE PHILOSOPHY OF HEGEL
G. R. G. Mure
ISBN 1 85506 237 2 : 1965 Edition : 224pp : £12.99/$

THE PHILOSOPHY OF KANT
John Kemp
ISBN 1 85506 238 0 : 1968 Edition : 138pp : £9.99/$

220

THE PHILOSOPHY OF NIETZSCHE
Abraham Wolf
ISBN 1 85506 353 0 : 1915 Edition : 120pp : £9.99/$14.95

PLATO'S PROGRESS
Gilbert Ryle
ISBN 1 85506 321 2 : 1966 Edition : 320pp : £16.99/$29.95

THE PRESUPPOSITIONS OF CRITICAL HISTORY *bound with*
APHORISMS
F. H. Bradley
ISBN 1 85506 214 3 : 1874/1930 Editions : 132pp : £12.99/$19.95

RELIGION AND PHILOSOPHY
R. G. Collingwood
ISBN 1 85506 317 4 : 1916 Edition : 238pp : £14.99/$24.95

THEORY OF GAMES AS A TOOL FOR THE MORAL PHILOSOPHER
bound with
AN EMPIRICIST'S VIEW OF THE NATURE OF RELIGIOUS BELIEF
R. B. Braithwaite
ISBN 1 85506 315 8 : 1955 Editions : 116pp : £12.99/$19.95

THREE ESSAYS ON RELIGION
John Stuart Mill
ISBN 1 85506 218 6 : 1878 Edition : 314pp : £14.99/$28.95

THE UNITY OF SCIENCE
Rudolf Carnap
ISBN 1 85506 391 3 : 1934 Edition : 102pp : £9.99/$14.95